WHEN THE HEAVENS FELL

Other North Star Titles
by John Koblas and Dave Page

F. Scott Fitzgerald in Minnesota: Toward the Summit

Other North Star Titles
by John Koblas

The Jesse James Northfield Raid:
Confessions of the Ninth Man

J. J. Dickison: Swamp Fox of the Confederacy

Faithful Unto Death: The James-Younger Raid on the First National Bank, September 7, 1876,
Northfield, Minnesota
(Published by the Northfield Historical Society Press)

Willow River Almanac:
A Father Copes with Divorce and Nature

Jesse James Ate Here: An Outlaw Tour and History
of Minnesota at the Time of the Northfield Raid

The Great Cole Younger and Frank James Historical Wild West Show

WHEN THE HEAVENS FELL

The Youngers in Stillwater Prison

John Koblas

For Dennis—
Some local
history, John J. Koblas
3-10-08

NORTH STAR PRESS OF ST. CLOUD, INC.

Library of Congress Cataloging-in-Publication Data

Koblas, John J., 1942-
    When the heavens fell : the Youngers in Stillwater
Prison / John Koblas.—1st. ed.
        p. cm.
    Includes bibliographical references and index.
    ISBN 0-87839-180-0 (pbk. : alk. paper)
    ISBN 0-87839-183-5 (cloth : alk. paper)
        1. Outlaws—West (U.S.).—Biography.
2. Imprisonment—Minnesota—Stillwater—History.
3. Prisons—Minnesota—Stillwater—History. 4. Younger,
Cole, 1844-1916—Imprisonment. 5. Younger, James,
1848-1902—Imprisonment. 6. Younger, Robert Ewing,
1853-1889—Imprisonment. I. Title.

F594.Y77 K63 2002
977.6'555--dc21   2002069237.

ISBN: 0-87839-180-0 Paper
ISBN: 0-87839-183-5 Cloth

First Edition
June 2002

Printed in the United States of America
by Versa Press, Inc., East Peoria.

Published by
North Star Press of St. Cloud, Inc.
P.O. Box 451
St. Cloud, Minnesota 56302

For my favorite literary group—The Lepers:

Kathy Anderson, Jon and Norma Arfstrom, Roger Brezina, Rolf Canton, Andy Decker, Joan Decker, Alison Decker, Bill and Mary Devitt, Doc Diezel, Walker Fischer, David Gatewood, David Goldman, Mark and Linda Goodman, Clark Hansen, Chris Hawes, Steve Heimbuch, Flensing Hlanith, Agris and Gail Kelbrants, Thea Kramer, Bill and Ann Lanoue, John Ledford, Shirlee Madow, Wayne McCloud, Andrea Dawn Miller, John Milton, Peter Morris, Jack Osander, Dave Page, Diana Pierce, Chris Roberts, Paul Roberts, Rachel Roberts, Wally Roers, Luke Rohde, Chris and Stephanie Rugg, Jeanne Scheffert, Ron Searby, Tim Sexton, Duane Stenzel, John Stevens, Chip Strobel, Jerome Wenker, Hans Werner, Joe West, and Ed Wilks.

Acknowledgments

This book could not have been completed without the kind assistance of the following persons. The author hereby expresses his gratitude to Bobe Boze Bell, *True West Magazine*; Brent Peterson of the Washington County Historical Society, Stillwater, Minnesota; Bonnie Wilson, Minnesota Historical Society, St. Paul, Minnesota; and to the following individuals: Ron Affolter, Pat Bantli, Chris Batchelder, Ada Bronaugh, Eugene Buelow, Armand De Gregoris, Chip DeMann, Ed and Diane Hannah, Beverlie Jones-Griffin, Emmett Hoctor, Lyndon Irwin, Thurston James, Randy Jones, Agris Kelbrants, Stephanie Koblas-Rugg, Donald W. Mickow, Andrea Dawn Miller, Jane Moline, Pamela Luster Phillips, Diana Pierce, Mr. and Mrs. E. Lisle Reedstrom, Corky Reynolds, Deeann Reynolds, Donna Rose, Hon. James R. Ross, Jeanne Scheffert, Kristin Scheffert, Donna Schurmeier, John Stevens, Ted P. Yeatman, Frank Younger, Sharon Younger and Wilbur Zink.

Contents

Prologue

"I've seen a good deal of the world anyway and might as well go into retirement. You know the indictment does not charge me with the murder of Heywood, simply with being accessory to it."

—Cole Younger[1]

n November 14, 1876, Cole, Jim, and Bob Younger were arraigned in Rice County District Court in Faribault, Minnesota. The three brothers had been part of a gang assault on the First National Bank of Northfield, Minnesota, on September 7, 1876. Two of their companions, Clell Miller and Bill Chadwell, had been killed in the street during the robbery attempt. A third, Charlie Pitts, was killed in a gunfight between the gang and loyal Minnesotans at Hanska Slough, near LaSalle, Minnesota, two weeks later. The Younger brothers all suffered serious wounds in the battle at the slough in which Pitts had been killed. Only two members of the gang—Frank and Jesse James—escaped capture.

During his interrogation following his capture, Cole was given a pen and piece of paper and asked to tell the authorities the name of the gang member who killed the bank cashier in the bank at Northfield. Cole, a master at twisting truths and protecting his confederates, wrote, "Be true to your friends if the heavens fall."

Be True To your friends
If the Heavens fall
Cole. Younger.

Note by Cole Younger concerning the Northfield bank robbery. (Courtesy of the Minnesota Historical Society)

A reporter from the *St. Paul Pioneer Press*, reporting on the incarcerated brothers, penned: "Here everything is quiet and settled, and there is but little talk about the great Northfield affair which took place two months ago. The excitement has passed way, and the people appear to feel that the law will provide the proper punishment for the notorious prisoners."[2]

Rice County Court House, Faribault, Minnesota. The three Younger brothers were sentenced to life imprisonment in this building. (Courtesy of the Rice County Historical Society)

A survey taken in St. Paul, however, proved that most Minnesotans had not forgotten the Northfield tragedy. The survey taken in St. Paul resulted in seventy-one citizens voting to "hang them," "six for don't hang them," and three people were undecided. One voted "hang them all but Bob."[3]

George W. Batchelder, who defended the brothers, later wrote:

> Feelings ran high both in Northfield and Faribault, and plans were laid to lynch the raiders, as under Minnesota law, a criminal could not be executed if he pleaded guilty. A posse of men came down from Northfield to carry out the lynching, but they met with so much opposition that they went away after one of their number was shot and killed as they approached the jail. Ara Barton, who had been a captain in the Civil War, was sheriff at the time, and he had mounted a cannon in the jail yard and had guards posted in every direction. The Youngers said they did not so much mind being shot, but they did not want to be hanged.
>
> From my contact with the boys, I do not feel that they were at all the criminal type of men that they have been pictured, and reports from their home town of Joplin, [sic] M[issouri] agree with this. They were born and brought up in that seething political section of the United States lying between the North and the South, where bitterness and bloodshed were part of their daily life and environment, and violence an everyday affair. As mere children, they had seen their father and mother dragged from their home and shot before their very eyes, and their home burned to the ground after being looted.[4]

The Youngers were shackled together with Jim on the left, Cole in the middle, and Bob on the right. Sheriff Barton, the chief of police, and one of his men, walked at their sides, an armed guard in front of them and another in their rear. Mutterings of a threatening nature were heard from the crowd, and although these whisperings frightened the brothers, there was no violence. Upon reaching the courthouse, guards moved to either side to admit the men and also keep out the entrance of any uninvited guests.[5]

The brothers appeared to be in fairly good health. Cole had hopes they would receive a light sentence. Willing to plead guilty to the charge of robbery, he did not consider him-

George N. Baxter, Rice County Attorney (and one-time mayor), assisted in the prosecution of the Youngers. (Courtesy of the Rice County Historical Society)

self guilty of murder. Jim did not enjoy such good spirits.[6]

Four indictments were handed down against the three Younger brothers: the first charged them with accessory to the murder of Joseph Heywood, the second with attacking Alonzo Bunker with deadly weapons. They were charged, of course, with robbing the First National Bank. The fourth indictment, with Cole as principal and his brothers as accessories, was for the murder of Nicholaus Gustavson, Northfield immigrant who died on the street during the robbery attempt.[7]

Judge Samuel Lord presided over the court, with George N. Baxter, County Attorney, assisted by Attorney General Wilson, conducting the prosecution. Batchelder & Buckham, a Faribault law firm, and Thomas Rutledge of Madelia represented the Youngers. The defense opened by challenging the grand jurors, resulting in the removal of five of the twenty-three.[8]

The courtroom filled with curious spectators, male and female, anxious to see the captured outlaws, who were brought into the room in irons. All three men were clean shaven and neat, leaving some of the spectators disappointed since they did not look like the desperate men they were supposed to be. Sheriff Barton commanded silence in the courtroom, and County Attorney Baxter read the indictments. The prisoners entered no pleas, having, under the statutes, twenty-four hours to do so.

Four days later, Monday, November 18, 1876, shortly before noon, the Youngers went to trial. Again, the courtroom filled with an enthusiastic, eager crowd, who leaned forward to catch every motion and every word. Handcuffed and chained together, Cole in the middle, Bob on the right, Jim on the left,

the Youngers were brought in through a side
door. Sheriff Barton, two deputies, and a
guard, the brothers' sister Retta, and their
aunt Mrs. Twyman accompanied the
brothers. Both ladies were veiled and
seated themselves with the prisoners
within the bar.[9]

The *St. Paul Pioneer Press*
reported: "The boys looked well—
they were neatly dressed and were
cool and collected, betraying nothing of nervousness. Bob smiled
serenely as he turned to make a
remark to Cole, at which the bald-
headed brother seemed somewhat
amused. Jim deferred to Cole, as
usual, and chatted now and then
with Mrs. Twyman, who sat fanning
herself with Jim's black felt hat. Upon
Miss Younger's face there was no other
expression than of unutterable sadness,
and with the exception of a glance now
and then at her three brothers, she seemed
oblivious to what was about her and taken up
with her own thought."[10]

Mrs. Fanny Twyman, aunt of
the Youngers. (Author's collection)

The court was called to order, and Sheriff Ara Barton
ordered everyone in the room to take seats. Barton, highly
respected, had been elected sheriff one year earlier after serving two terms in the state legislature. County Attorney Baxter
walked up to the judge's desk and read the indictments. Baxter
also stated that he felt the prisoners' wrist irons should be
removed.[11]

"The prisoners remained implacable, with no change
in expression, and only one or two nervous movements of the
hands upon the part of Cole," read the *Pioneer Press*. "Then
the counsel for the defense and the prosecuting attorney
entered into consultation for a few moments, at the conclusion
of which the irons from the wrists of the prisoners were
removed."[12]

The Youngers stepped to the bench one at a time,
with Cole first. He walked coolly up to the judge with his
hands behind his back and then dropping nervously to his

sides. Cole's plea of guilty "was uttered in a low but distinct tone of voice and was not heard beyond the railing inclosing the part of the courtroom set apart for the use of the attorneys. The judge moved his hand, and Cole marched coolly back to his seat and settled in his chair, while an expression of satisfaction and relief swept over his face. Then came Jim, and the same scene was gone through with, and lastly, Bob more cool and indifferent than ever. All pleaded guilty to the murder of Heywood."[13]

The brothers were asked if they had anything to say in their behalf, to which Jim and Bob answered no.

Cole, however, brought the room to tears by saying, "I feel responsible for leading my brothers into the deplorable situation we now find ourselves. I would willingly suffer death in any form—if, by doing so—my brothers could go free." The judge buried his face in his hands, and for several minutes, was incapable of speech.[14]

Addressing them, the judge said, "You have acknowledged your abetting in the crime of murder by entering pleas of guilty. There remains nothing for the Court, but to pronounce sentence upon you. It is general on such occasion for the Court to say something in explanation of its sentence. But I have no word of comfort to offer you and no desire to speak harshly of the deeds, which have brought you into your present positions. The sentence of the law leaves you life, but robbed of all its pleasures, hopes, and ambitions."[15]

Judge Lord addressed each of the men and sentenced them to life imprisonment in Stillwater Prison. Jim turned to Retta and put his arm around her.[16] In announcing the verdict, Judge Lord was so affected that he had trouble speaking. Women began crying; one spirited lady rushed up the aisle saying she wanted to kiss the prisoners.[17]

According to the *St. Paul Pioneer Press*, "The sentence was received by the three brothers without a movement of a muscle or change of expression. When Judge Lord had finished, they turned and took their seats, while an expression of satisfaction and relief swept over their faces. Jim sat next to his sister, a modest and rather handsome young woman, who, during all these proceedings had sat with sorrow depicted upon her face and occupied with her own thoughts. He leaned over to comfort her, and she burst into tears, dropping her head on his shoulder, while the only arm at liberty was thrown about her with rarest gentleness to support her. He made some remarks to Mrs. Twyman, who too had given way to her feelings, but there was no expression of giving way upon the faces of the three murderers. Their handcuffs had meantime been affixed and the brothers were led away while Messrs. Batchelder and Rutledge advanced and gave to the weeping women the support they so much needed. It was a touching scene, made even more touching in the jail, where secluded from the vulgar gaze the sister and aunt gave way to the full floods of grief which the unmoved and murderous brothers had brought with them."[18]

The Youngers' plea of guilty did not mean they suffered remorse for their actions. In 1868, legislation had been passed creating a new law stating that a person convicted of murder could only be hanged if the jury so determined the guilt. By a plea of guilty, a jury trial could often be avoided, and more significantly for the Youngers, they would escape capital punishment. Instead, the utmost would be life imprisonment.[19]

A local newspaper commented on the guilty plea: "By the plea of guilty, the prisoners saved the county the expense of a long and tedious trial; but it is exceedingly probable that by so doing they have saved themselves from the gallows."[20]

Bob Younger's arm wound continued to plague him the day of the trial as reported by a local newspaper: "The wound received by Bob Younger at Northfield having left him with a stiff arm, he a few days since took chloroform and had it broken again, as his physician thinks that by that means he can regain the use of the arm."[21]

On Wednesday morning, November 20, 1876, the prisoners were taken from the Faribault Jail and placed on the eight o'clock train accompanied by Sheriff Ara Barton, Fin Barton, Sheriff W.H. Dill of Winona, guards John Passon and Thomas Lord, Henrietta Younger, and Mrs. Twyman. A wagon was waiting in St. Paul to take the Youngers on the last leg of their journey.

Crowds waited at several stops along the way, and while many persons shouted in anger at the brothers, several others cheered them. The words of encouragement from faces in the crowd surprised the three men, making their plight perhaps just a bit easier.[22]

"Cole Younger looked around over the spectators inside and outside the car with an impudent and malignant stare, as if he was in a bad humor," penned the *St. Paul and Minneapolis Weekly Pioneer Press.* "He didn't appear at all like a saint or a bible-reading martyr, or even like a gentleman of leisure, who has traveled all over the world, and having seen all that is worth seeing, is glad to 'retire' to private life."[23]

Cole and Jim looking defiant and modest Bob with his head down, the three brothers approached their new home. Standing outside the prison walls, the three men stared at the small crowd that lingered to watch them pass through the gates of incarceration. A Madelia lady, who had helped nurse Cole back to health at the Flanders House, broke through the crowd and told the boys she was grateful they had fallen into her town's Christian hands. Cole smiled and replied they were sorry too but probably didn't deserve their kindness. He blamed the Civil War for making him who he was and added he may have amounted to something had it not been for that dreadful chapter in his life. Bob looked at her and muttered, "We are rough men, ma'am, and are used to rough ways."[24]

They had come a long, long way from Missouri.

Notes

[1] *St. Paul & Minneapolis Pioneer Press*, November 23, 1876.

[2] *St. Paul & Minneapolis Pioneer Press*, Thursday, November 16, 1876.

[3] Nancy B. Samuelson, "How the James Boys Fled the Disaster at Northfield and the Capture of Frank James," *The Journal*, Official Publication of the Western Outlaw-Lawman History Association, Spring-Summer 1993, p.7.

[4] Papers of Charles F. Batchelder in collection of Chris Batchelder.

[5] George Huntington, *Robber and Hero*, Minneapolis, Ross & Haines, Inc., 1962, pp. 76-77.

[6] Ruth Rentz Yates, editor, *Before Their Identity*, No publisher given, 1996, p. 20.

[7] *St. James Plain Dealer*, September 1926, "50th Anniversary of Northfield Bank Robbers and Capture of Four of the Bandits in this County," p.10.

[8] *Faribault Democrat*, Friday, November 17, 1876, "The Robbers."

[9]*Faribault Democrat*, Friday, November 24, 1876, "The Youngers."

[10]*St. Paul Pioneer Press*, November 20, 1876.

[11]Ibid.; *Faribault Republican*, November 9, 1898.

[12]*St. Paul Pioneer Press*, November 20, 1898.

[13]Ibid.

[14]Robert Barr Smith, *The Last Hurrah of the James-Younger Gang*, Norman, University of Oklahoma Press, 2001, p. 178.

[15]Ruth Rentz Yates, *Before Their Identity*, p. 20.

[16]Marley Brant, *The Outlaw Youngers: A Confederate Brotherhood*, Lanham, New York & London, Madison Books, 1992, pp. 212-213.

[17]Homer Croy, *Last of the Great Outlaws*, New York, The New American Library, 1958, p. 96.

[18]*St. Paul Pioneer Press*, November 20, 1876.

[19]J.A. Kiester, *History of Faribault County, Minnesota*, Minneapolis, Haiman & Smith, 1896.

[20]*Faribault Democrat*, Friday, November 24, 1876.

[21]*Mankato Record*, November 18, 1876.

[22]Marley Brant, *The Outlaw Youngers*, p. 213.

[23]*St. Paul and Minneapolis Weekly Pioneer Press*, Thursday, November 30, 1876.

[24]Will Henry, *Jesse James: Death of a Legend*, New York, Leisure Books, 1996, pp. 301-302.

Introduction

by Ted P. Yeatman

On November 22, 1876, the notorious Younger brothers, Cole, Jim, and Bob, partners in crime with Frank and Jesse James in the disastrous Northfield, Minnesota, bank raid, walked into relative obscurity behind the walls of the Minnesota State Penitentiary at Stillwater. While details of the attempts to have the Youngers pardoned over the next quarter century are often mentioned in accounts of their lives, a truly detailed history of their years behind bars has been lacking. In this work, John Koblas has done a remarkable job of research, giving precisely that detailed history of the Youngers' years of incarceration. This book fills a void in the history of the Old West and American penal history.

The sons of Judge Henry Washington Younger, a Missouri Unionist killed by renegade Union militia during the war, probably would have led far different lives but for their experiences during the conflict. Missouri was torn apart socially and psychologically by the guerrilla strife during the Civil War years. Cole and brother Jim eventually joined Confederate raiders under William Clarke Quantrill, and Cole eventually joined a regular Confederate unit. Brother Bob, only a child at the time, saw war from the home front, with his father killed, the family home burned and himself and his mother and sisters made refugees. That the war had its psychological impact is apparent in Bob Younger's comments after the trial: "We are rough men, ma'am, and are used to rough ways."

The Civil War in Missouri threw away the rule book as to what was and was allowable in warfare. It was as nasty a conflict as has ever occurred on American soil, not unlike the guerrilla conflicts of the 1990s in the former Yugoslavia. And just as in the Balkans and elsewhere where guerrilla wars have raged before and since, in the wake of formal peace some found it difficult to readjust and turned to banditry, or other illegal activity, to earn their livelihoods. It was from this milieu that the James-Younger Gang sprang.

Sympathy for the Youngers, particularly in Missouri, in the years following their capture was no doubt in part a result of the empathy of many who had experienced the upheaval of war and were trying to put it all behind them as well. Some saw the Youngers as merely trying to get retribution for what the family had lost during the war. In an era where incarceration in a penitentiary more often than not bordered on the barbaric, Minnesota had a remarkably progressive policy towards the treatment of prisoners. The Youngers became model prisoners, yet only one of the trio left the state alive. And the survivor would again team up with one of the James brothers for a "last hurrah" of sorts—but that is another story.

1831 to 1875

"It were long to tell and sad to trace
Their fall from splendor to disgrace—
[From honesty to crime]"
—Lord Byron

he St. Croix Valley, in the early nineteenth century, served as a dividing line at "the old trysting tree," between warring Dakota and Chippewa. Permanent villages could not be established by either tribe on land liable at any time to become a battleground, since the two Indian nations could not be restrained by any treaty from venting their hatred upon one another.[1]

A short distance above the future site of Stillwater, at a bend in the river, painted cliffs marked the land separating the two tribes. Tourists came up the St. Croix via the Mississippi River to enjoy the beautiful scenery of the rocky area. For several rods, the smooth surface of the cliff was decorated with colorful hues. Figures of animals were clearly delineated and symbols, almost a form of hieroglyphics, relating to battles and victories won dotted the cliff face. Whenever the tribes passed this sacred cliff, they would stop and perform ceremonies.

Zion's Hill, near the center of present day Stillwater, was the scene of an Indian tragedy. According to a manuscript of Thomas Connor, an old Indian trader, he, his Indian wife and many children had been accepted by both tribes of Indians. In 1831 he was the only licensed trader above the falls of the St. Croix, on the Minnesota side. Connor's manuscript relates the story of an Indian chief, who met his fate on Zion's Hill.

The war with no end between the Chippewa and Dakota had erupted into several battles with many men, women, and children mercilessly slaughtered. Both tribes, however, had become weary of war and agreed the two chiefs would fight a battle atop Zion's Hill in hand-to-hand struggle with only knives and tomahawks.

The two chiefs fought a bloody battle, which lasted over an hour. When neither could no longer stand, they were administered to by their people. One of the chiefs would be declared the winner when his adversary died. The Dakota chief, who had nearly won the battle, succumbed first, but his rival followed suit but minutes later. As he lay dying, the Chippewa chieftain called his warriors around him and warned:

> "This is a beautiful spot where I die. The white man is coming and will soon be here; then you must all go away. He will build buildings; one to settle his quarrels in, and not fight like the Indians, another will he build, where the children will learn to be good and not fight as I have done today. The Great Spirit will build another for the white man, and he will call it His tepee."[2]

In the few years between the consummation of treaties with the tribes in 1837 and the formation of the Territory of Minnesota in 1849, the white man did come. Parties of explorers pushed up the Mississippi and St. Croix rivers, and many points along the rivers were opened to settlement.

In 1838, Stillwater pioneer, Joseph Renshaw Brown, staked a claim on Grey Cloud Island, established a trading post and declared himself justice of the peace. Two years later, Brown laid out the first townsite at the head of Lake St. Croix, about half a mile above the original site of Stillwater. In 1840, he was elected a member of the Wisconsin legislature from Crawford County.

Jacob Fisher, Elias McKean, and Calvin F. Leach settled on the present site of Stillwater on October 11, 1843, and others soon followed suit. The name "Stillwater" was suggested by John McKusick, and the people of the village consented. McKusick's arguments for the name were the stillness of the water in the lake, the anomaly of building a mill beside still water, and by fond recollections of Stillwater, Maine. Still, no town was planned beyond a sawmill site.

In the spring of 1844, Anson Northrup came to Stillwater and erected the Northrup House—the first hotel in Washington County. Soon, a stable for the hotel was constructed, but it was quickly transformed into a store operated by Walter R. Vail. Quickly other entrepreneurs followed— Socrates Nelson, with a store and home under one roof; John McKusick built a boarding house, and Elam Greeley built a residence. Frank Roberts added a saloon, and John McKusick had a store.

Stillwater, like many Midwestern cities, took on several nicknames, including "Birthplace of Minnesota," "Queen of the St. Croix," and later, "the Prison City." The 1840s witnessed great strides in the lumber industry as numerous mills were constructed along the St. Croix River. John McKusick's sawmill at Stillwater was operational in 1844, and several others were established—namely by the Kent brothers at Osceola in 1845, the Mowers at Arcola in 1847, and James Purinton at Hudson in 1848 (all in Wisconsin Territory).[3]

When Henry Lewis, renowned English landscape painter, journeyed down the St. Croix River with a party in 1847, he noted "the pine forests along the St. Croix are no longer equaled on the entire continent except along the Penobscot and Kennebec in Maine." By 1855, seventeen mills dotted the river between St. Croix Falls to Prescott. In five years these mills processed twenty-eight million feet of lumber. By 1875, that figure more than tripled to 88,500,000 board-feet.

On February 3, 1843, Stephen A. Douglas introduced a bill to "establish the Territory of Minnesota." The bill came up for consideration but was recommitted. On August 8 of that year, Douglas added amendments to the bill, but Congress adjourned six days later without taking any action. The effort to establish a territory through the accepted channels failed.[5]

When Wisconsin was admitted as a state on May 29, 1848, a large section of St. Croix County, then in Wisconsin Territory, was omitted. The area became a no-man's land, without law or government. One politician, William Holcombe, wondered if a case could be made for the continued existence of the Wisconsin Territory in the area that had not been included in the state. Residents of St. Paul posed the same question, and decided to organize a convention to proclaim their right to representation. Before they could act, however, the people of Stillwater were already headed in that same direction.[5] The village of Stillwater was officially surveyed and platted by Harvey Wilson with the shoreline of Lake St. Croix clearly marked. Main Street was but a few blocks long with the original Stillwater mill at the north end and the huge bluff to the south.[6]

St. Paul newspaper editor, James M. Goodhue, in 1849, called the valley of the St. Croix "emphatically the best section of country in all the West." And he was far from being the first to call the valley the fairest in the land.[7]

The detached county quickly reorganized, with Stillwater selected as the county seat. In June, the first term of any court ever held in what is now Minnesota, was held in Stillwater, by Judge Charles Dunn of the United States District Court. Harvey Wilson, of Stillwater, was appointed Clerk of Court.[8]

The demand for a territorial government became general and was discussed in all the settlements in and around Stillwater. A public meeting was held in Stillwater on August 4, 1848, to discuss a convention to organize a territory. Attendance was poor, but the declaration was signed by eighteen men, stating: "We the undersigned citizens of the Minnesota Territory [sic] . . . respectfully recommend that the people of the several settlements in the proposed Territory appoint delegates to meet in convention at Stillwater on the 26th day of August inst. to adopt the necessary steps for that purpose."[9]

A convention organized at Stillwater, August 26, 1848, became the first step to establishing the Minnesota Territory. Sixty-one delegates—a loose assemblage of Yankee lumbermen, fur traders, and other frontier boosters—assembled and elected M.S. Wilkerson, president; David S. Lambert, secretary. John Catlin, secretary of the Territory of Wisconsin, declared himself governor of the portion of the territory not included in the new Commonwealth. Catlin established his capital at Stillwater and ordered an election to select a territorial delegate to Congress. Henry H. Sibley, who had also been chosen by the convention, was selected.[10]

These men believed that Congress would not recognize a Wisconsin Territory as existing and would never appropriate money for it. The Stillwater Convention decided to draft memorials to Congress and President James K. Polk.[11] The group laid out the new territory and named it "Minnesota," a Dakota word meaning "sky-tinted waters."

Sibley was seated in Washington as the delegate from the Stillwater Convention of January 15, 1849. With assistance from Stephen A. Douglas, the bill designed in Stillwater passed in Congress, and on March 3, 1849, the Territory of Minnesota was created. The population at the time was just under 6,000 people.[12]

Concerning his reception from the Washington set, Sibley wrote the State Historical Society: "When my credentials as delegate were presented by Hon. James Wilson of New Hampshire to the House of Representatives, there was some curiosity manifested among the members to see what kind of a

Henry H. Sibley. (Courtesy of the Rice County Historical Society)

person had been elected to represent the wild territory claiming representation in Congress. I was told by a New England member with whom I became subsequently intimate, that there was some disappointment when I made my appearance, for it was expected that the delegate from this remote region would make his debut, if not in full Indian costume, at least with some peculiarities of dress and manners, characteristic of the rude and semi-civilized people who had sent him to the capital."[13]

These "rude and semi-civilized" people, however, were making the St. Croix Valley the lumbering capital of the world. Sawmills were springing up along the river, and people were pouring into the valley to get rich in the lumber business. One settler described the valley thusly:

The St. Croix, with population on both sides of the river from point Douglas to the farthest point of the lumbering operations, will send to market this year nearly [sixty] million feet of sawed lumber and logs. Circumstances have greatly favored the lumbermen of the St. Croix this year. The high spring water has enabled them to send all of their logs down river. The boom was filled very early, and many millions have already reached the markets below. From Stillwater to the boom, six miles below Taylors Falls, you can see nothing but rafts and strings of logs. . . .[14]

St. Croix Timber Company, one of the early lumbering companies in the St. Croix area. (Courtesy of the Rice County Historical Society)

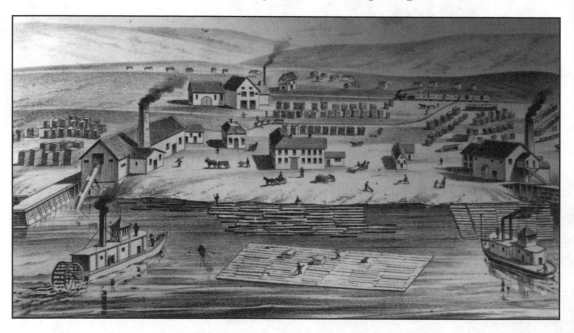

Much of the Stillwater lumber went down the Mississippi River in great log rafts, the raw materials needed to build up cities such as Dubuque, Rock Island, St. Louis, Omaha, Des Moines, Kansas City, and Topeka. Minnesota lumber also went east and to Europe, Brazil, and the West Indies.

On September 4, 1849, Governor Alexander Ramsey presented his first address to the Minnesota Territorial Legislature. He asked that a good road be built commencing at Point Douglas, going through Stillwater, "and thence, via the Marine Mills and St. Croix Falls, to Lake Superior."[15]

In that same address, Governor Ramsey declared the state lacked a suitable lockup controlled by civil authorities. Civilian lawbreakers had been held at Fort Snelling and Fort Ripley, but more often than not, they fled the territory before they could be sentenced. One year later, a St. Paul newspaper reporter rationalized that "probably this is the best way to dispose of our rascals so long as we are destitute of a prison."[16]

A suggestion that the prison be built in the village of St. Anthony was met with contempt by most of its citizens. Another location, farther up the Mississippi River in the center of the state—perhaps in Benton County—but this suggestion was rejected by the larger downriver cities, who found the site too far removed.[17]

A heated contest erupted during the second session of the territorial legislature over the location of the capitol and the prison. Since the temporary capitol had been established in St. Paul, general consensus was to leave it at that location. A bill to place the capitol in St. Paul and the prison in Stillwater united the delegations of those two communities, and they succeeded in overcoming a similar combination between St. Anthony and the Upper Mississippi delegates.[18]

The housing of the prison, government offices, and the university in buildings of their own faced several delays. The two houses of the territorial legislature met in joint session to hear Governor Ramsey's annual message at such sites as the Baptist Church in St. Paul and the Ramsey County Courthouse.[19]

Ramsey's suggestion, however, was approved by the legislators, November 1, 1849, and in June 1850, Congress appropriated $20,000 for the construction of a prison in the town of Stillwater, Minnesota. The institution, a wooden structure with a wooden wall, had the capacity to house a hundred prisoners. The new prison was built in Battle Hollow, a site named for a battle, which took place there July 2, 1839, when a band of Dakota attacked a group of Chippewa returning home from Fort Snelling. Fifty Chippewa were killed during the ambush.[20]

In May 1851, the Minnesota Board of Commissioners of Public Buildings, decided to construct the prison of stone. The Jesse Taylor Company, which included Francis R. Delano, Martin Mower, and John Fisher as partners, commenced construction of the facility. Located near the St. Croix River in a deep ravine in North Stillwater, the prison was enclosed on three sides by high cliffs and on the fourth by a twelve-foot masonry wall.[21]

The territorial legislature appointed Francis R. Delano, one of the contractors, as the first warden, and he assumed office on April 4, 1853. Delano had moved to Stillwater from Massachusetts in 1851 and had been engaged in a not-too-profitable lumbering business. Serving as warden was not a simple task for Delano, as he knew nothing of prison security. During his first few years at the prison, however, he set up a very profitable business on the grounds. With his own money, he purchased over $8,000 worth of steam-powered machinery for the manufacturing of shingles, sashes, doors, flooring, wagons, and plows and established his business within prison walls. He also hired fifteen Stillwater men to assist with special orders.[22]

The first prisoners were garbed in hickory-cloth shirts, gray pants, red-and-blue jackets, and blanket-wool caps. The heads of the inmates were shaved on one side only.

By early 1853, a three-story prison house with six cells and two dungeons for solitary confinement, a workshop, and an office were constructed of rock from nearby quarries. Within the enclosure was an area of approximately 280 square feet surrounded by the uninviting twelve-foot wall. Halfway up the south hill on the outside stood the warden's house.[23]

The entire cost of buildings and grounds, five thousand dollars, was paid by the United States government. The machinery, which cost eight thousand dollars, remained the property of the warden.

The sale of convict labor to privately owned industry was a commonly accepted practice, not only at Stillwater but at similar institutions across the country. Consistent with this policy were privately financed shops within prison walls in which shingles, sashes, doors, flooring, wagons, and plows were manufactured. Inmates and local residents worked side by side in these prison shops under non-prison supervisors and private management. Because the contract labor system placed almost exclusive emphasis on profit, with total disregard for the welfare and health of inmates, it became increasingly unpopular by the prisoners and some prison officials. Still, the system flourished until it was discontinued in the 1890s.[24]

The prison in Battle Hollow faced serious problems from the first. Poor architectural planning and the damp, swampy terrain made the structure anything but a working institution. Escapes were frequent, cells were damp, housekeeping difficult, and there was insufficient space within the enclosure to provide expansion of facilities.

Until the establishment of the Shakopee State Reformatory for Women (1920), Stillwater Prison received female as well as male convicts. The women were supervised by a matron (sometimes referred to as stewardess), who also attended to their needs. In addition, the prison sometimes received federal prisoners and was compensated for their maintenance.[25]

The prison was managed by a warden and a board of inspectors, whose three members were appointed by the governor to staggered three-year terms. This board met at the prison quarterly to audit the prison's financial records and report to the governor annually. The board also created prison rules and prescribed punishments for infractions committed by inmates. The warden was appointed by the governor for a two-year term and was responsible for day-to-day administration of the institution.

The first year, surprisingly, there were no convicts, and the second, there were but two, plus seven or eight persons from counties which had no suitable facilities for their confinement. In 1856, there was again but a single prisoner within prison walls, perhaps because during a ten-month period that year, seven men and one woman escaped. By 1857, there were none in confinement.[26]

Delano complained that the escapes were not the fault of the warden, and he blamed the prison, since the walls and buildings were not "of the most approved and substantial kind." There were several methods of escape, and each incoming prisoner concocted more during his tenure. The hall floor was pried up; an iron cell door was removed from rusted hinges; a burglar's bar was smuggled into the institution; locks and shackles were easily picked; iron bars in the windows were sawed; and holes were dug through the outside wall.[27]

In a meeting of the legislature, it was decided that the warden would receive all persons committed from counties having no suitable jail buildings. But several counties that sent prisoners to Stillwater failed to pay their lodging fees, and, try as he might, Delano could not collect from them. By 1857, these counties owed Delano $700. The prison committee of the legislature conducted an inspection and ruled that the warden was not responsible for prisoners whose fees had not been paid by the counties that had sent them there. A decree was approved on May 23, 1857, and Warden Delano immediately set free prisoners from those counties not paying fees— mainly Winona, Houston, and Nicollet Counties.

Besides the difficulties inside the prison, there was chaos outside the walls of prison in Minnesota that year as well. The bankruptcy of a New York financial institution, the Ohio Life Insurance and Trust Company, ignited a serious economic crisis that was national in scope. Cash dried up all over Minnesota, real estate speculators and merchants were ruined, banks closed, and people lost their jobs. So crippling was the depression that St. Paul lost half its population, and Ramsey County had to issue scrip.[28]

Following the 1857 escape of an accused murderer from LeSueur, who had been confined at Stillwater Prison for safekeeping pending trial, an editorial in a November 1857 issue of the *St. Paul Weekly Pioneer & Democrat*, declared: "There is something wrong about the territorial prison. Any person who desires it can escape from it, and the Warden does not even think it worth while to offer a reward, or notify the public." Two weeks later, the *St. Paul Financial, Real Estate & Railroad Examiner*, concurred, charging, "a canary bird in a [ten-]acre field, with the bar doors down at that, would be more safely caged."[29]

In early 1858, a new convict led three of his cronies in a successful jail break by chopping a large hole in the cell block's stone wall, and through the use of a ladder, climbed the wall while the guard had stepped out to attend church services. The federal government looked upon this incident as the last straw and decided changes needed to be made, the quicker, the better.

According to a *Stillwater Messenger* article, one writer penned: "Our penitentiary is a great humbug. There is no security about it—it is a cheat, a swindle, a disgrace."[30]

But with incoming prisoners entering Stillwater Prison at a record pace, the facility quickly began to fill, and new measures were already being adopted. A rule charging three dollars a week was implemented, and it required payment for five weeks in advance. Curiously, if at the expiration of that period, board was not again paid in advance, the prisoner was released. This ludicrous ruling led to considerable abuse of power and carelessness on the part of prison officials. The Grand Jury had to step in. The jury's investigation found that there had been eleven escapes on the part of prisoners since 1855, and five of those escapees had been discharged and set free. In all, there were eight infractions, and Warden Delano and Deputy Warden Michael McHale were found "negligent and careless."[31]

Delano, however, decided to fight the charges and challenged the moral character of the Grand Jury members. Although he did not offer names, he charged one of the men with "having been tried in a sister state for the highest crime known to the laws," and another of dealing "a little game of Chuck-a-luck" between sittings of the jury. Delano offered evidence that the inspectors had visited the cellblock for only twenty-seven minutes and checked only three cells. Most of their time, Delano contended, was spent with a saloon proprietor who was a member of the jury. They even went so far as to lock the saloon owner in a cell and refused to release him until he bought free drinks for everyone. Minnesota Governor Samuel Medary did not press charges against Delano and his men, and the Grand Jury charges were soon forgotten. Delano served his term out and left office honorably in 1858.

Francis Smith followed Delano as warden in 1858, but remained at the helm less than a year. The new warden was anything but welcomed by the departing Delano. Delano refused to turn over the keys to the prison to Smith until he received compensation for his machinery. The stand-off took months before the problem resolved.[32]

On August 19, 1859, Henry N. Setzer, a Stillwater lumberman and popular representative of the first territorial legislature, assumed the role of warden. He immediately closed the door to counties that used the prison as a common jail-house, and he clamped down on many of the lax measures enjoyed by Delano. Setzer recommended the prison be removed from the swamp at Battle Hollow, which, he contended, would never offer enough space for expansion. Then, in December of 1859, he resigned from office.[33]

Other changes were made during 1859. John B. Stevens, a Stillwater manufacturer of shingles and blinds, leased the prison workshop from the state and supervised the convict-labor system. A system of implementing the hiring out of prisoners was unpopular with the administration, but it would continue for another fifty-five years.[34]

J.S. Proctor, a Stillwater hardware merchant, accepted the job of warden in January 1860. Proctor served in that capacity for eight years under four Minnesota governors. Receiving a yearly salary of $750, Proctor was the perfect warden according to Alexander Ramsey.[35]

Because so many inmates continued to escape, Proctor introduced "penitentiary stripes" his first year, which made escapees easier to identify. The prisoners were issued hip jackets, trousers, and skullcaps of heavy blanket cloth with alternating horizontal black and white stripes.[36]

While the prison population continued to climb, the City of Stillwater, outside the walls, also saw an increase in citizenry. In 1860, Stillwater boasted 2,380 inhabitants, only slightly behind Minneapolis' population of 2, 564.[37]

John Stevens' mill burned to the ground in 1861, and he went bankrupt. George Seymour and William Webster, manufacturers of flour barrels, were awarded the prison labor contract, which had been initiated by Stevens. Dwight M. Sabin, later a United States senator, entered into partnership with Seymour later in the decade and their company controlled prison labor for the next twenty years.[38]

That same year, Governor Alexander Ramsey, in one of his official messages, drew attention to the increasing number of criminals and the overcrowding of inmates within state prison walls. "There are cells provided for twenty-two convicts," he said. "Fifteen of them are occupied, and the balance may be before the next session of the Legislature." A year later, he reported the prison would have to be enlarged.[39]

By 1862, the prison facility had reached its maximum capacity and steps were taken to enlarge the grounds and erect more buildings. During construction, the walls were extended, enclosing nine and one-half acres, and a dry house and shops were added with a cost of $14,500. Proctor left the prison in 1868, and was succeeded by Joshua L. Taylor (1868 to 1870), Alfred B. Webber (1870), and Henry A. Jackman (1870 to 1874).[40]

Warden Alfred Webber, an Albert Lea politician and former hotelier, was not highly regarded by the press. The *Stillwater Republican* quoted his defense of a pardoned convict in 1870: "I know he was not [guilty of any crime], for he told me all about it after he was pardoned."[41]

Under Warden Henry A. Jackman's reign, the tottering old territorial buildings of the prison were removed, leaving only the warden's house standing from the original prison. New accommodations were constructed to hold 158 prisoners, and Jackman called these new quarters "an honor to the State, a credit to the builders, and a blessing to the inmates." But faulty construction made it easy for a prisoner to crawl under his cell door and between the window bars.[42]

Governor Cushman K. Davis. (Courtesy of the Rice County Historical Society)

Jackman came under fire in 1874. Shortly after he relieved Deputy Warden Eri P. Evans of duty, his subordinate struck back, charging the warden with fraud, theft, neglect of duty, and infractions of discipline. The governor was handed 400 pages of testimony against Jackman, but the man was not immediately dismissed.

A St. Paul newspaperman visited the prison about this same time and reported that many of the newly built cells, bedding included, were damp and absolutely filthy. Faced with an ever-growing criticism, Jackman resigned in July 1874.[43]

Governor Cushman K. Davis appointed Jackman's successor on August 3, 1874. John A. Reed, of Sterling in Blue Earth County, would hold his the position of warden for thirteen years. The newspapers quickly labeled him the new warden of "that miserable basin."[44]

During Reed's tenure, the number of inmates more than quadrupled, and the state was faced with a problem of furnishing adequate living space for the prisoners. As Reed's administration worked on enlarging the facility, the prison received its most infamous prisoners: the Younger brothers.[45]

Notes

[1]J. Fletcher Williams, *History of Washington County & the St. Croix Valley*, Minneapolis, North Star Publishing Company, 1881, pp. 496-510.

[2]Ibid., p. 497.

[3]James Taylor Dunn, *The St. Croix Midwest Border River*, New York, Holt, Rinehart & Winston, 1965, p. 72.

[4]William Watts Folwell, *A History of Minnesota*, Volume I, St. Paul, Minnesota Historical Society Press, 1956, p. 236.

[5]Minnesota Beginnings Records of St. Croix County Wisconsin Territory, 1840-1849, Stillwater, Washington County Historical Society, 1999, p. 11.

[6]Brent T. Peterson & Dean R. Thilgen, *1843-1993 Stillwater A Photographic History*, Stillwater, Valley History Press, 1992, p. 6.

[7]A. Hermina Poatgieter and James Taylor Dunn, editors, *Gopher Reader*, St. Paul, Minnesota Historical Society and Minnesota Statehood Centennial Commission, 1966, p. 196.

[8]J. Fletcher Williams, *A History of the City of St. Paul to 1875*, St. Paul, Minnesota Historical Society Press, 1983, pp. 175-176.

[9]William Watts Folwell, *A History of Minnesota*, Volume I, p. 236.

[10]Willard E. Rosenfelt, Washington, *A History of the Minnesota County*, Stillwater, The Croixside Press, 1977, pp. 93-94; William E. Lass, *Minnesota A History*, New York & London, W.W. Norton & Company, 1983, p. 6.

[11]Minnesota Beginnings Records of St. Croix County Wisconsin Territory,1840-1849, p. 11.

[12]Dennis Brindell Fradin and Judith Bloom Fradin, *From Sea to Shining Sea*, Minnesota, Chicago, Children's Press, 1994, p. 19.

[13]Willard E. Rosenfelt, *Washington: A History of the Minnesota County*, pp. 93-94.

[14]Ibid., p. 132.

[15]James Taylor Dunn, *Marine on the St. Croix 150 years of Village Life*, Marine on the St. Croix, Marine Restoration Society, 1989, p. 21.

[16]*Minnesota Chronicle & Register*, April 20, 1850.

[17]James Taylor Dunn, *The St. Croix Midwest Border River*, p. 115.

[18]William Watts Folwell, *A History of Minnesota,* Volume I, p. 260.

[19]Bertha L. Heilbron, *The Thirty-Second State History of Minnesota*, St. Paul, Minnesota Historical Society, 1958, p. 75.

[20]*St. Paul Daily News*, Friday, June 26, 1936.

[21]Ibid.

[22]James Taylor Dunn, *The St. Croix Midwest Border River*, p. 116; Patricia Condon Johnston, *Stillwater: Minnesota's Birthplace*, Afton, Afton Historical Society Press, 1995, p. 61.

[23]James Taylor Dunn, "The Minnesota State Prison during the Stillwater Era, 1853-1914," *Minnesota History*, December 1960, Volume 37, Number 4, pp. 137-151.

[24]Charles A. Lamb, *Stillwater State Prison History*, Minnesota Historical Society.

[25]"Stillwater State Prison," Agency Record Group Administrative History, Minnesota Historical Society.

[26]J. Fletcher Williams, *History of Washington County & the St. Croix Valley*, pp. 533-536; James Taylor Dunn, *The St. Croix Midwest Border River*, p. 116.

[27]James Taylor Dunn, *The St. Croix Midwest Border River*, pp. 116-117.

[28]Virginia Brainard Kunz, *The First 150 Years*, St. Paul, the St. Paul Foundation, Inc., 1991, p. 34.

[29]James Taylor Dunn, *The St. Croix Midwest Border River*, pp. 116-117.

[30](Minneapolis) *Star Tribune*, August 2, 1998.

[31]James Taylor Dunn, *The St. Croix Midwest Border River*, pp. 116-117.

[32](Minneapolis) *Star Tribune*, August 2, 1998.

[33]James Taylor Dunn, *The St. Croix Midwest Border River*, pp. 116-117.

[34]Patricia Condon Johnston, *Stillwater: Minnesota's Birthplace*, p. 65.

[35]James Taylor Dunn, *The St. Croix Midwest Border River*, pp. 119-123.

[36]Patricia Condon Johnston, *Stillwater: Minnesota's Birthplace*, p. 61.

[37]U.S. Census for 1860; William Watts Folwell, *A History of Minnesota*, Volume II, St. Paul, Minnesota Historical Society Press, 1961, p. 64.

[38]Patricia Condon Johnston, *Stillwater: Minnesota's Birthplace*, p. 65.

[39]Theodore C. Blegen, *Minnesota: A History of the State*, Minneapolis, University of Minnesota Press, 1963, p. 255.

[40]William Watts Folwell, *A History of Minnesota*, Volume II, p. 64.

[41]*Minneapolis Star Tribune*, August 2, 1998.

[42]William Watts Folwell, *A History of Minnesota*, Volume II, p. 64.

[43]*St. Paul Dispatch*, June 24, 1874.

[44]*Stillwater Messenger*, May 22, 1874; *St. Paul Dispatch*, June 5, 1874; *St. Paul Pioneer Press*, January 20, 1874.

[45]Brent T. Peterson & Dean R. Thilgen, *Stillwater, A Photographic History, 1843-1993*, pp. 51-53.

Opposite: The Minnesota State Prison at Stillwater and two of its more famous prisoners, Bob and Cole Younger, ca. 1880. (John Runk Collection, Minnesota Historical Society)

THE OLD MINNESOTA STATE PRISON BUILT IN 1858
SITE - BATTLE HOLLOW

Most famous of all the thousands of prisoners who have come to Stillwater to spend time in the big institution which for so many years dominated the city from its position below the bluff on North Main street were the three Younger brothers. After becoming known as guerillas following the Civil War in Missouri, Kansas and Nebraska, they began branching out and covering more territory with their bank robberies. Finally, in 1876, they followed their leader, Jessie James, on the wild ride to Northfield, where their attempt to rob the bank met with such bitter repulse from the citizens that two bandits were killed and three Youngers were captured and sentenced to prison for life. Bob died in the old grey stone structure up Main street. Cole and Jim were instrumental in starting the Prison Mirror, they were active in the prison library work, and many Minnesotans worked for their release before they finally were paroled in the early 1900s. Neither man lived long after leaving prison, and neither succeeded in adjusting himself to enjoy the freedom he had been without so many years. The picture at the bottom of the page shows the old prison as it looked to those who gazed down on it from the Second street hill in winter; covered with a mantle of white over all the grey stone, the twine factory, the machine factory; with the grey watch towers looming up, and the river spread out before it. It is said that the two things the Youngers desired most to see when released were the river and the street cars. One they had not seen for 30 years, the other they had never seen. The prison was erected in Stillwater in 1858, and for many years women sentenced to prison had to be kept here. They were few and it was not possible to make much provision for their training. With the building of the Minnesota Reformatory for Women no more women were sent to Stillwater, and the big brick structure south of Stillwater now shelters more than 1,500 men serving sentences longer than a year.

BOB YOUNGER

The early days of Stillwater boasted of many fine homes and buildings. Among them were the old Minnesota State Prison, the Union Depot and the Isaac Staples property, that overlooked the town with its beautifully tiered vineyards. All these places were torn down, but could have been points of historical interest to our city and made to attract people from all over the world and brought in a substantial revenue.

COLE YOUNGER

Legend is that Stillwater was given the choice of the State Prison or the State University, and its business men chose the prison because at that time convict labor was available to carry on various industries operating in this city. The employment of convict labor was abandoned

Collected by John Runk, photographer, Stillwater, Minnesota U.S.A.
Historical Collection No. 436

Stillwater State Prison. (Courtesy of the Rice County Historical Society)

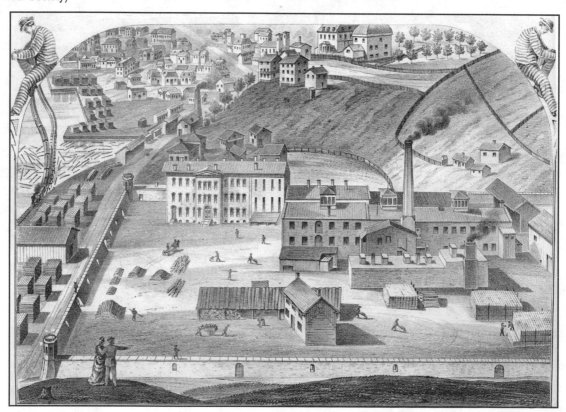

II

1876 to 1883

"I am proud to say to you we were raised by religious parents and attended Sunday school regular in our boyhood and I had charge of a bible class, while in Texas, at Seyene, Dallas County. I have always respected Christianity. I have known the right and endorse it. I condemn the wrong, but yet the wrong pursued."

—Cole Younger[1]

ays before the Youngers went to court in Faribault, officers of the Minnesota State Prison at Stillwater, anticipated that the Youngers would be sentenced to their facility and began preparations for their stay. In an interview with a reporter, Warden John A. Reed related that the cells had already been selected for them. He had decided to house them in apartments on the first floor, near the main entrance, which could easily be covered by the guards night and day. His plan was to remove them from communication with other prisoners so it would be simple to monitor their movements.[2]

On November 22, 1876, Cole, Jim and Bob entered Stillwater Penitentiary as Convicts #899, #900, and #901.[3] With them were Sheriff Ara Barton of Faribault and three deputies, who were handcuffed to the prisoners. This procedure was common with incoming prisoners considered "desperate fellows." The deputy warden frisked them, and their belongings were tied in a bundle and sent to the deputy warden's office where a receipt was issued. In the deputy warden's office, the men were weighed, questioned and read the rules of the institution.[4]

Walking into the prison yard, the three Younger brothers took a good look around, and one of the brothers was overheard to say he had found a home at last. Once placed in separate cells, they looked disappointed, and were quickly told they were not caged curiosities fed with luxury and leisure. Bob with his wounded stiff arm was handed a paintbrush.[5] Cole later wrote: "When the iron doors shut behind us at the Stillwater Prison, we all submitted to the prison discipline with the same unquestioning obedience that I had exacted during my military service."[6]

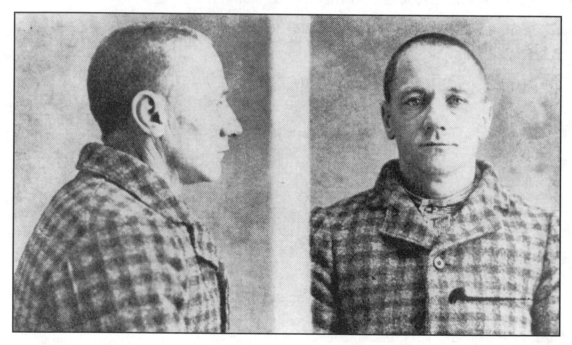

Cole Younger. (Courtesy of the Minnesota Historical Society)

A jubilant *St. Paul and Minneapolis Weekly Pioneer Press* reported that the outlaws were finally behind bars for good: "The three Missouri bandits and cut-throats, Cole, Jim, and Bob Younger, made their last appearance in St. Paul yesterday—at least it is hoped that we may never look upon their

ugly mugs again. Sheriff Barton, of Rice County, assisted by his
son and Messrs. J.H. Passon and Thomas Floyd, accompanied
the convicted scoundrels to the state prison, where they ha[d]
been sentenced to remain for life. The train containing their
unhung carcasses reached the lower levee at about eleven
o'clock, where a considerable crowd of people had assembled
to take a last or first look at the Missouri[ans] who have created such a sensation in Minnesota since the [seven]th day of
September last. Cole and Bob were shackled together and
occupied one seat, while opposite to and facing them sat the
genial Jim, who for safety was chained to the son of Sheriff
Barton."[7]

According to Cole, public opinion dictated that the
new convicts should be watched at all times, since many persons felt desperate men such as the Youngers could not be
held long behind prison bars.

The brothers were bathed and dressed in "penitentiary
stripes" of a third-grade prisoner. Prior to 1860, prisoners were
identified by having their heads shaved, but when John S.
Proctor had been appointed warden, he abolished the haircuts,
believing clothing made for easier identification.[8]

It did not take the three Youngers long to realize that
their new home was "not fit to keep hogs in, let alone human
beings." The buildings were poorly ventilated, damp and
uncomfortable, and overrun with roaches. Prisoners complained continually about the numerous bedbugs which drove
them "wild with pain and annoyance" and the prison stench
was "almost intolerable."[9]

The media thrived on the lack of glamour at the
prison and focused on the outlaws:

> So the romance is knocked out of all this murderous
> and horrible business, [declared a Twin Cities newspa-
> per.] Three vulgar and brutal ruffians, every one of
> whom richly deserves a gibbet, have passed from their
> reception rooms at Faribault—where they have been
> flattered and pampered for weeks, and where they have
> received their visitors with a benignity and patronage
> that was something royal in its style—to the penitentiary
> at Stillwater. Now let the warden at the prison see that
> they are kept there. The legislature of Minnesota has
> given these wretches their miserable lives—and it is
> hoped that an insecure prison will not give them their
> liberty also.[10]

Shortly after entering the penitentiary, Cole, Jim, and Bob were subjected to the Bertillion System for the Identification of Criminals. This system of measurement by means of anthropometric indications was anything but popular with the incoming inmates.

The first step measured the length of the head by caliper compasses. The operator placed and maintained the end of the left branch in the cavity of the root of the nose; then with his eyes fixed upon the graduation, he moved the right extremity up and down the middle of the back of the head until locating the maximum point. Then he was given a reading. The greatest width of the head was measured in the same fashion.[11]

Measurement of the left middle finger comprised the third step and was carried out by means of sliding compasses. This method was considered extremely valuable because it could be taken exactly independent of the subject.

A measurement of the left foot by sliding compasses comprised the fourth step. The prisoner was instructed to take a position standing and leaning forward on a firm solid bench. This position forced the "most stupid or wily person" to place himself in proper position so the measurement would be accurate.[12]

Fifthly, was the measurement of the left forearm by the same compasses. The operator demanded the prisoner stand in a leaning forward position. The operator then pressed the stationary branch closely against the point of the elbow, keeping the shank parallel to the axis of the arm.

Next, the right ear was measured by the compasses. Generally the measurement was taken after the length and width of the head, before using the large compasses, at a moment when the subject was standing erect. Operators of small stature, however, preferred measuring the prisoner in a seated position.

The Youngers were then subjected to measurement of height by means of the vertical and horizontal graduated measures. The test required the prisoner to be barefoot. Their outstretched arms were measured next via vertical and horizontal graduating measures. The measurement of the extended arms comprised the maximum length reached.

The prisoner was then seated well back on the bench and closely against the wall so his trunk could be measured.

The subject was told to hold his body erect against the wall. Other measurements were taken of eyes.

The men were fingerprinted, given complete physicals, and issued toiletries in their five-by-seven-foot cells.[13] Among the items each prisoner received were: a Bible, two cups, one small mirror, a spoon, face towel, dish towel, a comb, blankets, sheets, pillowcases, mattress, bedstead and springs, and a small bar of soap. Each cell contained a single cot and ventilation emanated from a six-inch hole in the wall. Narrow corridors frightened prison guards because they provided prisoners with an easy chance to attack their captors.[14]

The Youngers, as well as any other incoming prisoners, were issued three tickets entitling them to certain privileges as long as they followed the rules. Each week they were given one ration of tobacco, and they were allowed to write letters under grade rules. They could have visitors —family and friends, once every four weeks. All inmates were required to bathe once a week in summer and once every two weeks in winter.[15]

Officers from Missouri, who had come to Minnesota during confinement of the Youngers, were asked to file charges against the brothers, but they refused. Cole was a wanted man but Bob and Jim were not. According to the Missouri police, the Jameses and Youngers had been linked to several robberies, but they had never worked together.

Colonel and Mrs. H.W. Younger, parents of the Younger brothers. (Author collection)

"The Jameses are cold-blooded, deliberate murderers; the Youngers did hunt and kill the murderers of their father, who was waylaid, murdered and robbed of $5,000 by a party of Kansas jayhawkers," recorded a local newspaper. "They did not do this until after all efforts to bring them to justice through the law had failed. Since then Cole has been hunted like a tiger and has had no rest. He feels sorry for his brothers; but for himself he feels satisfied at being locked within prison walls."

Following a meeting with Warden Reed, the Youngers were given jobs making tubs and buckets in the prison basement with Ben Cayou as a special guard. Reed felt it was a sound idea to place the brothers together at one workstation where it would be easier to observe them. He had heard rumors that members of the James Gang might try to break the boys out at any time, so by putting the convicts together, he could concentrate key guards in one area. With Cayou watching over them, Cole dreamed about traveling to South America with Ben Butler's money. Union General Butler, despised by Southerners, had money in the First National Bank of Northfield, which may have led to the James-Younger Gang coming to Minnesota.[16]

Many of the inmates, working for Seymour and Sabin, commenced making threshing machines in 1876, and their product—the new Minnesota Chief, was called "the most successful thresher in the world." Seymour and Sabin became the largest manufacturers of thresher equipment in the country. The inmates at the Minnesota State Prison were anything but idle.[17]

News of the escape of Frank and Jesse James reached the prison on November 30 via a Twin Cities newspaper. The article summarized the flight of the robbers, the split between the Youngers and the Jameses, and touched on Jesse and Frank's ride to freedom. The Youngers were, undoubtedly, pleased that their confederates had reached home safely and no trace of their whereabouts had surfaced.[18]

Soon, the Youngers advanced to second-grade prisoners, were issued different uniforms, permitted to grow their hair to any preferred length, and allowed to visit with each other once a month. Assigned new jobs in the thresher factory, Cole made sieves, and Jim made belts. Since Bob could not straighten his injured arm, he was given the therapeutic job of painting walls. In their free time, the boys were given access to the prison library, and all three became enthusiastic readers.[19]

The prison library boasted about 6,000 titles with an emphasis on history, biography, science, art, fiction, poetry, and bound magazines. Works of fiction were most popular among the inmates, although they were carefully screened by prison personnel before being added to the library catalog. Thus, books of a sensational nature, such as the "Dead-Eye Dick" variety were considered in poor taste and were excluded from the library collection.[20]

By good behavior and adherence to prison regulations, prisoners could advance all the way to first-grade status in only six months. If any prisoner received two demerits in a single month, however, he would be sent all the way down to third-grade. He would then be required to keep a clean slate for three consecutive months before returning to second-grade status.

A typical meal at Stillwater called for boiled corned beef, mashed potatoes, two kinds of bread but no butter, and cabbage usually cut into slaw. The prisoners ate in long rows and were not permitted to speak to one another. Should a prisoner want an additional slab of corned beef, he had to raise his hand. Once they were finished with their meal, they were required to sit up and fold their hands.[21]

Every cell, as well as the corridors, was scrubbed and whitewashed every day. Most of the pictures hanging in the prisoners' cells were gaudy and cheap, but occasionally an inmate displayed a picture of Christ, a priest, or a boy at prayer.

A young reporter was allowed to visit Cole in the library. He quickly asked Cole what he thought had caused the birth of guerrillas in Missouri. Cole gave a lengthy answer after telling the young man the subject would take an entire volume in itself. He discussed the laying out of Independence by Joseph Smith and Brigham Young, and called his fellow Missourians born fighters. When asked to relate the circumstances surrounding the Northfield tragedy, Cole answered:

"I will give no details of that robbery or any other that is laid at our door. I tell everyone the same thing. I do this not out of unkindly feelings for your questions but not to say anything that might reflect upon our friends."[22]

When asked how long he received medical attention after his capture in the swamp, Cole explained they were still receiving medical attention and probably would for the rest of their lives. The reporter asked Cole if he and his brothers had specific duties in prison and Cole replied:

> No, Jim and I do very little as we are on the hospital list, but Bob performs various duties. I occupy much of my time in theological studies for which I seem to have a natural inclination. It was the earliest desire of my parents to prepare me for the ministry, but the horrors of war, the murder of my father, and the outrages perpetrated upon my poor old mother, my sisters, and my brothers, destroyed our hopes that any of us could be prepared for any duty in life except revenge.[23]

Most of their visitors that initial year in prison, however, were ladies from various Women's Clubs, who were always anxious to ask them if they wished they had led different lives. Cole, always polite and charming, assured them he wished he had.[24] Grace Yates, formerly of Madelia and a relative of one of the captors, made several visits to the prison to visit the Youngers. She always brought with her a bag of goodies for the three brothers.[25]

A representative of the St. Paul chapter of the Phrenological Society, who studied the "configurations of the human head," visited Cole that same year. The organizer of this strange group was a New Yorker named Orson Fowler, who had created a chart that showed from bumps just how the human head worked. Fowler's techniques were so popular with the public that many persons made the journey to New York to have their heads read.

Professor George Morris of St. Paul visited Cole at Stillwater to plumb the depths of his brain. Cole was seated in a chair in the warden's office when Morris opened his little bag, withdrew a tape measure, measured Cole's head, and recorded his findings. Morris produced a pair of calipers and then measured the bumps on Cole's head. Finally, the professor placed a paper-mâché mask over Cole's head and fitted it to the skull. When Morris left, Cole was as thoroughly mystified as when he had entered the room.

In February 1877, the Youngers had a surprise visitor. According to the *Stillwater Gazette:* "The brave young chap, Oscar Suborn [Sorbel], who gave prompt notice of the whereabouts of the raiders near Madelia, and was thus instrumental in the capture of the Younger gang, came over Saturday with the Solons, and took a look at 'poor Cole Younger painting pails.'"[26]

Since the Youngers' trial in Faribault less than a year earlier, public outrage demanded the law be changed that permitted the boys to escape death. While the brothers would continue to serve their sentences, a bill proposing "an amendment to our Penal Statutes, in reference to the punishment for murder committed in this state, which shall not leave it optional with the criminal to escape merited punishment by pleading guilty," passed the Minnesota House of Representatives in its 1877 session only to die in the Senate. The 1877 legislature also appropriated three thousand dollars to pay the expenses of the numerous posse members who had hunted the Youngers, and another four thousand for rewards. The legislature also saw fit to thank those who "resisted the attempt of the gang of brigands, commanded by Cole Younger, to rob the Northfield bank."[27]

In 1879, Dr. Clarke, the prison physician, tried to remove the bullet that lay close to the brain of Jim Younger; a wound that had been causing him unbearable pain. Dr. Clarke made an incision in the roof of the mouth, but his efforts to loosen the bullet were in vain. Still in pain, Jim convinced a hospital intern to try the procedure. The intern worked on the wound for two days and succeeded in dislodging it from near the salivary gland and throat muscles. The pain eventually disappeared, but Jim was left with a badly disfigured face and slurred speech. His jaw would not work properly, and he had to resort to drinking liquid gruel through a straw from a galvanized bucket.[28]

Jim dug deeper into the dogmas of socialism as he became more and more depressed and despondent. Because of his deep state of depression, many inmates and prison officials considered him on the verge of insanity.

In November 1879, the *St. Paul Pioneer Press* carried a story that Cole Younger denied being in any bank raid in Missouri since the Civil War. Cole's alleged statement read:

> Now I admit that I went east with fifty thousand dollars of U.S. bonds and exchanged them for greenbacks for other parties and they gave me five thousand dollars when I returned with their money. I ask[ed] no questions though I have an idea where they got it. They were all ex-Confederates that had been driven from their homes and they trusted to my honor and honesty gave me fifty thousand to exchange without the scratch of a pin, and when I returned from N.Y. with their money

they said there was not another man on earth they would have trusted and I never did give their names to a soul on earth nor never will. I know it was wrong but wrong or right I never betraid [sic] a friend.[29]

While the Youngers and other prisoners were working, Thursday, December 11, 1879, many of them witnessed a tragedy. A convict committed from Hennepin County, named John Clark, was reported to a guard as insubordinate. A few days earlier Clark had attacked a fellow convict named Ramsden with a putty-knife, and had it not been for the interference of others, would have killed the man. After being locked up in solitary confinement, Clark was eventually released and put to painting wagon wheels. Although a prisoner would easily paint forty wagons a day, Clark did only fifteen to eighteen. When he was told he had to paint twenty, he refused. Upon being informed by the guard of Clark's refusal, Deputy Warden Hall walked to the paint shop and ordered Clark and another shirker to their cells. The other prisoner followed orders, but Clark profanely refused to do so. Hall took out his pocket watch and told Clark he had only three minutes to do as instructed. At the end of five minutes, Hall drew his revolver and asked the prisoner if he would obey. Clark stated an emphatic, "No!" Hall shot Clark through the heart and killed him. A coroner's jury exonerated Mr. Hall from any criminality, as Clark was a desperate character, and at the time of the confrontation, was clutching a double-edged putty-knife, which he would have used on anyone coming near him. While many prisoners and guards were stunned, the Youngers had witnessed their share of violence over the years, and this killing perhaps did not affect them in many ways. Still, it was the talk of the prison for many weeks.[30]

Colonel and Mrs. George Gaston of Kansas City visited the brothers in 1880. According to Gaston, he and his wife were met by an officer with keys at the top of the stairs. The visitors were told to follow him into a square room with walls and ceilings of stone. After they were seated, Cole, Jim, and Bob Younger walked into the room through a side door and took chairs directly opposite. Gaston said the men looked very "genteel," despite their prison garb. Their faces were closely shaven and their hair cropped. Jim told the Gastons it had been so long since he had talked with anyone, he barely remembered how to speak.[31]

Cole conveyed that his health was poor, and he was feeling the ill effects of the wound in his head, received at the time of his capture. The rifle ball had entered his head near the right ear and had lodged under his left ear. It had never been removed. Jim, although he had been shot in the mouth, showed very few signs of pain or discomfort. Bob's jaw had been broken, but like Jim, he seemed to have recovered. Mrs. Gaston found Bob the handsomest of the trio.

Cole talked about his younger days, how at the age of nineteen, he had been promoted to captain in the Confederate army. He touched upon the murder of his father, his own career since the close of the war, and stated his outlaw career had been greatly exaggerated. Gaston called Cole a changed man and found him "positively entertaining."

View of the old state prison at Stillwater, ca. 1880. (Courtesy of the Minnesota Historical Society)

The visitors learned that none of the brothers were given much work to do; thus, they spent a great deal of time reading in their cells. Jim was studying law books, Bob medicine, and Cole theology. They related they prayed nightly that each month would pass quickly. What fascinated the visitors was the way in which the convicts looked up to them almost to the point of idolatry.

Cole asked about old army friends with tears in his eyes, and the Gastons related what they knew of each acquaintance. Cole was asked about the recent rumor that George Shepherd had killed Jesse James, to which Cole conveyed his fear that the news might be correct.

On May 1, 1881, Cole penned a letter to author J.A. Dacus in which he called the rumors of "The Black Oath" absolutely ridiculous. According to several persons, the oath was taken by new recruits into Quantrill's army, which Cole termed, "a myth originating in the brain of some irresponsible, badly informed and reckless chronicler." Cole also blasted the

Guards at the old state prison at Stillwater, ca. 1880. (Courtesy of the Minnesota Historical Society)

myth that Missouri guerrillas were not recognized by the Confederacy as Confederate
soldiers. These men took the same oath as
all Confederate soldiers and were recognized as soldiers of the South by all the generals in the Trans-Mississippi Department.
Cole maintained that the mix-up may have
occurred because the Confederate War
Department had refused to give Quantrill a
commission as colonel of partisan rangers;
but they did recognize him as captain with
all authority to recruit as many companies
for the Confederate service as he could.[32]

In July 1881, a pamphlet entitled,
"A Brief History of the Younger Brothers
and the Reasons Why They Should Be
Pardoned," was published by a group of ex-
Confederates. The piece, patterned after
John Newman Edwards' essay, "A Terrible
Quintet," focused upon the treatment of
the brothers during the war against the
South. Unfortunately for the Youngers,
the chapbook was riddled with errors, and
it made little effect on the general public.

William Clarke Quantrill. (Author's
Collection)

That same month, members of the James Gang held up
a Rock Island train near Winston, Missouri. The conductor,
William Westfall, had been taking tickets when three bearded
men leaped up with revolvers. One of the men stuck his face in
Westfall's, stared, and exclaimed, "You're the man I want!" The
man fired several shots at Westfall, as did a second robber, one
of the bullets tearing through his skull, killing him.[33]

According to several sources, it was Frank who fired
the initial shots at Westfall but Jesse who killed him. Gang
member Bill "Whiskey Head" Ryan was convicted for the slay-
ing and sent to the Missouri Penitentiary for twenty-five years.

That same year, the boys' uncle, Littleton T. Younger,
of St. Clair County, Missouri, came to Minnesota to work for
a pardon for his nephews. When he appealed to Governor
John S. Pillsbury, he was told in no uncertain terms, "When I
think of poor [Joseph Lee] Heywood, the cashier, refusing with
a heroism that has no parallel to forsake his trust, and when I
remember how your nephews murdered him in the coldest of

Young Jesse James. Photo by
B.A. Bottain. (Courtesy the
National Archives)

blood, intense indignation fills my breast, and instead of feeling that they have been punished sufficiently, I am more and
more convinced that death would have been a juster and more
righteous penalty."[34]

Littleton Younger returned later in the year for another private meeting with Governor Pillsbury. This time he was
armed with numerous letters written by influential persons in
Missouri, all requesting a Younger pardon. Pillsbury, however,
was adamant about the boys staying put, and he again denied
the request.[35]

On April 3, 1882, Jesse James was shot from behind
and killed by Bob Ford. Bob Younger was greatly affected by
the death of his friend Jesse. Jim, on the other hand, was probably relieved that Jesse's influence over his younger brother

was over. Cole believed that the reported death of Jesse was a hoax, another means of getting the Youngers to admit, at last, that the James brothers were involved in the Northfield robbery. He asked his sister Retta to visit St. Joseph, Missouri, and view the body to ascertain whether Jesse was really dead. Publicly, however, the Youngers gave no statements regarding Jesse's demise. They had earlier stated they had not been involved with the James brothers nor seen them since the close of the Civil War.[36]

Cole was conducted to the warden's office by a guard on April 4 and told of Jesse's murder. Cole, a model prisoner, had to be careful what he said as he still garnished the hope his sentence would be commuted. When pressed for a statement by the warden, he uttered, "I knew him when we were with Quantrill's Guerrillas. I have no sympathy for men engaged in the kind of things he is reported to have been in."[37] Cole never again mentioned the James boys while in prison, unless it was in a direct response to a question.[38]

On April 17, Bob Ford and his brother/accomplice Charlie, were indicted on charges of murder in the first degree. The brothers pled guilty as charged and were sentenced to death by hanging. Governor Crittenden, however, intervened and pardoned the boys.[39]

Frank James was with his family in Lynchburg, Virginia, when Jesse was killed. Only Frank had been able to stay away from crime, and even though Jesse had informed his family he was going to give up outlawry, Frank believed his brother would have had a difficult time leading a normal life.[40]

Bob Ford. (*Frank Leslie's Illustrated Newspaper*, April 22, 1882)

Jesse James house in St. Joseph, Missouri (Author's Collection)

Jesse James. (Courtesy of the National Archives)

The Judge, a satirical magazine in its first year of publication, proposed on April 22 that a monument be erected in Jesse's honor. While focusing on train and stage robberies, the monument would also feature a model of Jesse's home. Guns, daggers, and revolvers would be displayed within the house as well as three plaques bearing the messages: "Bless Our Home," "What is a home without a Revolver," and "What a Friend I Have in Jesus and My Revolver."[41]

During late summer, a blind woman stood before the courthouse in Springfield, Missouri, singing an ode to Jesse James. The song, composed by Billy Gashade shortly after Jesse's death, caught the attention of many passersby, who dropped coins in the blind woman's cup.

Frank and his friend, John Newman Edwards, met with Missouri Governor Thomas Crittenden and other state officials to discuss a surrender on October 4, 1882, in Jefferson City. They registered at the McCarty House, with Frank using the name "B.F. Winfrey" of Marshall, Missouri. The following morning, the pair took a stroll through the city while Governor Crittenden announced to a group of officials and newspaper reporters, he would have something important to show them at five o'clock.[42]

The meeting was held almost six months to the day of Jesse's death. When the governor remarked about the well-worn leather belt with a big bronze buckle in the shape of the "U.S.," Frank informed him it was a Union belt he had taken off a dead Federal soldier at Centralia, Missouri.[43]

Two days later, Frank was sent to the jail in Independence, Missouri, to await trial. Frank remained in official police custody for one year and two months while his participation in the Winston train robbery was investigated. Frank was charged not only with complicity in the robbery but for the murder of Frank McMillan.

During a train ride from the state capitol to Independence, spectators greeted him at every stop. For Frank, the train ride proved triumphal and the *Kansas City Journal* declared, "Had the train stopped long enough he would have

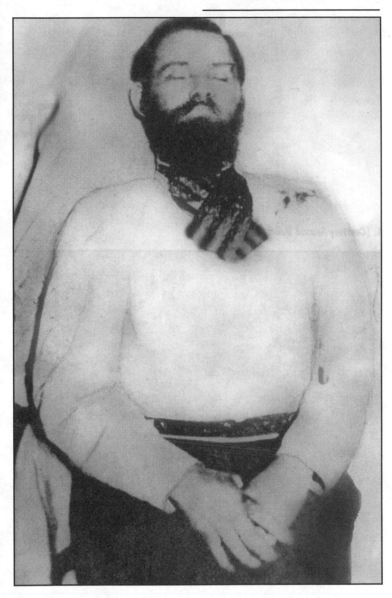

Jesse James after death. Photo by Uhlman. This photograph was used as an identifying photo, as Uhlman turned the hand to show the missing thumb on the right hand. (Courtesy of the National Archives)

been given an ovation at every station." Judge Henry of the Missouri Supreme Count was moved to remark, "He has won my sympathy already."[44]

Many people lined the tracks at Independence to greet the famous outlaw. Among the crowd of greeters were Frank's mother, Zerelda, his wife, Annie, and their four-year-old son, Robert. Frank and his family were allowed to spend some time together in a local hotel before he was taken to the jail.[45]

When Frank went to trial in the famous old courthouse in Gallatin, he was accompanied by eight lawyers; one of them later became a member of President Woodrow Wilson's cabinet, another a federal judge. Prosecutor William H. Wallace, who vowed to "Break up the James Gang," had eighty-nine witnesses backing him up. Frank James, on the other hand, had but thirty-nine. Frank finally went to trial on August 21, 1883. The trial was a sensation with even the governor called to testify, and General Jo Shelby nearly disrupted the court in taking the stand. The Missouri hero stepped from the witness chair and shook hands with everyone in reach, including the judge and the defendant. A sympathetic jury found Frank not guilty. Charges against Frank for the killing of William Westfall during the Winston robbery were dropped.

After walking away a free man, Frank was, however, arraigned in Huntsville, Alabama, on April 17 of the following year, where he stood trial for the Muscle Shoals robbery. After a ten-day trial, Frank was acquitted, although he was immediately arrested and charged with having been involved in the Rocky Cut robbery of 1876. But the charges were dropped by the governor of Missouri in February 1885, leaving Frank James a free man and forty-two years old.

Cole must have been elated in learning of his best friend's freedom, although his health was poor during this time. Throughout the fall of 1882, Cole and Jim were in sickbay, either in the prison hospital or confined to bed in their cells. This practice of inactivity via a real or feigned illness, continued well into 1884.[46] The period between October 1882 and January 1883 was especially tough on the Youngers:

October 9, 1882 to October 12, 1882—Cole in hospital.
October 18, 1882 to October 25, 1882—Cole and Jim in hospital.
November 1, 1882 to November 8, 1882—Jim in hospital.
November 11, 1882—Cole confined to bed in cell.
November 16, 1882—Cole and Jim in hospital.
November 27, 1882—Jim confined to bed in cell.
December 2, 1882—Cole in bed in cell.
December 13, 1882—Jim in bed in cell.
January 2, 1883—Jim and Cole in bed in cells.
January 5, 1883—Jim and Cole in bed in cells.

Prison physician Dr. Merrill examined the brothers. Cole was diagnosed with chronic pain and numerous microscopic organisms. Jim's report stated he was "erect and well

nourished with a few scars from bullet wounds." The examination also reported a bullet hole in the roof of Jim's mouth
[from his capture near Madelia] and the loss of his upper
front teeth. The mental health of both prisoners was listed as
good.[47]

During an 1883 legislative tour of Stillwater Penitentiary, the Younger brothers were visited, and a reporter from a
Twin Cities' newspaper interviewed the brothers. "Of the
prison celebrities, those life-term convicts, the Younger brothers, came in for a large share of attention. . . . Their cells,
which are on the ground floor in the second corridor, were surrounded continuously by a crowd of visitors. The chief interest to those familiar with the story of their crimes was in seeing how they bear their imprisonment, which has now ended
the sixth year of their sentence for life."[48]

The reporter was quick to note that the Youngers
received no special privileges. Cole was the only one of the
brothers in his cell when the journalist and others passed
through the cellblock as Bob and Jim were working. Cole
appeared to be in poor health, his close-clipped hair sprinkled
with gray. When the reporter said to Cole that the prisoner
looked more than age forty-five, the outlaw told him he was
only thirty-nine.

"I was shot quite to pieces," remarked Cole. "Here in
the face, in the neck here, behind the ear, and through my
shoulder. There is a ball still in my head, and one in my
breast." A visitor out of sight snapped that Cole did not like to
be addressed by simple curiosity hunters, but Cole answered,
"Someone says he doesn't want to look at me just out of
curiosity. Oh, I don't mind that. I'm used to it, and I used to
go see curiosities myself when I was a boy. . . ."[49]

A visitor in the crowd pushed his way forward and
asked Cole how long he was to be incarcerated. Cole told the
man he was serving a life term. "There isn't a requisition for
me in existence, that I know of," said Cole. "There was, I
believe, an indictment or two against me at Northfield, but
they found that two clerks were the only persons in the bank
where the cashier was killed. . . . I never had a trial except in
name. I was sentenced without a real trial. . . ."

Just then the dinner bell rang, and the prisoners filed
in from the shops. Among them were Bob and Jim Younger.
Bob sat with his back to the crowd of visitors, but Jim did not

touch his meal, preferring to talk instead: "The shot here in my mouth, and the one in my neck, is what's the matter with my voice . . . I got twelve different shots." Jim went on to explain he once weighed 165 pounds but was down to 149 in prison.

The reporter noted the prisoners' meal consisted of bread, coffee in a tin cup, meat (probably corn beef), baked beans, and a single raw onion. But the reporter added, "The Younger boys, if not other prisoners, seemed to have an addition of some nicely browned potatoes."

Bob became an accounting clerk, working with the prison steward, in 1883. This type of work was much easier for Bob, who had been plagued by illnesses. His chronic cough had depleted his energy, and procuring the clerk position was much to his liking.

Dr. Lydall Twyman, uncle of the Youngers. (Lyndon Irwin Collection)

Mrs. Frances Twyman, the brothers' aunt, became active in a parole drive for her nephews. Her husband, Dr. Lydall Twyman, was highly respected in Missouri, and the Twymans were considered society in Jackson County. She believed that if she could raise several prominent people in a parole plea, the brothers might be released. She also considered the many Minnesotans who had shown kindness in the past to the brothers. Sheriff Ara Barton of Rice County, according to Mrs. Twyman, was a good person to approach, but Bob sent her a letter stating that a plea to Barton was futile.[50]

During the fall of that same year, Lee Morgan, a former Quantrill man and friend of Cole's, visited the Youngers at Stillwater. Morgan had informed relatives in Carlisle, Iowa, that he and others were planning to liberate the three brothers. When Morgan returned to Iowa, he told his brother the boys wouldn't be in Stillwater long. Morgan's brother, a former Union man from the Twenty-third Iowa Infantry, was angry and told the conspirator, "Lee, if you and those Southerners try to liberate those killers and bank robbers, I'll tell you those Minnesotians [sic] will just shoot all kinds of hell out of all of you, and there won't be enough of you left to ship back in a pine box." Shortly thereafter, the plan was called off.[51]

As early as 1877, two ex-Quantrill men decided by getting into the prison, they could escape with the Youngers. Both men committed petty crimes for which they expected to be sent to Stillwater Prison. One of the men spent a brief term in the county jail, but the other did spend a year in the Stillwater penitentiary. During that entire year, however, he never sighted the Youngers, and their plan to free them quickly fizzled.[52]

But Morgan and the Quantrill may not have been the only friends of the Youngers planning on liberating the brothers. One account alleges that during their final months at the Peace Ranch, near San Angelo, Texas, even Frank and Jesse James were discussing plans to free their comrades from Stillwater Prison. No one had ever rescued anyone from the penitentiary before, but according to the Jameses, no one before them had ever robbed a bank or train either.[53] (The Reno Brothers of Indiana had, in fact, robbed trains before the Jameses.)

The rescue plan upon which they settled required twelve men and fifteen horses. Rescuing their comrades constituted only half the scheme; the James boys were determined to "defy the whole much-hated state of Minnesota." Jesse approved of eight men to attempt the rescue: He and Frank, Billy Judson, Jim Cummins, Stanley Little, Jim Reed, Jim Anderson, and Bill Ryan. He chose these men because they were completely unafraid, did not drink, and were willing to die in the attempt if necessary. He considered twenty other men but found them lacking in some of the required qualities. Ed Miller, brother of Clell, who had been killed in the streets of Northfield during the raid, was one of those who did not meet the requirements. Jesse felt, while he put up a good front, there was something furtive about him.

One of the men, Stanley Little, was to fill the role of a county sheriff, and the rest of the gang would ride in twos and threes to a short distance from Stillwater. A good team and a closed carriage would be waiting for them.

The plan called for Stanley to send a telegram to the warden at Stillwater Prison, conveying that as a country sheriff, he was bringing in

Billy Judson in 1885. (Courtesy of Hon. James R. Ross)

Jim Cummins (standing) with friend or relative. (Courtesy of the Armand DeGregoris Collection)

three prisoners. Since he had missed his last train connection, he would deliver them in a carriage; he did not want to hold them overnight. Stanley would explain the carriage would be holding the three convicts and three guards. Two other gang members were to ride on the rear of the carriage, drop off and cover the gate guards.

Once inside the institution, Stanley and his three "guards," would cover the officers, force one of them to the cells of the Youngers, and release them. The officers in the prison office would be tied up securely. The gang members would then trade clothing with the captured officers, but if that failed, they still could blast their way out with their guns. The outlaws outside the gates would be holding their horses, and a dash for Missouri would ensue with the Youngers among them.

The plan, if there is any truth in it at all, was canceled, however, before it could be executed. The continued physical deterioration of the three Youngers placed the plan at high risk, because the brothers were almost continually confined to the prison hospital with their multiple wounds. Not one of the Youngers had the physical stamina to withstand a long ride back to Missouri. The Jameses waited another year, hoping for good news of the Youngers' recovery but their status had not changed. Soon, they were confronted with other problems and the Stillwater raid never materialized.[54]

In 1883, a troupe of actors began performing a drama about Jesse James at Tootle's Opera House in St. Joseph, Missouri. Two horses that allegedly had belonged to Jesse were used on stage—one a roan charger said to have been in Jesse's stable, only yards from where he was gunned down by Bob Ford. A stage company spokesman said the second horse—Bay Raider—had also belonged to Jesse James.[55]

That same year, the State of Minnesota during a period of diversification of state institutions, realized that its prison, hospital, and school populations needed an upgrading. On the recommendation of Governor Lucius F. Hubbard, a central State Board of Corrections and Charities was organized. Although it lacked the authority needed to serve its purpose, it was responsible for the investigation of "the whole system of public charities and correctional institutions of the state."[56]

The new board was authorized to examine closely the management of prisons, jails, infirmaries, public hospitals, and asylums, and to offer recommendations for improvement and

advancement. Hastings Hornell Hart, a social-minded minister from Worthington was appointed secretary of the board. Hart reported "miserable, even horrifying" conditions in county jails and poorhouses and urged the need of uniform accounting in correctional facilities. A parole system was inaugurated at the Stillwater State Prison and a reformatory established in St. Cloud, with a youth rehabilitation school organized in Red Wing.

  For those individuals incarcerated in state institutions, reform was on the horizon. But for the Younger brothers, serving life sentences in Stillwater Prison, it would be years before that reform would be realized.

View of the state prison car shop and the St. Croix River looking south from the north bluff at Stillwater, Minnesota, ca. 1882. Photo by J.M. Kuhn of Stillwater. (Courtesy of the Minnesota Historical Society)

Notes

[1]*Martin County Sentinel*, September 29, 1876.

[2]Ruth Rentz Yates, *Before Their Identity*, p. 21.

[3]Document signed by Warden John A. Reed for receipt of prisoners from A. Barton of Rice County. Author's Collection.

[4]Dallas Cantrell, *Northfield, Minnesota Youngers' Fatal Blunder*, San Antonio, The Naylor Company, 1973, pp. 91-92.

[5]*Faribault Democrat*, Friday, November 24, 1876, "In Prison."

[6]Cole Younger, *The Story of Cole Younger By Himself*, St. Paul, Minnesota Historical Society Press, 2000, p. 90.

[7]*St. Paul and Minneapolis Weekly Pioneer Press*, November 30, 1876.

[8]Brent T. Peterson and Dean R. Thilgen, *Stillwater, A Photographic History*, p. 51.

[9]Patricia Condon Johnston, *Stillwater Minnesota's Birthplace*, pp. 65-66.

[10]*St. Paul and Minneapolis Weekly Pioneer Press*, November 30, 1876.

[11]Alix J. Muller, *A History of the Police and Fire Departments in the Twin Cities*, St. Paul, 1889, pp. 13-16.

[12]Ibid.

[13]W.C. Heilbron, *Convict Life at the Minnesota State Prison*, W. C. Heilbron, St. Paul, 1909, p. 13-16, 23-27.

[14]*St. Paul Daily News*, Friday, June 26, 1936.

[15]W.C. Heilbron, *Convict Life at the Minnesota State Prison*, pp. 115-116.

[16]Marley Brant, *The Outlaw Youngers: A Confederate Brotherhood*, Lanham, New York, London, Madison Books, 1992, p. 217; Cole Younger, *The Story of Cole Younger by Himself*, p. 90.

[17]Patricia Condon Johnston, *Stillwater Minnesota's Birthplace*, p. 65.

[18]*St. Paul & Minneapolis Pioneer Press*, Thursday, November 30, 1876.

[19]Cole Younger, *The Story of·Cole Younger by Himself*, p. 90.

[20]W.C. Heilbron, *Convict Life at the Minnesota State Prison*, p. 97.

[21]F.E. Stratton letter to daughter Alice, February 1904, published in *Historical Whisperings*, Washington County Historical Society, Vol. 9, No. 1, April 1982, pp. 1-2.

[22]Carl W. Breihan, *Ride the Razor's Edge: The Younger Brothers Story*, Gretna, Pelican Publishing Company, 1882, p. 238.

[23]Ibid., p. 239.

[24]Homer Croy, *Last of the Great Outlaws*, New York, The New

American Library, 1958, pp. 118-119.

[25]Buster Yates, *Seventy-Five Years on the Watonwan*, no publisher given, 1986, p. 157.

[26]*Stillwater Gazette*, February 7, 1877, p. 4.

[27]*St. Paul Pioneer Press & Tribune*, November 21, 1876; *House Journal*, 1877, p. 41.

[28]Dallas Cantrell, *Northfield, Minnesota: Youngers' Fatal Blunder*, pp. 95-96.

[29]*St. Paul Pioneer Press*, November 1879.

[30]J. Fletcher Williams, *History of Washington County and the St. Croix Valley*, p. 536.

[31]Dallas Cantrell, *Northfield, Minnesota: Youngers' Fatal Blunder*, pp. 93-95.

[32]Carl W. Breihan, *Younger Brothers: Cole, James, Bob, John*, San Antonio, The Naylor Company, 1961, p. 188.

[33]Paul I. Wellman, *A Dynasty of Western Outlaws*, New York, Bonanza Books, 1961, pp. 115-119.

[34]Walter D. Trenerry, *Murder in Minnesota*, St. Paul, Minnesota Historical Society, 1962, pp. 101-102.

[35]Marley Brant, *Outlaws: The Illustrated History of the James-Younger Gang*, Montgomery, Alabama, Elliott & Clark Publishing, 1997, p. 161.

[36]Marley Brant, *The Outlaw Youngers*, p. 225.

[37]Harry Sinclair Drago, *Outlaws on Horseback*, Lincoln & London, University of Nebraska Press, 1998, p. 84.

[38]Evan Jones, *The Minnesota*, Minneapolis, University of Minnesota Press, 1990, p. 241.

[39]Sybil Montana, *Bob Ford was his Name, Jesse James was his Game*, Springfield, Missouri, Sybil Montana, 2001, pp. 59-60.

[40]Stella Frances James, *In the Shadow of Jesse James*, Thousand Oaks, California, The Revolver Press, Dragon Books, 1989, p. 30.

[41]Roger A. Bruns, *The Bandit Kings: From Jesse James to Pretty Boy Floyd*, New York, Crown Publishers, Inc., 1995, p. 24.

[42]Marley Brant, *Outlaws: The Illustrated History of the James-Younger Gang*, p. 175.

[43]Homer Croy, *Jesse James Was My Neighbor*, New York, Duell, Sloan and Pearce, 1949, pp. 202-210; Thurston James, "Frank James—The Post—Outlaw Years," *James-Younger Gang Journal*, Spring 2001, p. 9.

[44]Betty Sterett, *Scenes from the Past*, 1985, p. 96.

[45]Marley Brant, *Outlaws The Illustrated History of the James-Younger Gang*, p. 175.

[46]Daily Medical Records. Northfield, Minnesota Bank

Robbery of 1876: Selected Manuscripts Collections and Government Records, Microfilm Edition, Roll 3, Minnesota Historical Society.

[47]Medical Examination File. Northfield, Minnesota Bank Robbery of 1876: Selected Manuscripts Collections and Government Records, Microfilm Edition, Roll 3, Minnesota Historical Society.

[48]"Life in Minnesota in St. Paul's First Hundred Years," undated newspaper article, Northfield Public Library collection.

[49]Ibid.

[50]Marley Brant, *The Outlaw Youngers*, p. 231.

[51]C.W. Deaton, "Plot to Free the Youngers Failed," published in *Northfield Independent*, Date Unknown, Collection of Northfield Public Library.

[52]Dallas Cantrell, *Northfield, Minnesota Youngers' Fatal Blunder*, p. 97.

[53]James R. Ross, *I, Jesse James*, Dragon Publishing Company, 1989, pp. 221-224.

[54]Ibid.

[55]Roger A. Bruns, *The Bandit Kings*, pp. 24-25.

[56]Theodore C. Blegen, *Minnesota: A History of the State*, Minneapolis, University of Minnesota Press, 1963, pp. 435-436.

A view in Stillwater, Minnesota, in 1882, showing the Minnesota State Prison and the St. Croix River. (John Runk Collection. Courtesy of the Minnesota Historical Society)

III

1884 to 1885

"On the border of our state, where the red lightning of murder played the fiercest among the western sky and the dogs of war were turned loose on innocent women and children, I saw it all; where torch, and fire, and sword and rapine, and pillage, and plunder, and robbery, and murder, and assassinations were abroad in the land; when sabred horsemen shot across the prairies and devouring flames leaped from house to house, until both earth and sky seemed ablaze with living horrors."

—Hon. W.H. Wallace
at the trial of Frank James[1]

hile rumors circulated regarding an assault on the prison by friends of the Youngers, other stories spread just as quickly that gang members were searching for Oscar Sorbel, the youth who had ridden into Madelia and alerted people to their presence in the Madelia area. While he was directly responsible for their capture, he received little for his efforts. Young Sorbel was paid only a seventy-eight dollar reward, and his dash into Madelia had ruined his father's horse. This was but small compensation compared to that of the seven men who made the actual capture. Each received $240.[2]

Friends of the Youngers supposedly hunted Sorbel and allegedly found him on two occasions living in Montana. When the young man was asked if he was the one who had ridden into Madelia, Sorbel immediately sensed danger and insisted it had been his brother.

With friends of the Youngers contemplating violence, near disaster at Stillwater came, not from an attempted prison break, but through fire. On January 8, 1884, at about 10:45 P.M., flames were discovered in the sash, door, and blind shop. Within minutes, the fire spread through the hardwood and wagon shops, boiler room, engine, blacksmith and cooper shops, all of which were totally consumed. Fireman fought to save a building containing a large amount of valuable moldings and manufactured lumber and an ironclad building full of casting patterns.[3]

Gus Lindahl, a watchman responsible for monitoring the steam heating and water supply, discovered the blaze in the third floor glazing room of the wood shops. Another guard, John Walton, joined Lindahl in an attempt to put out the flames, but the two men met with no success and quickly sounded the alarm. By the time the St. Paul Fire Department arrived, flames were shooting out of the windows of the four-story building.[4]

A local newspaper described the blaze: "The gutters became babbling brooks, then increased to rapid streams and a few seconds later had swollen to rivers that carried everything before them irresistible at the speed of a mill race . . ."[5]

The fire did not reach the cellblock, but there was a genuine concern for the prisoners when the flames spread to within fifty feet of the inmates. The convicts were not removed from the building, although Warden Reed had them taken from their cells and chained together in gangs. Reed then called out Company K of the state militia, and fifty men under Captain Merry arrived to watch the prisoners. The inmates remained docile and did not panic.[6]

A problem occurred when the firefighters failed to properly connect the penitentiary hose with the city hydrants, and the valves originally opened by Lindahl and Walton reduced the pressure on the stand pipes on the inside of the prison yard. The woodworking shops contained a large amount of flammable materials, and before the firefighters could get started, the shops were ablaze.

Prison officials believed the blaze was deliberately set by convicts, although no one was charged. Damages caused by the fire amounted to about $300,000 and 300 men lost their jobs.

On January 25, disaster struck again. About 11:45 P.M., O.A. Watler was passing by the prison on his way home from a professional visit when he noticed a bright light in the basement beneath the car company's offices. Watler immediately rode to the engine house and notified the watchman. The alarm was sounded, and an engine, hose cart, and hook-and-ladder truck rushed to the scene. Initially it appeared the fire would be contained, but before long it was apparent the flames were spreading, and the prisoners inside the cell blocks were in danger.[7]

Cole Younger described the situation: "My cell is on the ground floor, on the south side of the building. I went to sleep about nine o'clock and had just wakened when I heard the alarm whistle. I smelled a faint odor of smoke but thought it was gas escaping into the corridor. I looked out of my window, which faces south but could not see any fire. I was wondering why the whistle had been blown, when the guard, Mr. Cayou, informed me of the fire and told me to hurry. I did not apprehend any danger, but he told me how bad the fire was, and I hastened to follow him."[8]

Cole was sorry he could not remove his pictures from the wall or take his books along to safety. A pair of worsted wristlets, given him by Mrs. Cayou, sister of St. Paul Mayor O'Brien, as a Christmas gift, was all he could salvage. Two books, *Wit and Humor* and *God's Book of Nature,* given him by General Henry Sibley, were the two possessions he regretted losing the most. Cole was thankful he had only two weeks earlier sent his book on General Sibley's military campaigns home to Missouri.

"We were taken to the storeroom, where it was very cold, but it is very comfortable here," recalled Cole. "I have nothing to complain of in my treatment here. It certainly isn't like stopping at a hotel, but it's not very bad considering the place. We are all sorry for Warden Reed. This fire is a terrible misfortune to him. I'm a little dubious also about the prospects for food and sleeping quarters tomorrow—or, today, rather. I

View of the state prison at Stillwater after the fire of 1884. Photo by J.H. Kuhn of Stillwater. (Courtesy of the Minnesota Historical Society)

wish they'd send me back to Rice County until they rebuild. Sheriff Barton always treated me excellently."[9]

About 12:45 A.M., an alarm whistle called out Company K, and at the same time a telephone message brought assistance from St. Paul firemen. Once Company K arrived, most of the prisoners were taken from their cells, chained and shackled, and taken to a large lumber warehouse in the rear.[10]

Cole Younger may have been an exception. Said Cole: "Attempt to escape? Why, we are on our parole. When the guard opened our cells, he was going to take me down chained, but I told him to spare himself the trouble. I would give my word of honor to make no attempt to escape. No, sir. I have been here too long for that and will never go out until I can go out honorably."[11]

By the time the prisoner evacuation had begun, the cell building, containing nearly 400 cells, was filled with a dense cloud of smoke. The flames had been sucked under the roof of the building, and quickly burst through the roof in every part, preventing any hopes of containing the blaze. As the prisoners were ushered into the foundry, the 350-by-sixty-foot building was consumed in flames.[12]

Guard Ben Cayou, who was in charge of the Youngers, described the scene: "The last time I started down the south side of the gallery, the smoke had grown so thick that I had to grope my way on my hands and knees. I opened a number of the doors and sent the men back to the stairs where they were met by guards. I succeeded in reaching the front end and had just started back down the north side when, as I stood up to open a door, I lost the sponge which protected my mouth and nose. For a moment I was almost stifled, and fell prostrate upon my face. The smoke was not so dense within a few inches of the floor, and I managed to crawl along a few feet at a time."[13]

One of the prisoners, Con Riellen, insisted on being left behind, and after most of the convicts had been evacuated, the guards returned to his cell and found him locked in. One of the guards took a crowbar and battered the door. Riellen was removed and dragged to safety. Fire Chief Frank Joy also had a narrow escape when he was knocked down by a hose stream in the basement and nearly smothered to death.[14]

Convict Henry Lempke was not so lucky. Several prisoners had heard cries for help during the evacuation, but no one could tell from which direction the sound was coming. Warden Reed and two of his guards searched the passages beneath the hanging ice-coated rafters to the upper gallery. They found cell 212 locked. Unlocking the cell door, they found Lempke's body covered with a coating of ice. The victim's head was resting upon the bed, eyes wide open glaring up at the rafters, one arm raised in an attempt to protect the face.[15]

While the Youngers sat in a vacant room awaiting their removal from the prison, head guard George Dodd appeared. Dodd was to select twenty-five trustees to help evacuate fellow prisoners. As Dodd entered the room, Cole asked if the brothers could be of help. Dodd decided to take a chance on the boys and handed Cole a revolver, Jim an ax, and Bob an iron bar. Dodd asked them to relocate the female prisoners and also the women's matron, Dodd's own wife. Although Dodd was criticized for his decision by Stillwater res-

View of the state prison before the fire of 1884. Stillwater, Minnesota. Photo by J.H. Kuhn of Stillwater. (Courtesy of the Minnesota Historical Society)

idents, the boys led the women to safety, returned their weapons, and were highly praised by Warden Reed and his staff.[16]

Dodd later stated, "I was obliged to take the female convicts from their cells and place them in a small room that could not be locked. The Youngers were passing, and Cole asked if they could be of any service. I said: 'Yes Cole. Will you three boys take care of Mrs. Dodd and the women?' Cole answered: 'Yes, we will, and if you ever had confidence in us place it in us now.' I told him I had the utmost confidence, and I slipped a revolver to Cole, as I had two. Jim, I think, had an ax handle and Bob had a little pinch bar. The boys stood before the door of the little room for hours and even took the blankets they had brought from their cells and gave them to the women to try and keep them comfortable, as it was very cold. Of course I felt uneasy as the prisoners were all loose in the cell room. Deputy Warden Hall, having recovered, came long about the time the boys were guarding the women, and ordered them with other prisoners out of the cell room, but Cole explained that I had put them there to protect my wife and her charges. When I could take charge of the women and the boys were relieved, Cole returned my revolver."[16]

William H. Pratt, prison physician, later gave a slightly different version of the Youngers' role in the fire. Pratt said he spent the night of the fire with the prisoners and had an opportunity to observe them closely. The convicts kept to their cells when the fire broke out since the smoke was not dense enough to harm them. When it became necessary to remove the men from their cells, they were arranged in double file.

"Cole was at the right of the procession; when everything was ready, Deputy Warden Hall, brought out handcuffs for part of them," recalled Pratt. "Seeing this, Cole asked Mr. Hall if he thought it necessary to put men in irons. Mr. Hall replied that he disliked to do so, but the yard was full of smoke, and the gates frozen open. Cole then said, 'Mr. Hall, I give you my word of honor that if you will leave them off, neither I nor my brothers will give you the least trouble, and I do not think anyone else will. We will do all in our power to help you.' Mr. Hall replied, "Well! I will trust you.' With the gates wide open, the yard full of smoke, and very few guards, the convicts were marched down to the foundry where they remained during the night. I was with them until morning, and can say that Cole Younger did much to keep the men quiet and keep down any insubordination."[18]

Following the prisoner evacuation, a reporter was allowed to enter the foundry and interview prisoners. In one corner of the three rooms was a group of ten or twelve black prisoners, some wrapped in blankets, others stretched fully on the floor, singing old-time ballads under the leadership of a lifer. In the opposite corner was a smaller group consisting of the most well-known felons in the prison. Bob Younger sat on a box, his brother Cole leaned against the wall opposite him, and Jim was lying on the floor between the two. Lifer J.B. Coney, Faribault murderer L.M. Sage, and other less notorious convicts sat beside them as did guard Cayou.[19]

Sage related his story to the journalist: "I was in cell 236 on the upper floor, just over the Younger boys. The smoke was stifling. I had difficulty in breathing. The men near me were greatly alarmed and were pounding on their cell doors and crying for aid. I could hear the fire roaring below. The heat became unbearable. The atmosphere was stifling. As I was beginning to succumb, I heard a rattling outside, and my cell door was thrown open by Coney. A number of others were released at the same time I was. The smoke and heat in the upper gallery were terrible, and I don't wonder, that, many of the boys fell on their knees to pray. You fellows can smile at it now, but you would have smiled rather differently if you had been in that gallery."[20]

Newspapers argued the origin of the fire. The *Stillwater Messenger*, in its January 26, 1884, edition, stated: "The origin of the fire is wrapped in mystery, but there seems little doubt that it was the work of a citizen incendiary. The room in which it originated was filled with hardware and advertising matter belonging to the company, and no convict could have gained access to it, as we are informed by Warden Reed."

The same newspaper, one-week later, stated: "The striped sojourners in our city seemed to have enjoyed the episode as they have been able to talk with each other quite freely, play games, and read at will."[21]

The *St. Paul Pioneer Press* for January 26, 1884, expressed the opinion the fire was not set by convicts but did state that there were several rumors suggesting certain inmates were responsible. Other sources suggested an insurance scheme. Total damage from the fire amounted to $30,000.

Telegrams poured into the office of Warden Reed and newspaper headings sizzled: "Keep close watch on the Youngers"; "Did the Youngers escape"; "Plot to free the Youngers." Reed went to his chief deputy, Abe Hall, and suggested irons be placed on the Youngers to satisfy the public. Hall refused to do so.[22]

The day following the fire, there were no quarters for officers or prisoners; few provisions were available; and all utensils, hospital equipment, furniture, and library books had been destroyed. Among the few objects saved were the prison records. Governor Lucius F. Hubbard visited Warden Reed, and they decided to house a few of the inmates on the prison grounds. Most, however, were transported to county jails in St. Paul, Minneapolis, Winona, and Hastings, where they were to remain until the damage in the cellblock had been repaired. The Younger brothers were taken in a sleigh to the Washing-

Ruins of the Minnesota State Prison after the fire of 1884. Photo by J.M. Kuhn of Stillwater. (Courtesy of the Minnesota Historical Societ)

ton County Courthouse by Abe Hall and Judge Butts where they spent four weeks; the only time during their incarceration that they were outside the prison walls.[23]

According to a St. Paul newspaper, a large crowd of convicts pushed and pulled and elbowed its way in front of the barred gates during their removal from the damaged prison compound. "The appearance of the prisoners chained two and two, dressed in their striped clothes . . . created quite a sensation" as they marched down Main Street to the railway depot.[24] While the matron and six female convicts, three of whom were serving terms for murder, waited for the Winona train, they were guests of the warden and his wife. When the prisoners later returned to the prison, they found their home a temporarily roofed and fire-scarred cellblock.

The Union Depot at Stillwater, Minnesota, about 1885. The locomotive at the far left is from the St. Paul and Duluth Railroad. Following the fire, many prisoners were transported from Stillwater to the Twin Cities, Winona, and Hastings. (Courtesy of the Minnesota Historical Society)

Cole Younger later stated: "I can say without fear of contradiction that had it been in our minds to do so we could have escaped from the prison that night, but we had determined to pay the penalty that had been exacted, and if we were ever to return to liberty it would be with the consent and approval of the authorities and the public."[25] The Youngers probably could have escaped during the turmoil, as it was night and the darkness would have hidden them.

Following his return to Stillwater Prison, Cole went back to work as a librarian. Only two prisoners were employed in the prison library, and it was their duty to circulate the various books and papers among the inmates. Cole was also in charge of the "exchange box." Material that came under subscription by inmates could be exchanged for other such material. Papers would circulate ten days from the date of issue and magazines every thirty. Cole then delivered the materials to the room numbers indicated.[26]

The library was a large, well-lighted room, featuring a bay window overlooking the prison yard. Keeping him company were two cages of singing canaries, which Cole fed and cared for. On the walls were autographed pictures of famous people, and he received his visitors in the library. Adoring ladies sent him flowers, and he always wore a straw hat should visitors catch him unaware. When a lady entered the library, he removed it but replaced it after she had left. Because he was growing bald, Cole believed that drafts could be injurious to his health.[27]

When Cole became a hospital trustee, Jim took over his position in the library, and he eventually became head librarian. Always a voracious reader, Jim kept to himself and did not interact with other prisoners, with the exception of his brothers.[28]

On June 12 and 14, one year later, the community of Stillwater was devastated by a flood caused by heavy rains. The town's largest hotel, the Sawyer House, and another, the Pitman House, were hit with three feet of water in their dining rooms. At the former, a hundred-pound boulder crashed through the hotel's barbershop, landing on a stove in the next room. Although the Stillwater Prison inmates were aware of the disaster around them, there was little to fear behind the protection of high prison walls.[29]

In February 1885, the last charges against Frank James were finally dropped, and the newspapers were competing with one another with stories of the James-Younger Gang. Several former members of the gang were in hiding, but when lawman Frank Canton learned that a Buffalo shoemaker was Jim Cummins, he jailed him. Canton wired the Clay County sheriff, but Cummins told him, "I never did anything worse than Frank James did, and if they reprieved him they surely will me." He was right; the Missouri authorities refused to send a requisition for Cummins, and Canton released him.[30]

In March of 1885, Cole Younger wrote M.J. Franklin of Dallas asking that he and other old friends in the area assist in procuring him and Jim a pardon:

"Should we ever be released," wrote Cole, "rest assured there will be nothing on our part to cause anyone to regret having

Frank James. (Courtesy of the National Archives)

extended a helping hand to us in this dark hour. Eight years is a long time to be shut up in a prison. I received a letter from major J.N. Edwards a few days ago. He will do all he can for us. I was in hopes my friends in Texas could get the help of the representative men in that state to use their influence in our behalf. I think Col[onel] Cockrell of Missouri could do much. Of course, everything rests with Gov[ernor] Hubbard of this state, but the more influence that is brought to bear the better prepared he would be to satisfy his constituents, should he feel so disposed to grant our petition for pardon. Senator Frank Cockrell told my friends in Jackson County last fall he would do all he could for us. He and my oldest brother were at college together, though I never knew him personally, though I soldiered under Col[onel] Vest and helped him in two of his hardest fights of the war. But I lay no claim to anyone's help; still I would feel very grateful for the help of all and would, as far as in my power, return all favors. You will please call and ask Mr. I. Jones and family, and my sister Hettie Younger. Our health is only tolerable, as Jim and I suffer with rheumatism most of the time. I hope Cleveland, Lamar, and Garland will bring a change in everything. I will again thank you for your kind favors, and wishing you a long and happy life. . . ."[31]

On April 12, a Nevada, Missouri, newspaper reporter learned that Frank James was in town and found him at the Hotel Mitchell seated at a table, writing a letter. Frank was well dressed, wearing a heavy fur-trimmed overcoat and looked to be in excellent health. The newsman introduced himself to Frank and begged for a short interview.

"With all due respect for you and your profession, I must decline to be interviewed," stated Frank politely. "The subject has been exhausted. There is not an indictment standing against me, and I am a free man. I desire to travel and be treated as the ordinary citizen; therefore you will please excuse me."[32]

The reporter asked Frank if he would merely tell him how long he had been in the county, and how long he expected to remain.

"I am stopping with some friends—Duncan and Shepherd—near Moundsville," replied Frank. "I arrived in the county last Saturday. I came here this morning and return to Moundsville this afternoon. Do not know how long I will stay in the county."

In the fall of 1885, Warren Carter Bronaugh of Clinton, Missouri, a former Confederate, was staying at the Merchants Hotel in St. Paul with his new bride, Eva Blankenbaker, daughter of Mr. and Mrs. Andrew Blankenbaker of Franklin, Missouri, on their honeymoon. Because he was in the state where three fellow Missourians, all ex-Confederates, were being held, he decided to visit the Youngers.[33]

One account alleges that Bronaugh knew the Youngers in his boyhood days. They supposedly "fished and hunted, courted pretty country girls and together they went into the service of the Confederacy. Attachments were formed such as exist only between men who marched many weary miles along dusty or rainy roads, who stood elbow to elbow in the stormy ranks of battle, who suffered in prison and hospital."[34] It is extremely doubtful, however, that this account is valid.

Warren Carter Bronaugh. (Courtesy of the Lyndon Irwin Collection)

A letter from Bronaugh to Frank James after the meeting, however, suggests that Frank may have engaged Bronaugh's assistance in regard to his old friend, Cole Younger. Bronaugh wrote that he had a great deal more to tell Frank after the visit but would wait until they met in Clinton, Missouri.[35]

Captain Bronaugh was born in Buffalo, West Virginia, in 1841. He was the son of Christopher Columbus Bronaugh and Ann Waters, a descendant of Lieutenant Edward Waters of the English army. Born of French and English stock, he was the grandson of William Bronaugh, a hero of the French and Indian War, Revolutionary War patriot, and member of George Washington's council.[36]

After his family moved, "Wal," as he was nicknamed, grew up in Henry County, Missouri. According to Bronaugh family history, an elderly black woman and former slave, who stayed with C.C. and Ann, remarked about their three sons, Wal, Frank, and Sam. She stated that Wal would talk his way into heaven, Frank would buy his way in, but poor Sam . . . "There just ain't no way."[37]

In 1861 at the age of twenty, he enlisted in the regular Confederate army at Springfield, Missouri. At the Battle of Lone Jack, in Jackson County, Missouri, August 6, 1862, he fought under Colonel Vard Cockrell, whose brother, General Francis Marion Cockrell, had served for thirty years as a United States Senator from Missouri. Following Lone Jack, he fought at the battles of Prairie Grove, Helena, Pleasant Hill, and Jenkins' Ferry, under Confederate General Sterling Price, before surrendering in June 1865 at Shreveport, Louisiana.[38]

William Yelverton "Buck" Bronaugh, born 1821, married Martha Newman September 23, 1847, died 1862 in Henry County, Missouri. (Courtesy of the Pam Luster Phillips Collection)

Wal was the nephew of Civil War hero William Yelverton "Buck" Bronaugh, born in 1821, who was killed leading a band of irregulars behind northern lines. Following Buck's death, the band was taken over by John Rafters and Buck's body was hidden for fear it would be hanged in effigy.[39] Buck's home was destroyed by Union troops. Bronaugh family member, Clara Miller-Dugan, later recalled that, when she was a small girl during the Civil War, two men knocked at their door and asked for breakfast. As they sat down to eat, one of the men looked out the window and yelled, "There's Buck Bronaugh. Let's go get him!" They rushed out the door and jumped behind a rail fence at the edge of the yard. As Buck rode into range, they both opened fire on him, inflicting a mortal wound. He rode on for several miles before he died. Clara planted a tree with a spoon in memory of Buck Bronaugh.[40]

While most of Wal Bronaugh's Civil War activities have not been documented, those of his uncle Buck and Buck's son, Yelveton M. Bronaugh, still survive. Fourteen-year-old Yelverton helped the irregulars after his father was killed by bringing them food and supplies. One night he went to meet two fellow irregulars in a grove of trees. Approaching the grove, one of the men ran out waving his arms pointing behind Yelverton. Turning, he saw a band of Union soldiers and he spurred his horse and rode for his life. The soldiers killed the two irregulars and pursed Yelverton to a neighbors barn where he was hiding. After the soldiers conducted a vote whether to hang him or let him go, he was released.

At the close of the war, Wal and his brother Frank, moved to Texas where they raised cattle, but they went broke during a drought in the early 1880s. The Texas ranching property was called the Concho Land and Cattle Company, and comprised about 10,000 acres. Bronaugh's Texas property also boasted a historic landmark—Paint Rock—with 200 to 300 yards of Indian drawings.[41]

The brothers moved to an area south of Nevada, Missouri, and commenced a new cattle operation, shipping a great number of cattle out of the area. In October 1884, Bronaugh met with his partners, an A. Duncan of Moundsville and a Mr. Hasting, in Nevada. The three gentlemen jointly owned a fine bunch of two-year-old cattle—175 in number— and met to discuss their well-being. Duncan had recently lost 110 head of hogs to cholera, and the men wanted to make sure their cattle were safe from disease.[42]

The meeting between Duncan and Bronaugh is significant because this is the same A. Duncan that Frank James met with in April of the following year in Nevada and Moundsville. Bronaugh undoubtedly was involved in Frank's

This tree was planted beside the Bronaugh home in 1862 in memory of "Buck" Bronaugh. Photo taken in 1973. (Courtesy of the Pam Luster Phillips Collection)

later move to Nevada, and he may have, in fact, put up some, if not all, of the money. Because Bronaugh and Frank James were "working together," it is more than possible that Frank was the real force behind Bronaugh's bid for a Younger pardon.

While W.C. Bronaugh worked his cattle, a nearby town in Vernon County was named for him because he had given the right-of-way to the railroad at that location. Soon, however, W.C. departed from the new town of Bronaugh, returning to Henry County, Missouri, eight miles northeast of Clinton, where he resumed farming and stock-raising operations. His large, pretentious, country home was christened Bronaugh Place. Wal and Frank were instrumental in building Bronaugh Church near their home and always paid the preachers' salaries and entertained them in their home.[43]

Bronaugh, apparently an adept land speculator, was involved in various land troubles in 1885. On March 6, he was in Nevada investigating a matter connected with a Barry-Chase trade. Prior to his appearance in the city, he and Hasting had sold a Mr. Barry 320 acres of land, and each received $500 as an initial payment, leaving a balance to each man of $2,700. The deeds were left in the Thornton Bank with an order to deliver upon payment of the remainder of the money. Barry, in turn, despite having no valid deed, gave a warranty deed to the land to Chase, causing Bronaugh and Hasting legal trouble.[44]

Bronaugh home northeast of Clinton, Missouri, photographed in 1973. (Courtesy of the Pam Luster Phillips Collection)

Although Bronaugh carried a letter of introduction to Warden Reed from a St. Paul Merchants Hotel owner, Captain Allen, the warden was suspicious of anyone from Missouri. Bronaugh was immediately aware of Reed's contempt toward him, stating later, "I was painfully aware that I was in the enemy's country and must use all the cool judgment and nice diplomacy at my command."[45]

Reluctantly, Reed did allow Bronaugh to visit, but only on the condition he kept his arms bared to the elbow. A deputy warden presided over the visits, listening carefully to every word spoken. Bronaugh was first taken to Jim's cell, and when he approached, Jim extended his hand through the bars in friendship. According to Bronaugh, Jim's speech was greatly impaired, and he had a little trouble understanding what the Missourian said.[46]

He was next taken several cells away and introduced to Cole. After only a few minutes, Bronaugh realized he and Cole had met before. He recognized him as the Confederate picket, who in 1862 had stopped him and another soldier from riding into Lone Jack, Missouri, which was held by Union General Blunt and 1,500 Jayhawkers.

Following the gory Battle of Lone Jack, Bronaugh and his friend had ridden a few miles out of camp to forage for breakfast. When they returned, they found their camp deserted, and galloped away to find their unit. In encountering another Confederate force, a picket [Cole Younger] informed them that Colonel Cockrell was on the east side of town in full retreat as Union General Blunt was in town with 1,500 Kansas Jayhawkers and Redlegs. For nearly an hour they talked with the picket who had saved them from capture or death.[47]

Bronaugh remembered the young picket, Cole Younger, as an exceedingly handsome young man, "stalwart, alert and intelligent, and every inch a soldier." At his waist, the picket who had saved their lives carried a brace of fine revolvers, and his face was never forgotten by Warren Carter Bronaugh. He recalled too that during the Battle of Lone Jack, Union Major Emory S. Foster had recounted that during the heaviest fighting, Cole rode up and down in front of the lines distributing ammunition.

Bronaugh thanked Cole for saving him from a dreadful peril, and then and there, decided to do everything humanly possible to secure a pardon for the brothers. He planned to write reams of letters and set up meetings with prominent politicians or people of power with the hope of swaying them toward working for a Younger pardon.

Bronaugh left Cole when the noon whistle went off. He asked the deputy warden about Bob and was told that he was at work in the prison factory. Surprisingly, the officer said he would take him to see Bob. Bronaugh spent only a few minutes with Bob, enough to be impressed by his tender youth.

Cole soon wrote Bronaugh a letter referring to his role in the Battle of Lone Jack. Younger had read Major Foster's account of the battle in a recent issue of *Weekly Republic* and related to Bronaugh that he had discovered some errors in the article. According to Cole, Foster had overrated the number of Confederates although his account of the fighting was accurate. Foster, however, referred to Confederate regiments that were not at the battle. As to Cole's gallant ride within thirty feet of Union guns, the rousing cheer he was given by the Yankees, was not because of his courage but because the enemy thought they had killed him when his horse jumped a fence.[48]

Cole wrote at great length to Bronaugh, and although prison rules limited the number of letters a prisoner could write, he made up for it by writing extremely lengthy ones. He wrote in very small letters and was a master at crowding the lines close together. His penmanship and composition improved with time, and although he touched upon many topics of interest, he wrote mostly about measures being taken to grant him a pardon.[49]

With the ten-year anniversary of the Youngers' incarceration coming up, a period which marked their eligibility for parole, the Missourian was determined to do everything he could to get the boys home. He outlined his plans to the brothers for securing them a parole and left. Although Bronaugh did not impress Warden Reed, he did receive support from former Minnesota Governor William R. Marshall and Missouri Governor Thomas Crittenden.[50]

Returning to St. Paul where his wife waited for him, he began stopping citizens on the street, in the hotel lobbies, in their homes, and places of business. Pleading the Youngers' cause, he was met with opposition from everyone he addressed and was told his idea was ludicrous at best.[51]

During the spring of that year, Bronaugh began a correspondence with the wife of Dr. L.W. Twyman of Blue Mills in Jackson County, Missouri. Fanny C. Twyman, the brothers' aunt, meanwhile, had accumulated many letters of support from prominent Missourians. Among these letters was one from former Minnesota Governor William R. Marshall with whom she had been corresponding for about a year. When Bronaugh visited Mrs. Twyman at her home near Independence, she showed him several letters from prominent Minnesotans who favored a Younger pardon. Many were from Governor Marshall, and these, plus others, she turned over to Bronaugh.

Word may or may not have reached the Youngers regarding a near fatal fall of Frank James in Nevada, Missouri. Frank, employed as a driver to a Mr. Bigelow, was passing down South Main Street in a wagon drawn by a team of horses when a street sprinkler directly in front of them frightened the horses. The flow of water caused the team to turn east with a sudden jerk, which snapped the carriage tongue. Frank was thrown to the ground, striking his head and shoulders, and was rendered unconscious. As the horses dashed down the street, Frank was presumed dead. Although such was not the case, he did suffer severe bruises.[52]

During 1885, Cole and Jim became avid woodworkers, and the pair produced several fine pieces of wood sculpture, which they gave away as gifts. Cole carved magnificent leath-

Nevada, Vernon County, Missouri, looking north. (Courtesy of the Lyndon Irwin Collection)

er-and-wood walking canes and Jim beautifully adorned wood-
en boxes and chests. Both of the brothers were adept at creating beautiful picture frames. Bob, on the other hand, could not
use several fingers of his right hand, and, therefore, could not
share the hobby with his brothers.[53]

In October, the *Nevada Daily Mail* reported: "The
Chicago Herald says the Younger brothers, who were sent to
Stillwater, Minnesota, Penitentiary for life, for robbing the
Northfield bank, and murdering the cashier, are in a fair way
to receive pardons. Wealthy relatives of the Youngers at
Marshall, M[issouri], and a wealthy aunt, who lives in the
southern part of Minnesota, are working to secure their release
from prison. Cole Younger is studying medicine, and the other
boys are reading up on the law at odd times. It is also reported that Cole is doing a medical practice, in a small way, among
his fellow convicts."[54]

Frank James made the news in November: "Frank
James has accepted a position as salesman of the Huff &
Simon stock and is doing admirable work for his employers. As
superintendent of the gravel hands at the track, he has
demonstrated during the past two weeks that he is a thorough
businessman."[55]

Biding their time, the three Youngers remained model
prisoners. There was still little hope for an eventual parole or
pardon, but friends like Warren Carter Bronaugh and others
had begun the fight for their freedom. While waiting for a mir-
acle, Cole incurred what may have been his sole infraction at
Stillwater Prison. He was written up for blowing kisses to
ladies walking across the prison grounds.[56]

Notes

[1]James D. Horan, ed., *The Trial of Frank James for Murder with
Confessions of Dick Liddil and Clarence Hite and History of the
"James Gang,"* New York, Jingle Bob/Crown Publishers, Inc.,
1977, pp. 194-195.
[2]Ruth Rentz Yates, *Before Their Identity*, p. 25.
[3]*St. Paul and Minneapolis Pioneer Press*, Wednesday, January 9,
1884, "Fire Within Prison Walls"; *Stillwater Messenger*,
Saturday, January 12, 1884, "Minnesota State Prison Fire."
[4]Brent T. Peterson and Dean R. Thilgen, *Stillwater: A*

Photographic History, p. 57.

[5]*Stillwater Gazette*, May 10, 1894.

[6]*St. Paul and Minneapolis Pioneer Press*, Wednesday, January 9, 1884; *Stillwater Messenger*, Saturday, January 12, 1884.

[7]*Stillwater Messenger*, Saturday, January 26, 1884, "Another Pion Conflagration."

[8]*St. Paul and Minneapolis Pioneer Press*, Sunday, January 27, 1884, "Painting the Town Red."

[9]Ibid.

[10]*Stillwater Messenger*, Saturday, January 26, 1884.

[11]*St. Paul and Minneapolis Pioneer Press*, Sunday, January 27, 1884.

[12]*Stillwater Messenger*, Saturday, January 26, 1884.

[13]*St. Paul and Minneapolis Pioneer Press*, Sunday, January 27, 1884.

[14]*St. Paul and Minneapolis Pioneer Press*, Saturday, January 26, 1884, "The Prison Again Ablaze."

[15]*St. Paul and Minneapolis Pioneer Press*, Sunday, January 27, 1884.

[16]Marley Brant, *The Outlaw Youngers*, p. 227; Brent T. Peterson and Dean R. Thilgen, *Stillwater: A Photographic History*, pp. 59-60; *St. Paul & Minneapolis Pioneer Press*, Sunday, January 27, 1884.

[17]*St. Paul Pioneer Press*, Thursday, July 11, 1901, "Prison Doors are Opened."

[18]Dr. W.H. Pratt letter to Board of Pardons dated July 3, 1897. Northfield, Minnesota Bank Robbery of 1876. Selected Manuscripts Collections and Government Records, Microfilm Edition, Roll 3, Minnesota Historical Society.

[19]*St. Paul & Minneapolis Pioneer Press*, Sunday, January 27, 1884.

[20]Ibid.

[21]*Stillwater Messenger*, February 2, 1884.

[22]Cole Younger, *The Story of Cole Younger by Himself*, p. 91.

[23]Brent T. Peterson and Dean R. Thilgen, *Stillwater: A Photographic History*, pp. 57-59; James Taylor Dunn, "The Minnesota State Prison during the Stillwater Era, 1853-1914," *Minnesota History*, December 1960.

[24]*St. Paul Daily Globe*, January 27, 1884.

[25]W.C. Heilbron, *Convict Life at the Minnesota State Prison*, p. 147.

[26]Ibid., p. 97.

[27]Homer Croy, *Last of the Great Outlaws*, pp. 119-120.

[28]Marley Brant, *The Outlaw Youngers*, p. 229; Carl Hage, interview with author, Madelia, Minnesota, February 27, 1982.

[29]Brent T. Peterson and Dean R. Thilgen, *Stillwater: A. Photographic History*, pp. 57-59.

[30]Robert K. DeArment, *Alias Frank Canton*, Norman and London, University of Oklahoma Press, 1996, pp. 62-63.

[31]*Nevada* (Missouri) *Daily Mail*, March 23, 1885.

[32]*Nevada* (Missouri) *Daily Mail*, April 13, 1885.

[33]*Kansas City Times*, February 27, 1923; Warren Carter Bronaugh obituary, February 1923, Louis Woodford Bronaugh/Pamela Luster Phillips Collection; Dr. William A. Settle (ed. Marley Brant), *Cole Younger Writes to Lizzie Daniel*, James-Younger Gang, Liberty, Missouri, 1994, p. 1.

[34]Kathleen White Miles, *Annals of Henry County, Volume 1, 1885-1900*, 1973, pp. 219-220.

[35]Marley Brant, *Jesse James The Man and the Myth*, New York, Berkley Books, 1998, p. 244.

[36]*Kansas City Times*, February 27, 1923; Warren Carter Bronaugh obituary, February 1923, Louis Woodford Bronaugh/Pamela Luster Phillips Collection; *The History of Henry and St. Clair Counties, Missouri*, St. Joseph, Missouri., National Historical Company, 1883, pp. 296-298.

[37]Pam Phillips, "The Bronaugh Family," unpublished manuscript from the papers of Louis Woodford Bronaugh.

[38]Lyndon Irwin, "Bronaugh, Missouri History." Unpublished manuscript.

[39]His grave has never been found.

[40]Pam Phillips, "The Bronaugh Family," unpublished manuscript from the papers of Louis Woodford Bronaugh.

[41]Louis Woodford Bronaugh/Pamela Luster Phillips Collection; Pamela Luster Phillips letter to author dated August 4, 2001.

[42]*Nevada* (Missouri) *Daily Mail*, October 7, 1884.

[43]Lyndon, Irwin, "Bronaugh, Missouri History;" Lyndon Irwin letter to author dated August 5, 1901; Frank Bronaugh Obituary, January 1937, Louis Woodford Bronaugh/Pamela Luster Phillips Collection; Robertus Love, *The Rise and Fall of Jesse James*, Lincoln & London, University of Nebraska Press, 1925, pp. 400-401.

[44]*Nevada* (Missouri) *Daily Mail*, March 6, 1885.

[45]Dallas Cantrell, *Northfield, Minnesota Youngers' Fatal*

Blunder, p. 100.

[46]Ibid., p.101.

[47]Robertus Love, *The Rise and Fall of Jesse James*, p. 141.

[48]W.C. Bronaugh, *The Youngers' Fight For Freedom*, Columbia, Missouri, E. W. Stephens Publishing Company, 1906, pp. 35-37.

[49]Ibid, p. 306.

[50]Carl W. Breihan, *Outlaws of the Old West*, New York, Bonanza Books, 1957, p. 36; Marley Brant, *The Outlaw Youngers*, pp. 231-236.

[51]W.C. Bronaugh, *The Youngers' Fight For Freedom*, p. 47.

[52]*Nevada* (Missouri) *Daily Mail*, September 23, 1885.

[53]Carl W. Breihan, *Outlaws of the Old West*, p. 36.

[54]*Nevada* (Missouri) *Daily Mail*, October 6, 1885.

[55]*Nevada* (Missouri) *Daily Mail*, November 6, 1885.

[56]*Minneapolis Star Tribune*, Sunday, August 2, 1998.

Frank James raised Light Brahma chickens. (Courtesy of the
Lyndon Irwin Collection)

IV

1886 to 1888

"I have known the true character of Cole Younger for many years. At a critical time, while he wore the gray, he did brave and unselfish things for those who were dear to me, now dead and gone . . . . I have learned from the lips of the just dead the true nobility of his inward character."

—Lizzie Daniel[1]

hile the Youngers languished in a Minnesota prison, their friend Frank James began raising Light Brahma chickens. Frank purchased his first three Brahma birds from Thomas W. Ragsdale of Monroe County, Missouri, and quickly decided they were more than just a hobby.[2]

Stories were circulating through Missouri newspapers that Frank James was living in St. Louis and also in the town of Mexico, but he still resided in Nevada, Missouri, raising his chickens. According to a Missouri newspaper:

"Frank James is registered at the Ringo. He is looking quite well and says that he is enjoying the very best of health. . . . Frank has been engaged in business in Nevada, Missouri, where he says he is succeeding finely. . . ."[3]

In June 1886, Warren Carter Bronaugh set up a meeting with Governor Marshall in Jefferson City, Missouri, at the Madison House. The two gentlemen had breakfast together while discussing plans for a Younger pardon. In the afternoon, they visited former Confederate General John Sappington Marmaduke, then governor of Missouri. During the course of the meeting, Governor Marmaduke declared that he and his associates would recommend a pardon for the Youngers at any time his visitors thought advisable.[4]

Honorable William R. Marshall. (Courtesy of the Rice County Historical Society)

Marshall and Bronaugh had been convinced that Marmaduke, who had been elected governor on March 18, 1885, would back their movement to secure freedom for the Youngers. One year earlier, he had assured Frank James' friend John Newman Edwards that he would never surrender Frank to the authorities in Minnesota. He related to Edwards:

"Tell Frank James from me to go on a farm and go immediately to work. Tell him to keep away from any sort of display, like that Moberly business.[5] Tell him to keep out of the newspapers. Keep away from fairs and fast horses, and to keep strictly out of sight for a year."[6]

Marmaduke was aware that, according to rumors, Bronaugh had purchased a house for Frank in Nevada, Missouri, at 520 South Cedar Street for $1,200 from the M.E. Church South. In settling down in Nevada, Frank took on an air of pseudo-respectability. The house was easily recognizable with its round pillars in front. On the inside, the original sandstone fireplace with wrought iron mantelpiece, captured the eye of visitors. An old covered cistern under the house probably held nothing but water, but the curious talked of hidden booty.[7]

Frank was described as a "slender, sandy-haired man, [who] minded his own business, took the family to church on Sundays and worked during the week in the McGowan & Jordan Shoe Store" on the south end of the square. A Nevada neighbor later recalled that he walked "stealthily, like a cat."

Frank's wife, Annie Ralston James, was a pleasant, pretty little lady but not inclined to be neighborly. Their son, Robbie, was only six when the family moved to Nevada, and he attended the old Franklin School.[8]

Presumably, Frank took up residence in Nevada because he had been offered a job in McGowan & Jordan's Shoe Store. His employer, Robert J. McGowan, was a veteran of the "cause," having served under Kentucky's John Hunt Morgan. Pro-Union newspapers sarcastically linked Frank's move to Nevada to the campaign to locate the new state hospital there. The *Springfield Herald* quipped, "Gov[ernor] Marmaduke and the commission have conspired in placing the asylum there to resurrect the defunct Southern Confederacy in the locality!"[9]

By 1887, Frank had changed professions, as evidenced by a news article, which appeared in the *Nevada Daily Mail:*

"It cannot be said that like Othello, Frank James' occupation's gone, for he is achieving considerable fame at Nevada, M[issouri], as a poultry fancier, having for sale a handsome strain of purebred Light Brahman. Since his surrender to the authorities, friends have presented him with a small place valued at $2,000."[10]

Frank James home, 520 South Cedar Avenue, Nevada, Missouri. (Photo by Lyndon Irwin)

M E Church South
TO
Alex F James

WARRANTY DEED.

Know all Men by these Presents, That B S M Clack, J F Harber, H F Jones, John S Clack, D Nixon, C N Conrad, F H Lacy, C Hurd and F P Anderson Trustees of the M E Church South of the City of Nevada of the County of Vernon in the State of Missouri have this day, for and in consideration of the sum of Twelve hundred DOLLARS, to the said Trustees in hand paid by Alexander F James of the County of Vernon in the State of Missouri Granted, Bargained and Sold, and by these presents do Grant, Bargain and Sell unto the said Alexander F James the following described tracts or parcels of land situate in the County of Vernon in the State of Missouri, that is to say: all of Lot (3) Three and (8) Eight feet off of the north side of Lot (4) four all in Block (10) Ten of Hights addition to Nevada City according to the recorded plat of said Addition: also with the privilege of passway (10) ten feet in width across the west end of lot four (4) of said Block (10) Ten of Hights Addition until an alley is opened running North and South through the center of said Block

TO HAVE AND TO HOLD the premises hereby conveyed, with all the rights, privileges and appurtenances thereto belonging, or in anywise appertaining unto the said Alexander F James his heirs and assigns, FOREVER. WE, the said B S M Clack, J F Harber, H F Jones, John S Clack, D Nixon, C N Conrad, F H Lacy, C Hurd and F P Anderson Trustees of the said M E Church South hereby covenanting to and with the said Alexander F James his heirs and assigns, the ourselves as Trustees as aforesaid and their successors heirs, executors and administrators, to Warrant and Defend the title to the premises hereby conveyed, against the claim of every person whatsoever. Except taxes for 1886

In Witness Whereof, the have hereunto subscribed our names and affixed our seals this 19th day of Feby 1886

C N Conrad (Seal)   B S M Clack (Seal)
F H Lacy (Seal)   J F Harber (Seal)
F P Anderson (Seal)   D Nixon (Seal)   H F Jones (Seal)
C Hurd (Seal)   John S Clack (Seal)

STATE OF MISSOURI, } ss.
COUNTY OF   On this   day of   and   188 , before me personally appeared his wife, to me known to be the persons described in and who executed the foregoing instrument, and acknowledged that they executed the same as their free act and deed.

In Testimony Whereof, I have hereunto set my hand and affixed my official seal at my office in , the day and year first above written.

my term expires   18

STATE OF MISSOURI, } ss.
COUNTY OF Vernon   On this 19th day of February 1886, before me personally appeared J F Harber, F H Lacy, D Nixon, C N Conrad, B S M Clack, H F Jones, John S Clack, C Hurd and F P Anderson to me known to be the persons described in and who executed the foregoing instrument, and acknowledged that they executed the same as their free act and deed. And the said further declared to be single and unmarried.

In Testimony Whereof, I have hereunto set my hand and affixed my official seal at my office in Nevada , the day and year first above written.

(Seal)

E T Davis
Notary Public

term expires Dec 18th 1889

Filed and Recorded 29th day of Feby 1886 at 5 o'clock minutes P M.

A J King Recorder.

Henry County home of W.C. Bronaugh. (Courtesy of the Lyndon Irwin Collection)

His benefactor, Warren Carter Bronaugh, was also living in the area. A local newspaper carried a notice that he and partner Duncan sold 110 head of hogs which averaged 312.5 pounds apiece.[11]

Years later it was disclosed that W.C. Bronaugh had, in fact, purchased the house for Frank. In 1891, when Frank sold the house, the *Kansas City Times* reported the house had been bought for him by "sincere admirers." According to a neighbor, Walter Wilson Mayes, a Nevadan of the mid-1880s, Frank James was anything but a clerk by nature or occupation.

Frank made national headlines during his Nevada residency when he received a mysterious letter believed by the public to have been a "detective's dodge to throw suspicion on an innocent man." Outside the Nevada post office where Frank was talking to both the mayor and city marshal, he opened a letter disclosing some crisp new banknotes. The letter read:

"St. Joseph, MO., October 31, 1886.

Frank James, Esq:

Sir: Please accept the enclosed as a 'memento' of the late 'Frisco train robbery of October 25, 1886.

Jim Cummins."

Opposite: Frank James deed to Nevada, Missouri, home. (Courtesy of the Vernon County Deed Book 36)

James Andrew "Dick" Liddil. Photo by E.B. Snell, traveling photographer. (Courtesy of the Armand DeGregoris Collection)

The letter, addressed in lead pencil, was in a bold, business hand, and showed an attempt at disguise by writing a slanting backhand. The money contained in the envelope consisted of one twenty-dollar banknote and three ten-dollar notes, of the Merchants' and Planters' National Bank of Sherman, Texas. Frank was at a loss to explain the situation.

"I think it is an outrage for any scoundrel to take advantage of me in that manner, situated as I am, striving as I am to make an honest living for my wife and little boy," Frank told the local press. "I am satisfied that some scoundrel of a detective put up the job on me in order to get the reward, thinking I would keep the letter and money on my person without informing anyone that I received it. He would then arrest me and apparently discover my guilt. On the other hand they might have thought I would open communication with their 'Jim Cummings,' [sic] but they were badly mistaken. . . ."[12]

The town of Nevada seemed to draw persons affiliated with the James-Younger Gang. In 1876, the year of the Northfield robbery, James Gang member, James A. "Dick" Liddil had moved into a house at 403 South Main. His father, James Liddil, also lived in Nevada and was a prominent citizen in town circles. The younger Liddil was arrested for horse stealing in Vernon County a year later. The court tried and sentenced him to ten years in prison.[13]

After their meeting with Marmaduke, Marshall and Bronaugh met with several local politicians who favored a Younger pardon before moving on to Kansas City where they spoke with ex-Governor Crittenden, Colonel L.H. Waters, and other prominent men. Crittenden, a Democrat, and Waters, a Republican, had both served the Union during the Civil War but were favorable toward a pardon. Upon returning to Minnesota, Marshall found that he was being attacked in the newspapers for his championing of the Youngers by numerous politicians.[14]

General John B. Sanborn spoke out against a Younger pardon in the July 23, 1886, issue of the *Pioneer Press.* Sanborn had commanded a Union brigade in the Civil War that had fought Frank James, the Youngers, and other guerrillas who had "infested" southwestern Missouri near the close of hostilities. According to the general:

> Those bands of Quantrell [sic], West, and Anderson conducted their operations in the most barbarous and ferocious style, and entirely at variance with the principles of civilized warfare. They granted no quarter to their prisoners, and their malice did not even end with the death of their prisoners, whom, they mutilated in the most frightful manner. The younger of the brothers was a companion of his brother during part of this time, I believe. Since the war, and until their incarceration, a period of thirteen years, they lived lives of robbery and bloodshed, and nothing else. I don't know how many they killed themselves, but their gang killed, I know, scores if not hundreds in their raids. What are their lives worth compared with that of Cashier Heywood, whom they killed? I haven't seen any reason advanced for their release except that, while in prison, where it is impossible for them to commit crime, they have not attempted it. But

General John B. Sanborn. (Courtesy of the Rice County Historical Society).

James A. "Dick" Liddil home at 403 South Main, Nevada, Missouri. (Courtesy of Lyndon Irwin)

is that any reason why they should not attempt it after they are out? I shouldn't feel safe if they were released, and I do not think society ought to hazard itself by turning loose upon its self, men with such records. Remembering the scenes I saw in the war, and the career of crime of these men since that time, I think it is an outrage to even think of releasing them from their bondage. Gov[ernor] Marshall was responsible more than any other man for the repeal of the law making hanging the punishment for capital offenses. The repeal of that law; in my judgment, has been the ground of many of the lynchings, which have occurred since. This tender-heartedness of Gov[ernor] Marshall does him great credit, but, I think, is disastrous to the state.[15]

Representatives from the city of Northfield also protested any means of setting the Youngers free. The letter writers were shocked that a movement was in progress to parole or pardon the boys and stated "the horrors of that bloody affair" were too fresh for them to ever consider freedom for the prisoners. The article concluded:

Just why Sheriff Barton and ex-Governor Marshall should become interested in their behalf is unexplainable. It is not probable that their bumps of magnanimity have been enlarged for this especial purpose. It is very strange, indeed a matter of much inquiry, why a few men in Minnesota favor a pardon of the Youngers, and an explanation would be in order. It is hoped that every citizen who loves the enforcement of the law and the peace of his own fireside will enter a solemn protest against the pardon of the Younger boys.[16]

The citizens of Madelia spoke out against a Younger pardon in the following day's *Pioneer Press*. The author of the piece admitted that the boys had been model prisoners in Stillwater but felt it was unfair to commit depredations, become good prisoners, and be freed. According to the article, time softens all things and the petitioners in favor of a pardon had forgotten about much of the treachery committed by the Youngers. The people of Missouri, in fact, would make them honored citizens if released.[17]

Another piece, "Don't Deserve Clemency," appeared in the same issue. The writer recapitulated an April 29, 1872, robbery by five outlaws in the village of Columbia, Kentucky. The men made small purchases in some of the stores, mounted and rode to the bank. Three of the men entered the bank, drew guns, and ordered cashier R.A.C. Martin to open the burglar-proof safe. Like Joseph Lee Heywood, Martin refused and was shot to death. The outlaws took $4,000 from the cash drawer and some special deposits in the outer vault. The men, wrote the author T.T. Alexander, were the James and Younger boys. Alexander, a staunch believer in "an eye for an eye," ended his article with the quote, "Who so sheddeth man's blood, by man shall his blood be shed."[18]

Still another piece in this same issue presented what the newspaper called an "almost unanimous opinion in favor of keeping the Youngers at Sillwater for life." Several persons spoke out against the outlaws when asked their opinion in an "impartial" poll taken by the newspaper:

STATE AUDITOR BRADEN: "If they let them out, they ought to let out every prisoner who has been there ten years and who has behaved himself. Don't believe in it."

DEPUTY ATTORNEY GENERAL MARTIN: "No danger of it. It's ridiculous."

CHIEF CLERK TREASURER'S OFFICE SANDERS: "I am entirely opposed to it. I am opposed to pardoning any man found guilty of murder or rape—such men ought never to see daylight again. This was not the only murder they were interested in. Am opposed to their pardon."

ADJUTANT GENERAL MACCARTHY: "I think they ought to be hung before they are let out."

STATE LIBRARIAN WILLIAMS: "It would be a perfect outrage to let these men out. They ought to be kept there for life. Ten years? Why, what's ten years when you come to consider what they have done. The people never would stand it."

CLERK OF THE SUPREME COURT NICHOLS: "On general principles, I am opposed to pardoning in such cases. It might be in this case they would become good citizens if let out."

ASSISTANT SUPERINTENDENT INSTRUCTION PENDERGAST: "I think they ought to stay there for life. If Missouri can't take care of her criminals, when they come up this way, Minnesota can."

RAILROAD COMMISSIONER BECKER: "It would be a very great stretch of the pardoning power and a false use of it to let these men out. There's no doubt of their guilt. It's not claimed they are innocent. They are simply undergoing the penalty of their crime. They are in the right place, and I can't conceive of any reason why they should be let out."

W.P. Murray: "They ought to keep the Younger boys just where they are."

Chief of Police Clark: "They ought never to liberate the Youngers."

Captain Starkey: "I don't think the Youngers ought to ever leave Stillwater alive."

Captain Peter Berkey: "These Younger boys were bad men, and were professional robbers and murderers. And for this reason I say they should be kept in prison for life. In many of the states, they would have been hanged for the crime they committed here. They should stay in the penitentiary forever."

Harry Horn: "I am decidedly opposed to the pardon of the Younger boys. They came to our state and committed murder, and to let them loose now would be but to give them new opportunities for murder."

Alderman Minea: "It is my opinion that society in general and the Younger brothers themselves will be better off if no pardon is granted."

County Commissioner Hazzard: "I don't like the idea."

Professor Phelps: "It would be a travesty on justice. If a man is sentenced for life for such atrocious crimes as those committed by the Youngers, he ought to serve it out."

Judge Wood: "I think they are safer in the prison than out of it."

Colonel William Leip: "It would be the —dest shame ever heard of to let those men out."

Major Newson: "I am rather lenient in my feelings, but I should never consent to a thing of this kind."

Commodore Davidson: "Every other man now in the penitentiary ought to be pardoned out first."

J.T. Magnes, City Editor of the St. Louis Post-Dispatch: "We don't want 'em down our way."

H.R. Morrison, Waseca: "If the Younger boys are pardoned, it will be a disgrace to the judiciary of the state that has condemned them to prison for life. I do not believe that Governor [Lucius F.] Hubbard will ever pardon them."

C. H. Waite, Albert Lea: "Gov[ernor] Marshall is an amiable old gentleman, but he has made a mistake in endeavoring to secure the pardon of the Younger boys. Minnesota will never consent to that."

GEORGE R. PATTEN, CROOKSTON: "The candidate for governor this year who will announce that he will never pardon the Younger brothers will be elected."[19]

The *Pioneer Press,* however, declared on July 26 that, according to ex-Governor Marshall, his chances for a proposed release for the Youngers were not as bleak as painted. Marshall contended that the brothers were not the evildoers people considered them to be. In his lengthy article, he produced evidence that Cole Younger was not in Missouri in 1864 and had nothing to do with atrocities cited by General Sanborn in his article published in the same newspaper. Marshall stated that Cole was at that time a captain in the regular Confederate army in southern Arkansas, Mississippi, and Texas. Early in 1864, at Bonham, Texas, he was ordered by General McCullogh to go under command of General Jackson into New Mexico to recruit a regiment for the Confederate service. This expedition left Texas on May 1, and when the plan failed, Cole went on to Arizona and into Sonora, Mexico. Cole and his men sailed from the port of Guyamas to San Francisco and remained there until the surrender of Lee's army.[20]

Cole Younger. (Courtesy of the Lyndon Irwin Collection)

Marshall scolded Sanborn for his errors of history and related that while Cole served in the regular army under General Jo Shelby's brigade of Sterling Price's army and in the division of General John Sappington Marmaduke, he was never guilty of a cruel or unsoldierly act. He added that the Youngers had nothing to do with the killing of cashier Joseph Lee Heywood in the First National Bank of Northfield. While wandering in the woods west of Northfield while making their escape, Cole allegedly gave an elderly poor woman his last gold coin for giving him and his brothers something to eat. Marshall continued by quoting Byron and the Bible and praising the virtues of the brothers. In answer to the list of persons condemning a would-be pardon in the newspaper, two days earlier, Marshall presented the names of popular Minnesotans, including that of Warden Reed, who were in favor of pardon. Reed was a busy man at the time, but he did what he could to secure a pardon for his prisoners.

Cole wrote Marshall a letter of appreciation, and the letter was published in the *Pioneer Press*:

Your kind favor of July 29 was received with many thanks. I do not take the *Pioneer Press* and have not seen the interview with Colonel Fladd. I understand there are several so-called histories of the James and Younger brothers, but I had nothing to do with them. I never knew or ever had any interview with anyone engaged in getting up these histories. I have steadily refused all applications for information in getting them up. As for the war, I have said that I was engaged in the bloody warfare on the border of Missouri and Kansas. As you truthfully said in your letter to the *Pioneer Press*, it was little better on both sides than murder. That is the original cause of my being in prison today. In all that time of service in Missouri, I was either a private or sub-ordinate officer, acting under orders. In 1862-1863, I was a lieutenant in Captain Jarrette's company, Shelby's brigade of Price's army. All soldiers. Whether they wore the blue or the gray, know that they take an oath to obey officers appointed over them, and all good soldiers obey the orders of their superior officers. As for the kind of soldier I made, I leave that to the honorable federal and Confederate soldiers that I fought against and with, who now live in Missouri. I know that no one will ever say that he knew me to be guilty of any individual act of cru-elty to the wounded or prisoners of our foe. I do not believe there is a brave federal soldier in Minnesota today who, if he knew every act of mine during the war, but what would give me the right hand of a soldier's recognition. I was engaged in many bloody battles where it was death or victory. I tried to do my part; any true sol-dier would. All articles, such as referred to, are false when they charge me with shooting unresisting men or wounded prisoners. No man who has respect for the truth will say that I ever ordered the execution of a citi-zen at any place during the war—at Lawrence or any-where else. Not one of my brothers ever soldiered with me a day. As to a story going the rounds that during the war I captured fifteen men, tied them together and tried to shoot through them all, it is false from beginning to end. I never heard of anything like it having being com-mitted during the war, in Missouri, Kansas, or anywhere else. I know of no foundation for the falsehood. The whole thing was so absurd that I never supposed any sensible man would believe it. I have always supposed the story was gotten up by some reporter as a burlesque on sensational newspapers.[21]

But Marshall was far from finished. On August 9, he wrote again to the editor of the *Pioneer Press* stating that he felt compelled to aid the Youngers, whom he termed "helpless to defend themselves." He attacked the newspaper for publishing an improbable history of the Youngers in an earlier edition. The story claimed Cole had lined up Union prisoners in a straight line just to find out how many men one ball would penetrate. He asked that Cole be allowed to testify as to the vicious lies and reiterated that the warden, deputy warden, and chaplain of the prison all regarded his word as one to be depended upon.[22]

Isaac Staples. (Courtesy of the Rice County Historical Society)

During the early 1880s, Benjamin Franklin Butler, controversial Civil War army officer, former governor of Massachusetts, and old enemy of the Youngers, purchased some land near St. Croix Falls. In September 1886, his son-in-law Adelbert Ames, also regarded as a nemesis by the boys, went to St. Croix Falls to appraise the situation and arrange for the sale of the land to Stillwater lumber baron, Isaac Staples. In a letter to his wife, Ames described the twin towns on the St. Croix:

"Great expectations have been their bane. Instead of being flourishing manufacturing places they seem dead and alive in spots, the dead spots being the most numerous. There is no water power here utilized. The only dam ever built here has long since passed away, and only slight traces of the foundation remain."[23]

Butler and Ames may have been the catalysts that brought the James-Younger Gang to Minnesota. Prior to the Northfield raid, Cole Younger had overheard a conversation that General Benjamin Butler of the Union army had taken $300,000 from the South and deposited it in a Northfield, Minnesota, bank. Indignation that a Union general was profiting from the loss of the South filled his heart with rage. It was afterward

Residence, lumberyard, and mills of Isaac Staples. (Courtesy of the Rice County Historical Society)

learned that the money had not been taken from the South but Cole's belief that the money was Southern loot was sincere.

No Northern officer was more fiercely detested in the South than Butler, known to Southerners as "Silver Spoons" Butler and the "Beast" of New Orleans. Placed in charge of the city in May 1862, Beast Butler quickly moved to banish or jail Confederate activists and confiscate their property. Butler sparked an international furor by seizing $800,000 in hidden Confederate silver from the office of the Dutch consul. When a local citizen desecrated the United States flag in public, Butler had him hanged. Butler was also reputed to have appropriated furniture and silverware for his own use.[24]

In 1874, his son-in-law, Adelbert Ames, was elected governor of Mississippi with a black running mate, A.K. Davis as lieutenant governor. Ames had hoped to remake Mississippi into the model of New England. Ames despised the South, writing to his wife "slavery blighted this people." Ames, however, held his fellow carpetbaggers in no better regard, calling

82

them "an audacious, pushing crowd" who were out to loot the state, and he grew disillusioned by the ignorance and corruption of the blacks with whom he worked. His connection with Beast Butler and his own high-strung personality made him anything but popular with Southerners.[25]

It is unlikely that the Younger brothers learned of the Butler-Ames-Staples land transactions in the St. Croix Valley. Since the boys regarded these men as carpetbaggers, these real estate dealings would only have enforced their position that these Yankees were getting rich off the poor.

The *Nevada Daily Mail* reported in August:

> Mr. Stevens [managing editor of the *Kansas City Journal*] says ex-Governor Marshall of Minnesota is working hard to secure a pardon for the Younger brothers. Gov. Hubbard's official organ in a recent issue says, 'No governor of Minnesota will ever pardon the Younger brothers; it would be political death to him in any view of the case. There are hundreds of other prisoners that should be pardoned before them.' This is undoubtedly Gov. Hubbard's own expression. Efforts have been made to induce the Youngers to testify against Frank James, in case he should ever be brought there for trial, but even the promise of pardon has failed to induce them to say he was there.[26]

Governor Marshall and his son George visited Bronaugh in Clinton, Missouri, in October 1886, after vacationing in Hot Springs, Arkansas. George, twenty-three years old, was in ill health, and he and his parents had visited the springs, hoping the medicinal waters would provide some improvement. Governor Marshall remained ten days with the Bronaughs, although his son stayed on as a guest for seven weeks.[27]

Considerable reconstruction in the prison was completed under Warden Reed by mid-1886, with 582 cells and ample shop room and machinery to employ over five hundred workmen. With the prisoner population of 387, there was more than enough room for years to come. The contracting company, however, faced financial setbacks following the fire and was placed in the hands of a receiver. Still, all available prisoner labor was employed making engines and threshing machines. The State Board of Corrections and Charities reported, "Careful observation has confirmed our good opinion of the administration of Warden Reed."[28]

Three prison inspectors, however, attacked Warden Reed and his staff in 1886 regarding their management of the institution. According to the inspectors, "Ambitious men, disappointed, scheming demagogues, cannot understand why it is that businessmen will accept such positions as these unless it is to ally themselves to rings and assist in defrauding the State."[29]

When Andrew R. McGill became Minnesota's governor in 1887, he chose not to reappoint Warden Reed to his post. Instead, he selected Halvor G. Stordock, a farmer from Rothsay in Wilkin County. Two of the three prison inspectors resigned, however, charging the governor with giving the post to a political friend. Their actions may or may not have been responsible for a change in state policy as Stordock was the last warden in the state appointed by a governor.

Stordock and his staff immediately launched an investigation of what they called prison "irregularities and immoralities" under the Reed administration. Many scandalous charges and countercharges were alleged by Reed and Stordock. During hearings, Govornor McGill temporarily suspended Stordock. Mrs. Sarah E. McNeal, a matron highly regarded by Reed, became the principal witness against him. Several prisoners also testified against Reed. The committee later reported that none of the charges against Reed were sustained; Warden Stordock and Mrs. McNeal were reprimanded, and Reed was greatly censured. Stordock was restored as Warden but Mrs. McNeal did not return. In June of the following year, Reed attempted suicide in his Minneapolis home.

Bob Younger. (Courtesy of the National Archives)

Governor McGill, however, took a personal interest in the Youngers and even visited them in Stillwater. He was a good listener when they told him why they felt they should be paroled, and he promised to look into the matter. Although McGill studied the matter, no parole was forthcoming.[30]

In February 1887, the Youngers were visited by a party of legislators. One of the legislators, George P. Johnston, had been one of their captors in Hanska Slough in 1876. Surprisingly, Bob Younger presented Johnston with a leather cane, which he had made. Johnston told Younger he planned to have the cane mounted in gold, and he would keep it as a souvenir of the memorable event.[31]

Jim Younger, continued to suffer with his bouts of depression. He did, however, turn to writing and began putting his ideas down on paper. He even went so far as to create a mock newsletter complete with illustrations. Jim was urged to continue his writing endeavors by those who had read some of his work. Some even suggested he form a newspaper to be circulated throughout the prison, but Jim rejected the idea. He refused to share his ideas with strangers, and stated that his writings were for his own amusement and nothing more.[32]

While the Youngers greeted the legislators, Zerelda James talked with the press. A newspaper reporter described her as being portly, graceful, and nearly six feet tall. She talked freely of Jesse and Frank, and even of Bob Ford and the Pinkerton bomb that killed her eight-year-old son Archie and blew off part of her arm. When asked if she missed the use of her arm, she replied:

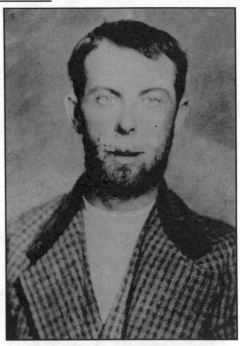

Jim Younger. (Courtesy of the National Archives)

"Yes; more, I believe, as I grow older. But there is another loss that I suffered on that memorable, cold January night, that I feel more—they robbed me of much sunshine—the loss of my fair, sweet young boy. He was eight years of age, and he often would say to me: 'Mama, isn't it strange that both the men I was named after were killed?' His name was Archie Payton, Jesse having christened him after two of his guerrilla friends who were killed. And the poor little fellow was killed too—the James boys were not at home that night."[33]

She still kept part of the hand grenade in her possession. When asked how often Frank and Jesse came to see her, she answered:

"Not very frequently. Frank was away once for four years; that was while he was in Tennessee. Eighteen months was the longest period Jesse ever remained away. He would come home and say: 'Mother, I could not stay away longer without coming to see you and the home a little bit.' They would always come during the night and only remain a day or so. I would never know when they were coming, nor did I ever hear from them when away. My mail, of course, was always watched."

She was asked if any officers came to the house when the brothers were there.

"Yes, twice," she recalled. "Once Capt[ain] Thomason and son Oscar, present sheriff of the county, came here and Jesse was at home. They inquired for Jesse, but I kept talking to them and trying to delay them as much as possible. Jesse, in the meantime, was going out at a back window across to the barn and making for the woods. They discovered him and followed in hot pursuit and engaged in a sharp encounter, thirty shots being exchanged. Capt[ain] Thomason's horse was killed while he was standing behind it shooting. Jesse told him he did not want to kill him though he could and would if he followed farther. He returned to the house and rode a favorite horse of Jesse's away. Jesse came back shortly afterward, and when he learned that the horse had been taken, he was very angry, and followed, vowing he would kill Capt[ain] Thomason if he overtook him, though he did not wish to do so before. Jesse told me often afterward these two men were as brave men as he ever met.

Zerelda Samuel and unidentified man, both seated on a bench under the old coffee bean tree at the James farm. (Courtesy of the Armand DeGregoris Collection)

"Another time Sheriff John S. Grooms, sheriff of this county at the time, came here when Jesse was at home, but his presence was not discovered.

"I know that the James boys have done wrong, or done things that they should not have done, but they were driven to it by that cruel and bloody war, and then outlawed and not permitted to settle down and live the lives of peaceable and orderly citizens. Jesse wrote to three governors, McClurg, Woodson, and Phelps, asking if protection from mob violence would be guaranteed should he surrender. He was willing to be tried for all charges that might be brought against him. He never received any reply from any of them. I have often regretted that I did not go personally to see the executives, especially after I visited Gov[ernor] Crittenden, after Jesse's death, to make terms and conditions for Frank's surrender. I think since Frank's surrender his conduct and citizenship have been such as to win approval and respect."

She spoke of those who had came miles to see the farm, the "curiosity visitors," and laughed. "When they come, most everyone will say that they 'just happened to be passing through the country, and thought we would stop for a few minutes.' Of course, I don't say anything, but know they may have come for miles purposely to come here, led by curiosity. Anyone is always welcome, even if brought by curiosity; for I know that people, especially strangers at a distance, had naturally a curiosity to see the place, and I always try to treat everyone kindly and politely and make their trip as pleasant as possible, although during summer there are many days that crowds come and occupy my time all day. Sometimes some of these smart people come that I don't care about coming. For instance, one day I carried all the pictures out on the porch to dust them off, not being fixed up much myself. Suddenly I heard a rustling of silk, and, looking around, beheld a young woman arrayed in silk and satin, and almost lost in the ribbons that were flying around her. She tripped up to me and said, 'Can you tell me where Mrs. Samuels is?' I straightened myself up and replied, 'She stands before you, Madam, look and behold.' She threw up her hands and screamed with astonishment. I called the hired girl to bring the camphor quick, and I began asking Mrs. Bonneshaw if she thought she would survive. I suppose she thought I was Bridget.

"When coming over from Kansas City on the train one evening, a gentleman from Vermont sought the services of the conductor to get acquainted with me. The conductor asked if he might introduce a gentleman to me. I told him I had no objections to being introduced to a gentleman, and no one but a gentleman would seek an introduction to a lady. We conversed until it came time for me to leave the train. He said the conversation was worth [twenty-five dollars] to him. I told him I would only charge [twenty-five] cents, and he would be $24.75 ahead, which he could contribute to some institution for the poor, if he desired. He looked a little blank, but handed me the [twenty-five] cents, which I took."

Producing a leather duster, she said, "Here is the duster that my poor boy had in his hand when the fatal shot was fired that ended his earthly existence." She then commenced talking about her own youth.

"I remember, well, when I was the age of you young people, how my beaux used to come see me. Oh, what happy days, then; but, alas, what sad days have I experienced since that halcyon period! The trouble and anxiety that I have suffered! Two boys out in the world, liable at any time to meet with a tragic death! Could I forget or forsake them? Could I possess a mother's heart, or is there a mother in this world who would forsake her offspring under any circumstances, and isn't it the case that the parents, especially the mother, exhibits the greatest attachment for the erring or wayward boy?"

Frank James also gave an interview to the press, and as per usual, avoided any mention of the Youngers. Having moved to Dallas, he talked with a reporter shortly after taking up residency in Texas.

"Yes, I am living quietly enough here, and I think the balance of my life will be passed peacefully," stated Frank. "I have never carried a weapon since I surrendered my revolvers to Gov[ernor] Crittenden in Missouri. I do not carry any arms because I do not want to have any trouble with anyone. I do not think anybody wants to kill me unless it might be some crank who wanted notoriety, and a gun would be no protection against such a man, for he would shoot me in the back or at some time when I was not expecting."[34]

When asked if he was a good shot, Frank replied: "No, I am nothing extra, but there was a time when I thought that no man on earth could draw a gun quicker than I could. I practiced it for twenty years, and always felt safe when talking with a man who had not already drawn his weapon. I knew that whenever he made a motion I could kill him before he could draw."

Frank was asked what kind of gun he preferred:

"Well, I always used a Remington .44. The same cartridges used in this six-shooter fit a Winchester .34 rifle, so there is no danger of a man getting rattled in a fight and putting the wrong cartridge in his gun. It is a bad plan to carry two kinds of ammunition when you use it in a hurry sometimes."

The former outlaw was asked if he had met any people in Dallas whom he had known before. He replied:

"No, I meet a great many who claim to know me, but the fact is I really knew very few people anywhere, and fewer still knew me. One reason I was never captured was because I never made a confidante of anyone and I never placed perfect confidence in any human being. There was a time when no man on earth could have killed me without a fight. I never let those who were with me handle my guns, and if anyone asked to look at my pistols I always took out the cylinder before handing it to him."

Frank was then asked if he knew any of the noted people who tamed the West. "I know them by reputation," he answered, "but never have met any of them. I always made it a point to keep away from bad men. These killers are always seeking quarrels, and I always tried to avoid them as much as possible. I always hated to kill anybody, and never did unless I had to. No reasonable man wants to take the life of another if he can help it. I always tried to keep away from the western country, where the detectives supposed me to be. I lived east of the Mississippi River most of the time, and always among quiet people who carried prayer books in their pockets instead of six-shooters. I found it much safer." Frank ended the interview by insisting he never touched liquor.

Mrs. James, and to a much lesser degree, Frank, continued to live in the past, while the Youngers looked to the future. For quite some time, Cole had entertained the idea of establishing a prison newspaper, but he did not have the funds for such a daring enterprise.[35] But on August 10, 1887, his dream came true when on that day the first issue of the *Prison Mirror* rolled off the presses. With contributions from fifteen inmates, including twenty dollars each from Cole and Jim, and ten dollars from Bob, the first edition was distributed to 412 inmates and a handful of outside subscribers. The *Mirror* was unique for two reasons: it would become the oldest continuously published prison newspaper in the United States, and it was the only prison publication launched with funds from inmate shareholders. Since the Younger brothers were among the founders, the newspaper gained wide acceptance from its inmate readers.[36]

Lew P. Schoonmaker became the publication's first editor. The first masthead also included the names of two compositors, and because of his outlaw notoriety, Coleman Younger was listed as printer's devil. It was not customary to cite a printer's devil since the position was nothing more than a shop cleanup person, but Cole's name did attract subscribers.[37]

Cole Younger. (Courtesy of the National Archives)

In the first issue, the *Mirror* ran the following information: "Cole Younger, our genial prison librarian, has received new honors at the hands of the *Mirror* by being appointed to the honorable position of 'printer's devil,' in which he will in the future keep flies off the gift of 'wedding cake,' and other editorial favors of like nature which may find lodgement in our sanctum sanctorum."[38]

The goals of the *Mirror* were to dispel rumors and to inform inmates on policies, procedures and upcoming events. For its outside readers, the journalists hoped to present a correct understanding of the realities and problems of prison life and prisoners. The negative headlines printed by outside news sources usually dwelled on sensational violence, reporting on escapes, beatings, killings, lockups and riots. The *Mirror* was, and still is, a positive experience, reporting on realistic positive issues.

The investors who "funded" the venture would get their money back, but only at the rate of three percent a month. Once the men were paid in full, all claims upon stock, material and shares would cease, and one hundred percent of profits would be given the prison library for the purchase of such books and periodicals as the warden selected. The treasurer of the *Mirror* was George Dodd, head prison guard who had helped the prisoners to safety during the fires two years previously.[39]

"Cole's" paper was issued every Thursday and boasted a circulation of 1,500 subscribers. The *Mirror* was distributed with no charge to the inmates of Stillwater Prison. These same inmates were permitted to send the newspapers to relatives or friends free of charge as well. The general public, however, paid one-dollar for a yearly subscription, and there were readers in nearly every state of the Union.

A prisoner submitted chase proofs of the following day's issue to the warden for approval every Wednesday. Rarely, however, did the warden exercise his power of censorship as the inmate editor always eliminated sensational material. All inmates were allowed to contribute articles to the *Mirror*, providing they met the publication's standards. Some of the topics were quite tongue-in-cheek, as evidenced by the following headlines: "It makes a man awful hot under the collar to accuse him of having cold feet" and "I do not know whether there are any lady 'bugs' in here or not, but there are quite a number of the other sex."[40]

The August 10, 1887, installment of the *Mirror* focused upon a letter Warden Stordock received from a critic and the "practical information free of charge" he sent back to the man. The letter writer said he had a "reformatory full of boys as one of my hobbies," and asked Stordock if he believed using the rod for punishment. The writer, H. Wilson, of Newport, Rhode Island, said there was nothing as beneficial to boys and men as a good whipping. Wilson said he disagreed with other disciplinarians who whipped their prisoners on the shoulders; he preferred the back just below the waist. He asked Stordock if he conducted beatings regularly and about his methods.[41]

In his reply, Stordock told Wilson he was sorry that a reformatory of boys served as his hobby. He was, he insisted, not sorry for Wilson but for the boys. The angry warden related to Wilson that he never used a rod because he was not interested in murdering anyone. As for beating below the waist, he replied, "Nature has provided a place for brains in all human beings, but sad to reflect on the vacant places in some craniums, even among men with 'hobbies.'"

The next issue carried an article entitled, "A Monument to the Younger Boys." The piece related what the newspaper's goals were and called it "the birth of a new era in prison reform in this country." The principal shareholders were listed as Cole, Jim, and Bob Younger. The article concluded with a word for Cole:

"Cole Younger is the librarian of the prison, and, as he is an inmate for life, the unfortunate fellow is making the richest atonement within his power for the errors of his past life. The good that the *Mirror* will do for his fellow prisoners will be a monument to his memory that many a more fortunate person that Cole Younger might envy."[42]

While Cole worked diligently inside the walls on the newspaper, supporters outside the walls continued to work for a Younger pardon. The efforts of Bronaugh, Newman, and Marshall had encouraged others to work independently on a "Free the Youngers" campaign, and several enthusiasts rallied around a new leader. In 1887, W.H. Harrington, former chaplain of the Minnesota State Prison at Stillwater and then chaplain of the Minnesota House of Representatives, authored a brochure called "Justice," advocating a pardon for the brothers.

Harrington had known the brothers intimately over the past seven years. In talking with the Youngers and from trips to Missouri where he interviewed their former neighbors, he was convinced they were victims of a troubled time trapped in the violence of the Kansas-Missouri Border War and American Civil War. According to Harrington:

"Against every prejudice, sectional, political, military, and religious, I have been driven to the conclusion that the Youngers are not bad at heart, that they are not of choice criminals and are in every way worthy, after ten years of prison service, to regain their liberty, and in pleading for their release I act voluntarily, from a sense of simple justice, for here as everywhere justice and mercy are really one. A prison is maintained, according to all modern theory, for two simple purposes, first, to protect society, and second, to reform the criminal."[43]

Harrington's "Justice" was well received, and it quickly orchestrated another Younger pardon campaign. On August 17, 1887, T.J. Younger, the brother's uncle in Warrensburg, Missouri, wrote Harrington a grateful letter, and the campaign was in motion:

"I hope I am not too familiar when I address you as my dear friend. Let me assure you that any and everyone who has the largeness of heart and magnanimity of soul to help my unfortunate nephews feel like a very dear friend to me. I get my mail at Warrensburg [she lived near Osceola, Missouri] hence the delay in this answer. Am very busy at present—and frustrated about business, therefore can't say much at present, but will have a number of letters sent to you and Governor Hubbard, can use as in your judgment—seems best. Will see what I can do in the way of money to pay your expenses. Cole wrote me of you, and I feel as though I know you personally. You can assure everyone who helps you that our hearts will go out in gratitude to them. We only ask that our nephews be understood and as you say justice will be done. Hopeing [sic] I may be able to reciprocate—the kindness of the good people of Minnesota."[44]

Six days later, William O. Mead of Osceola wrote Harrington a letter of support:

"I learned that you were the chaplain of the penitentiary of the State of Minnesota for several years after the incarceration of the Younger brothers. Therein, I have read your circular [Justice] carefully and heartily endorse every word you have given to the public in so far as their crimes before their confinement as far as it goes is correct. I have lived in Missouri for thirty-seven years and know them and their family very well and am intimately acquainted with two of their uncles T.J. [Thomas Jefferson] and C.F. [Charles Frank] Younger both of this county. I knew the grandfather of the Younger brothers and knew the father by reputation, and up to the time of the trouble of these boys, the whole family have born [sic] a good reputation as good law abiding citizens, and their trouble is the result of the tumultuous days between 1856 and 1866 on the border of Missouri and Kansas."[45]

Mead wrote that the Youngers' father had been a good Union man, and when the Civil War erupted, was a candidate for the office of delegate to the state convention to determine whether the state should concede or not. Mead told of his murder by abolitionist border ruffians, Younger property confiscated, and their house put to the torch. The boys became desperate and turned to crime, all the while searching for the murderer of their father.

He offered a long history of the Younger brothers' actions during the war and justified some of them whenever he could. He concluded his letter by writing:

"I was for four years a soldier in the federal army and have never voted any other than the Republican ticket, fought the Youngers in many conflicts during the Civil War and deprecate their acts as much as any man in Minnesota but under all the circumstances it does seem to me that the law has been vindicated and that [neither] law nor society can be further subserved by their further imprisonment, and I do hope in common with thousands of good citizens of Missouri that the executive department of your state can see its way clear to release these boys, and I feel quite certain that should such be done no one will ever have cause to regret it."[46]

Others rallied behind Harrington. On August 31, Robert M. Culloch, register of lands, and Michael K. McGrath, Missouri secretary of state, wrote a joint letter to Harrington:

"We are fully aware of the circumstances surrounding the case for which Coleman Younger and his brothers are now paying the penalty by [being] in the Minnesota Penitentiary, but we do not hesitate to join in the request to the governor of Minnesota in asking for their pardon, restoration to liberty and their homes. We believe that Justice has been satisfied by the long confinement and when their good behavior and exceptional conduct are also taken into consideration, it is clear to our minds that theirs is a case for the rightful exercise of Executive clemency, and we trust the governor of your state will pardon these unfortunate men, and thereby satisfy the demands of both Justice and humanity by this benevolent act."[47]

During late spring 1888, Warren Carter Bronaugh received a telegram from John Newman Edwards requesting he come to Kansas City immediately. Arriving in that city, Edwards introduced him to Kansas City newspaperman Liberty Hall. The man with the patriotic but very real name was a Minnesota native who volunteered to aid in the cause of a Younger pardon. Hall was given money to fight for the cause and soon departed for Minnesota.[48]

In 1888, a petition signed by several Missourians reached the office of Minnesota Governor William R. Merriam requesting parole for the three Younger brothers. The petition, composed by Younger supporter John Newman Edwards and carried out by Warren Carter Bronaugh, was signed by

Liberty Hall. (Courtesy of the Rice County Historical Society)

twenty-eight members of the General Assembly of Missouri. Bronaugh, however, was disappointed that Missouri Governor D.R. Francis did not join the campaign.[49]

In August, a reporter from the *Nevada Daily Mail* hopped a train for Minnesota after being told by W.C. Bronaugh, "Don't fail to go out to Stillwater and see the Younger boys." When the young man arrived at the prison, he found he had come on a bad day, as the warden and deputy warden were both absent, and the officials on duty were under orders to admit no one to see the Youngers. He was taken on a quick tour of the facility, however, and saw Bob at work as postmaster and Cole in the library. Jim was not seen since he was visiting the steward about his facial injury.[50]

"We have no fault to find with the Youngers as prisoners," said an officer of the penitentiary. "Their behavior is invariably good and no fault can be made of their attention to duty."

Inquiries at various points revealed there was considerable diversity of opinion relative to the propriety of pardoning the Youngers. The recent legislature of Minnesota inaugurated a doubtful change in the conduct of the prisoners by abolishing all manufacturers. The prisoners, previously engaged making threshing machine engines and separators, suddenly they found themselves with idle time on their hands. The prison officials told the reporter they felt it necessary to double the force of the guards during the coming month.

Later in the year, renowned actor/playwright, Hal Reid, visited the ailing Bob Younger. When asked how he felt, Bob answered he would be finishing his sentence before long. Reid told him he still thought a governor would release him before that. Bob replied it had better be soon or it would be too late for him.

Reid left Bob and went to the post office where Jim was in charge, only to find him sitting back in his chair strumming a guitar. Jim got to his feet and offered Reid, as well as Deputy Warden Westby, a chair. Reid jokingly asked Jim if he had been offered a postal commission in Missouri, and Jim quipped that Westby would not accept his resignation. Reid, concerned about Bob's condition, asked Westby and Jim how Bob was really feeling. Westby related that hospital steward Frank Hall and prison physician Pratt were doing all they could for him.

Reid continued on to the library where he shook hands with a nervous Cole. The prisoner asked him if he had seen Bob and conveyed he was very worried about his brother. Cole said he wished he could die in Bob's place and reminisced about the days when Bob was a boy.

Reid, in the company of Westby, left the library. There was very little hope that his friend Bob Younger would go on living.[51]

Notes

[1]Dr. William A. Settle, *Cole Younger Writes to Lizzie Daniel*, Liberty, Missouri, James-Younger Gang, 1994, p. 20.

[2]*Nevada* (Missouri) *Daily Mail*, January 25, 1886.

[3]*Nevada* (Missouri) *Daily Mail*, April 2, 1886.

[4]W.C. Bronaugh, *The Youngers' Fight For Freedom*, p. 54.

[5]During Frank James' trials, while he was out on bond, Missouri Republicans decided to hold their convention at Moberly. Frank asked to be race starter for the Moberly Fair Association, which angered Republicans. Because of this, the state committee voted to move their convention to Jefferson City.

[6]Ted P. Yeatman, *Frank and Jesse James: The Story Behind the Legend*, Nashville, Cumberland House, 2000, p. 289.

[7]Betty Sterett, *Scenes From the Past (of Nevada, Missouri)*, 1985, p. 89; *Nevada* (Missouri) *Herald*, October 24, 1971; Deed for Frank James house, Vernon County Missouri Deed Book 36, p. 595.

[8]Ibid, pp. 89-90.

[9]*Nevada* (Missouri) *Daily Mail*, Thursday, June 18, 1992.

[10]*Nevada* (Missouri) *Daily Mail*, February 28, 1887.

[11]*Nevada* (Missouri) *Daily Mail*, March 1, 1887.

[12]*Nevada* (Missouri) *Noticer*, November 11, 1886.

[13]*Nevada* (Missouri) *Daily Mail*, June 18, 1992..

[14]Dallas Cantrell, *Northfield, Minnesota: Youngers' Fatal Blunder*, pp. 101-102.

[15]*St. Paul Pioneer Press*, Friday, July 23, 1886.

[16]Ibid.

[17]*St. Paul Pioneer Press*, Saturday, July 24, 1886.

[18]Ibid.

[19]Ibid.

[20]*St. Paul & Minneapolis Pioneer Press*, Monday, July 26, 1886.

[21]*St. Paul Pioneer Press,* August 1, 1886.

[22]*St. Paul Pioneer Press,* August 13, 1886.

[23]James Taylor Dunn, *The St. Croix: Midwest Border River,* p. 95.

[24]Dick Nolan, *Benjamin Franklin Butler: The Damnedest Yankee,* Novato, California, Presidio Press, 1991, pp. 166-170; *Time-Life Books,* "Long Cruel Roads," pp. 114-115.

[25]Bob Warn, "Historical Bank Raid Centered on Ames Family," in "Nuggets from Rice County, Southern Minnesota History," *Golden Nugget,* May 17, 1972, p.11; *Time-Life Books,* p.145; Ted P. Yeatman, *Frank and Jesse James,* pp. 171-172.

[26]*Nevada* (Missouri) *Daily Mail,* August 21, 1886.

[27]W.C. Bronaugh, *The Youngers' Fight For Freedom,* pp. 81-82.

[28]James Taylor Dunn, "The Minnesota State Prison during the Stillwater Era, 1853-1914," *Minnesota History,* December 1960.

[29]Ibid.

[30]Marley Brant, *Outlaw: The Illustrated History of the James-Younger Gang,* p. 185.

[31]*Stillwater Democrat,* February 19, 1887.

[32]Marley Brant, *The Outlaw Youngers,* p. 236.

[33]*Nevada* (Missouri) *Daily Mail,* May 2, 1887.

[34]*Nevada* (Missouri) *Daily Mail,* June 10, 1887.

[35]Carl Hage interview with author, February 27, 1982.

[36]*The Mirror,* Anniversary Edition, Vol. 103, No. 1, August 11, 1989, "Mirror Turns 103."

[37]*Stillwater Evening Gazette,* Friday, November 9, 1979, "Younger Brothers Play Role in First Prison Paper."

[38]Ibid.

[39]*The Mirror,* August 11, 1989.

[40]H.C. Heilbron, *Convict Life at the Minnesota State Prison,* p. 101.

[41]*Prison Mirror,* Wednesday, August 10, 1887.

[42]*Prison Mirror,* Wednesday, August 17, 1887.

[43]W.H. Harrington, "Justice," Northfield, Minnesota Bank Robbery of 1876: Selected Manuscripts Collections and Government Records, Microfilm Edition, Roll 3, Minnesota Historical Society.

[44]T.J. Younger letter to W.H. Harrington dated August 17, 1887. Northfield, Minnesota Bank Robbery of 1876. Selected Manuscripts and Government Records, Microfilm Edition, Roll 3, Minnesota Historical Society.

[45]William O. Mead letter to W.H. Harrington dated August 23, 1887, Northfield, Minnesota Bank Robbery of 1876. Selected Manuscripts and Government Records, Microfilm Edition, Roll 3, Minnesota Historical Society.

[46]Ibid.

[47]Robert M. Culloch and Michael K. McGrath letter to W.H. Harrington dated August 31, 1887. Northfield, Minnesota Bank Robbery of 1876. Selected Manuscripts and Government Records, Microfilm Edition, Roll 3, Minnesota Historical Society.

[48]W.C. Bronaugh, *The Youngers' Fight For Freedom*, pp. 86-87.

[49]Marley Brant, *The Outlaw Youngers*, pp. 237-238.

[50]*Nevada* (Missouri) *Daily Mail*, August 28, 1888.

[51]Dallas Cantrell, *Northfield, Minnesota: Youngers' Fatal Blunder*, pp. 117-118.

V

1889

"I do not attempt to deny my own part in the affair. I was one of the number who went into the bank. It is not for me to say who shot the cashier; the parties there could probably tell him should they see him. But it was a bad piece of business, and very foolish. It was not our intention to kill him; we have not wanted to kill anyone. It would of course do no good to kill the cashier, because then we couldn't get into the vault anyway. Of course I cannot say what the motives of the man were when he shot, but I suppose he thought that the cashier was reaching down under his desk for his revolver."

—Bob Younger[1]

 n February 5, 1889, Cole was called to the warden's office. Upon entering the room, he was greeted by a reporter, who informed him that his old friend, Belle Starr (Myra Belle Shirley) had been killed. Rumors had circulated that Cole and Belle had married shortly after the Civil War and he had fathered a daughter, Pearl. Shortly thereafter, she left him for another outlaw, Sam Starr. The reporter asked Cole directly if he had, in fact, been married to Belle.[2]

Cole insisted he had never married anyone, and he certainly knew no one by the name of Belle Starr. He did admit, however, that he had met a lady named Belle Shirley in Seyenne, Dallas County, Texas, in 1869. She eloped with a man named Reed, and the couple left Texas for California. They returned in 1872, and Reed was later killed in a brawl.

Cole wrote W.C. Bronaugh on March 1, conveying to him that Bob was not well, and should their release not be achieved soon, he would never recover. Cole wished that Bronaugh was in Minnesota to get something done in their behalf as he had not a single dollar to pay someone else. As to the money to hire someone, Cole insisted he was good for it and would rather spend forty years in prison than cheat a person out of his fee. Cole ended his letter stating that he was blue.[3]

Cole Younger did an interview with an Ohio newspaper reporter on April 17, 1889. He did all he could to convince the public that all the men who had robbed the Northfield bank with him were now dead. But this statement indicated Frank James had not been involved, and since Frank was then living, most people considered it a sham to protect his good friend from prosecution. Some very prominent Minnesotans, however, were not turned off and eagerly sided with those favoring a Younger pardon.[4]

Cole wrote Bronaugh again on May 17 stating that he had instructed a relative, Jeff Younger, to visit Bronaugh and offer his services. He said when he learned of the petition being circulated in Jefferson City in support of a pardon, he felt like he had many times during the Civil War, when the fight was going on and he and his fellow soldiers could hear it, but, as reserves could not go to the aid of their comrades.[5]

Former Governor of Minnesota Henry H. Sibley eagerly joined Bronaugh's campaign in 1889. Sibley had enjoyed a long and distinguished career. He had served as Minnesota's first delegate to Congress, and it was Sibley who secured passage of the act creating the Minnesota Territory. He was the first justice of the peace in what had become Iowa, the Dakotas, and Minnesota. He had helped frame the state's first constitution and was the state's first elected governor (1858 to 1860). Sibley led the government troops to victory during the Dakota Uprising of 1862 and devoted his later years to civic and business pursuits. He and his family moved to St. Paul in 1862.[6]

Warren Carter Bronaugh visited the general in his St. Paul home. While there, Bronaugh met several Dakota Indians who trusted the general and no other white man. Bronaugh was impressed. He had heard many stories about the hero Sibley, and he was moved even more by the awe he inspired in the Dakota.

On behalf of the Youngers, Sibley penned the following letter on July 8, 1889:

> I feel it to be my duty to join in the appeal for pardon to the three convicts known as the Younger brothers, who have been incarcerated in the state prison at Stillwater for the past thirteen years. In so doing, I depart from the rule which has governed me, not to interfere with the course of justice, except under very exceptional circumstances.
>
> Believing the ends of justice to have been fully answered by the long and severe punishment inflicted upon the convicts mentioned, and taking into consideration the excellent record made by them during their confinement, I am persuaded that their release from further punishment would be favorably regarded by a majority of the people of the state, as an exercise of the comity toward a sister state which has appealed to your Excellency, through many of her high officials and other representative citizens, to pardon these young men and restore them to their friends, guaranteeing that in such event, they will prove to be law-abiding citizens.
>
> Minnesota has shown her power to punish malefactors, let her now manifest her magnanimity, by opening the prison doors to the men who have so long suffered for a violation of her laws, and bid them 'go and sin no more.'[7]

During the spring of 1889, a Younger support group met with Governor William R. Merriam in his St. Paul executive mansion. Representing a Younger pardon drive were former Minnesota Governor William R. Marshall, ex-warden Reed, Sheriff Ara Barton, Colonel E.F. Rogers, Colonel Stephen C. Reagan, Frances Twyman, Retta Younger, and Warren Bronaugh. Merriam dismissed the delegation from his office, refusing to discuss the subject any further.[8]

Bronaugh and Marshall visited the governor again a couple months later. Before being asked to leave once more, Bronaugh offered to take Cole's place in prison if the Youngers could be allowed to visit their Jackson County home for thirty days. He even ventured to produce a bond of a million dollars as a guarantee of faith if the boys could be pardoned. Marshall also offered to take Cole's place in prison. Merriam asked the two men to leave.

Former Stillwater Prison Warden John A. Reed approached Merriam supporting a Younger pardon. In an 1889 letter to the governor, Reed penned:

> I was warden of the Minnesota State Prison at the time the Younger Brothers were committed and for ten years thereafter, and I cheerfully testify to their good conduct during that time. I never had occasion to even reprimand them for they were always obedient and gentlemanly. They have now served more than an average length of time for a [sic] life prisoners. Believing as I do that the ends of justice do not require longer imprisonment and that they would settle down to be good citizens if liberated and the long imprisonment is telling on them as it such upon all long term prisoners and that mercy is not strained in asking for the release of those that are worthy but rather that humanity requires it. I join in with their friends in petitioning your Excellency to grant clemency and pardon them."[9]

Governor Merriam also received seven petitions from various government offices in the State of Missouri. These included petitions from officers of the State Missouri; members of the Thirty-fifth General Assembly, House of Representatives, State of Missouri; members of the Thirty-fifth General Assembly, Senate, State of Missouri; Clerks of the Thirty-fifth General Assembly, State of Missouri; Enrolling and Assistant Enrolling Clerks of the Thirty-fifth General Assembly, State of Missouri; Engrossing and Assistant Engrossing Clerks of the Thirty-fifth General Assembly, State of Missouri; and Chief and Assistant Chief Clerks of the Thirty-fifth General Assembly, State of Missouri.

Several of the petitions listed seven reasons why the Youngers should be pardoned:

"First. That they have now been in the penitentiary very nearly thirteen years.

"Second. During this entire period their behavior has been so excellent as to win not alone the respect but the perfect confidence of the prison authorities.

"Third. Every intention of the law has been fulfilled in this, that the punishment for the violation of it has been ample and complete.

"Fourth. If restored again to freedom almost the entire population of this state would stand security as a mass to their becoming law-abiding, peaceful, upright and worthy citizens.

"Fifth. To a certain extent they are the last victims of the Civil War, having been so unfortunate as to live upon the border at a time when bad blood was hottest, and evil passions most fully aroused.

"Sixth. Despite whatever may have been said to the contrary, those of the three who were in the Confederate army were always merciful in combat and also in victory. If they could be reached, hundreds of gallant federal soldiers would speak gladly out today and bear generous testimony to the truth of the declarations hererin made.

"Seventh. Your petitioners are of either military service. They simply come to you as one united whole asking for their pardon in the name of mercy and humanity. In so doing your petitioners will ever pray for your health, happiness, and high fortune."[10]

Colonel E.F. Rodgers, Captain Stephen C. Reagan, and Warren Carter Bronaugh visited the Youngers in Still-

Old prison ruins. (Photo by Author)

water Prison in June 1889. William R. Marshall advised the trio they should visit Judge Rodney A. Mott of Faribault, a distinguished community leader who could help their cause. Judge Mott served as Judge of Probate Court House and later as mayor of Faribault. He was also the first superintendent of the Minnesota State Academy of the Deaf. The three Younger supporters stayed at the Brunswick Hotel, formerly the Barron House, in Faribault while they conducted their visits to Judge Mott.[11]

Old prison ruins. (Author photo)

Mott read their letter of introduction and was sympathetic. His answer: "During the three months of the Younger brothers' trial and imprisonment in the county jail at Faribault, our people, strangely enough, became attached to them. The conduct of the prisoners was so excellent, their manners were so pleasant, and their intelligence so marked that they easily won over to themselves many persons who had been their bitter enemies and who had clamored for revenge. On returning home, after the Youngers had been convicted and life sentences had been passed upon them, my wife asked me the result of the trial. I told her and also added that it was my purpose to use my influence toward having them released. And now, to know that, after thirteen long years, I have not kept my promise."[12]

The following day, Judge Mott assembled twenty-five of Faribault's leading citizens. Before leaving the meeting, they drafted twenty-three letters of recommendation. On June 22, ex-Governor William Marshall received the following letter from Judge Mott:

> My wife reminded me last night of an incident I had forgotten, i.e., when I came home from court in 1876 and told her of the sentences of the Younger boys, I remarked, "If they continue to behave for ten years as well as they have here in jail and during their arraignment and sentence, I pledge myself to join a movement for their release."
>
> I now trust that Governor Merriam may see his way clear to send them all home, rejoicing, to their friends, after these weary years to them. The clamor that their pardon might evoke can only emanate from a spirit of revenge, unworthy of our civilization. We have vindicated the power and majesty of the law, let us now manifest its mercy; for executive clemency, in all deserving and proper cases, is as the verdict of the jury, or the sentence of the court, and is it not the crowning glory of all to say, "Go and sin no more!"
>
> It does not seem that our Governor can hesitate to send poor Robert home at once, to die among his friends. If you think my opinion of any value, you are at liberty to show this letter to Governor Merriam, who, I know, has nerve enough to stand the nine days howl that might follow a pardon.
>
> I have met with great pleasure Colonel Rodgers, Reagan, and Bronaugh from Kansas City—they are true gentlemen, every one.[13]

Rodgers, Reagan, and Bronaugh visited multi-millionaire miller George A. Pillsbury on what they called a mission of mercy. Bronaugh set his grip, which he called his "Cole Younger Bag," on the floor and withdrew letters and testimonials. He also extracted a letter of introduction from a Baptist minister, who was Pillsbury's pastor, in Kansas City. Pillsbury was giving the church $20,000 a year, and Bronaugh felt he could soften the wealthy aristocrat. But Pillsbury became angry when asked to contribute a letter of pardon for the Youngers and refused to cooperate with the men on such an outrageous request.[14]

The trio next visited milling magnate and soon-to-be-elected Senator William D. Washburn. Washburn became indignant because the men had come to his home rather than his office. They fared better, however, in their meeting with Senator Cushman K. Davis, who agreed to work with them for a Younger pardon.

Bob Younger in 1889. (Courtesy of the National Archives)

During that year, Bob's health began to decline, and following examinations, he was diagnosed with tuberculosis.[15] A.K. Doe, a prominent Stillwater resident, who had already signed his name to several petitions for a Younger pardon, wrote Governor Merriam:

"I observe that there is a petition in circulation for the pardon of Robert Younger, now confined in the state prison here.

"From conversation with a number of physicians of repute, particularly Doctor Pratt, prison physician, I am satisfied that Robert Younger's term of life is short. H[is] having been confined so long, I am satisfied that the ends of justice have been met, and that he is worthy in every respect of executive clemency."[16]

Former prison chaplain W.H. Harrington continued his efforts for a Younger release. In June, he wrote Governor Merriam again:

"I take the liberty of representing to you my most earnest wish that you would liberate from the State Prison immediately Robert Younger and thus allow him to be cared for among his friends in what seems to be his last sickness. Even should he by some unlooked for help, recover there is nothing to fear.

"You are perhaps aware of my persistent efforts to secure some commutation of the sentence of the three brothers as a matter of justice. I shall offer you my reasons with corroborating papers, letters."[17]

On June 12, Colonel A.W. Edwards, editor of *The Argus* in Fargo, North Dakota, wrote Cole Younger, offering to help in securing a release for him:

> I fully appreciate your situation, and while I have no hesitation in feeling the wrong originally committed, I have no hesitation in saying that the punishment, has, in my judgement, been meted out to the full extent of all necessary requirements, and I trust that the agitation now going will result in your benefit.
>
> I believe sincerely that if you and your brothers were restored to freedom and citizenship, you would be worthy of confidence, and for this reason I have taken occasion to so express myself.
>
> At any time I can assist you in any honorable manner do not hesitate to call upon me. Governor Merriam is a strong man, and it seems to me if you can get your case properly before him, he will have the nerve to do the right thing. Ex-governor Marshall has in years past, taken much interest in your matter, and I like him for it.
>
> Please say to Mr. Benner [prison steward] that I remember him well, and at the first opportunity I shall call upon him. I do not visit St. Paul very often and when there am very much pressed for time, but I hope soon to have an opportunity of shaking him by the hand and if ever I can visit Stillwater, shall certainly call upon you.
>
> Keep up your courage, maintain the good record you have established, and although it may seem tedious and a long time coming, I feel assured that you will yet be restored to liberty, as I believe you should be.[18]

Younger nephew, Harry Jones, of Pleasant Hill, Missouri, wrote Governor Merriam on June 14. Like Harrington, Doe, Edwards, and so many others, his request for a pardon for his uncles fell on deaf ears.

Over the summer of 1889, Bob Younger was nearing death. Many persons considered his illness a sham being acted out to get him released from prison. Ex-Governor William R. Marshall journeyed to Northfield and paid a visit to First National Bank President George Phillips in hopes of obtaining a pardon for the brothers. Phillips, however, doubted the seriousness of Bob's illness but brought in a doctor whom he trusted to examine the patient and satisfy everyone interested in the case.[19]

The physician, Dr. Benjamin H. Ogden, was a young, well-known surgeon who had moved to St. Paul from Northfield and set up a practice in the Germania Bank Building. Phillips contacted Dr. Ogden and arranged for him, along with Stillwater Prison physician Dr. William H. Pratt to examine Bob within the prison walls. Doctors Ogden and Pratt conducted a thorough examination of Bob and diagnosed him with only weeks to live, or if he was lucky, two months. Dr. Ogden sympathized with Bob's wishes to die outside the prison walls, and he penned a letter to Phillips requesting a pardon for all three brothers. The plea, however, was turned down.[20]

When physicians told Bob he was dying, he accepted his fate, but he would not discuss his situation with anyone other than his brothers. Meanwhile, he continued to work toward a possible parole.

Sometime prior to receiving his diagnosis, Bob wrote his sweetheart Maggie that he did not want to see her again until he was back in Missouri a free man. Bob had met Maggie, a New Englander, in Missouri while coming home to visit his brother John's grave. Together they began working a farm in Jackson County, and the short-lived romance began to flourish. Bob had fallen head over heels in love with Maggie but only after he was able to put aside his initial distrust of a Yankee. In spite of Bob's decision to cut ties, she refused to accept the rejection and maintained that she was ready to make a home for him upon his return to Missouri. While Maggie was described as a "gentle, beautiful woman" by those who saw her in Bob's company, her last name was never revealed.[21]

A May 1889 *Stillwater Messenger* article discussed the failing health of Bob Younger: "The many friends of Coleman, James and Robert Younger, who have spent nearly thirteen years in the state prison of this city, will regret to learn that Robert (familiarly called 'Bob'), who has been in impaired health for several years, is rapidly failing, and little hope is entertained that he will survive many months. There are thousands of excellent citizens of Minnesota who are familiar with the facts connected with the Northfield tragedy who would gladly see the Youngers restored to freedom and who would be especially pleased to see Robert released in view of the expected, speedy and fatal termination of his illness."[22]

The author of the article assured his readers that if released, the brothers would never resort to a life of crime. According to the piece, the brothers had never in two decades of confinement, wanted anything but an "opportunity to lead quiet, peaceable, law-abiding lives." The Youngers were not murderers, the article implied, although they were guilty in participating in the robbery of the First National Bank in Northfield. In Stillwater, their conduct had been exemplary, and they had encouraged hundreds of convicts to lead better lives during confinement and after their release.

"If society will suffer no harm from their release," the author wrote, "it is hard to see what is to be gained by their continued imprisonment, as it is not pretended that they will be made any better for life or death thereby. If the victims of the deplorable crime at Northfield could be restored to life by their ending their days in prison few would question the justice of their punishment. But as every object of imprisonment (except unrelenting vengeance) has been accomplished in this case, it is difficult to see why they should not be allowed, after this long atonement for a crime for which they were only indirectly responsible, to spend a few years, or months, or weeks in the enjoyment of the blessings of heaven, which descend alike upon the just and the unjust."

The writer stated that the citizens of Minnesota should have no fear of a Younger release for they would return home to Missouri. Thousands of Missouri's best citizens, including the governor, state officers, nearly every member of the legislature, and hundreds of prominent Union ex-soldiers, had signed a petition requesting executive clemency. He added:

"But in case Governor Merriam will not let them all go, it is to be hoped he will allow Robert, the youngest, who is now slowly dying, as a result of his first, and only serious offense, to breathe his last and be buried in the state which gave him birth."

According to prison physician William H. Pratt: "At that time, Bob Younger was sick and going to die, and (the officers of the prison) tried hard to get him pardoned so that he might die with his friends around him, and Cole and James told me if Bob was allowed to go home and die, they would never ask for a pardon for themselves."[23]

Governor Merriam, still refusing to let Bob go home, received a petition to pardon Bob due to his poor health. The petition was signed by several prominent citizens: A.K. Doe, Andrew D. Stowe, M.E. Murphy, J.C. O'Gorman, G.M. Seymour, J.H. Albert, E.G. Butts, Isaac Staples, R.M. Anderson, and John A. Reed. The petition read:

"The undersigned respectfully ask for the pardon of Robert Younger, now in the State Prison under life sentence.

"The grounds of this application are the fact that said Younger is wasting away from Consumption and in the judgement of physicians will not live many months or even many weeks if continued in confinement. Added to this is the fact that he has now served nearly fifteen years (if allowance of time for good conduct be reckoned). Also that his conduct has been without exception good. He was but [twenty-two] years of age when implicated in the crime for which he was sentenced. We earnestly pray for you to extend Executive Clemency to this man, that he may go to his relations before his life ends."[24]

Also writing Governor Merriam with a request to free Bob was Rice County Sheriff Ara Barton, who had held the brothers in the jail at Faribault and, following their trial, accompanied them to Stillwater Prison. Barton wrote:

"I take the liberty of writing you a line asking you to pardon the three Younger Brothers now confined in the prison at Stillwater. From what I know of their pain surely they would make good Christian citizens if they had their liberty I think. I think for Minnesota to capture the boys and keep them and make good men of them and return them to their friends and state would be a great feather in the hat of Minnesota of its power that dare to do right though the heavens fall will be the cause that the people will stand by, from what I know of the feeling of the people of the state, I think they are of the affirmation that the boys ought to have their liberty. If you cannot see it in that light for God's sake pardon Robert and let his aunt and sister take him home to be with his friends what few days he has to stay on earth."[25]

Younger supporters were probably banking upon securing a pardon from the government in the same manner that Stillwater murderer Joseph Marco had four years earlier. On July 7, 1877, one-year after the Youngers' Northfield crime was committed, farmhand Marco had shot and killed Olive Enos with a shotgun when she caught him stealing. When her husband, Joseph, came home, Marco killed him as well. He placed their bodies in the cellar and set the house on fire to cover up his vicious crimes. Like the Youngers, Marco pleaded guilty to murder to escape a hanging and was sentenced to life in Stillwater Penitentiary.[26]

During the summer of 1883, Marco's father received word that his son was dying of consumption (tuberculosis). He began a campaign to get his son pardoned so he could die at home with family and friends. Petitions were circulated, and even County Attorney James Brian, who originally tried the case, signed in favor of a pardon. The records of pardon included letters from the warden and the doctor at Stillwater who stated that Marco was in the final stages of consumption, and it was but a matter of days until his death. On September 10, 1883, Governor Hubbard pardoned Marco. He went home to LaCrosse, his health improved, and he went back to work. Later, Marco committed suicide by eating lye soap.

The Marco-Younger situation was a purely identical one. Both were lifers, both were dying of consumption, and supporters in both cases were circulating petitions and sending letters to the governor. Although Bob's crime was of a less brutal nature, he had served more time than Marco. Still, Marco was sent home, and Bob languished in his cell with little hope of redemption.

On June 12, 1889, an article appeared in the *Butler* (Missouri) *Times* stating Bob's "former florid complexion had faded to an ashy paleness. His cheekbones stand out prominently, and his whole face is that of an invalid. He has lost much flesh, his arms and limbs are narrowed down almost to bones, and his hands are thin and shallow. He is but a shadow of what he was up to a year ago. As he speaks, his voice is husky, and he once in a while coughs. His steel blue eye is yet bright and restless. He knows he is far from well, but his iron will, so the attendants say, does not for an instant weaken, and he says he is sure he will be better."[27]

That same month, the Youngers were visited by a Stillwater newspaper reporter, who penned, "I saw the celebrated Younger brothers, too, and, although Bob is in a very precarious condition physically, they still have something of a distinguished air about them, something that marks them as being different from the ordinary convict."[28]

Elsewhere in the same article, the author wrote: "Looking on the emanciated [sic] form of Bob Younger, I

WHEN THE HEAVENS FELL

could only ask myself the question, 'What end of justice is being subserved by keeping this wreck of a once physically splendid man here to die?' If he had been a Chicago alderman and robbed the poor of the city of a million dollars he would long ere this [have] paid the penalty of his crime with a few thousand of the money he had stolen and would have been in the legislature by this time making laws for the punishment of other thieves. There can be little doubt that the Northfield robbery was Bob Younger's first real offense against society, and if it were left to a vote of the people I am positive that four-fifths of the citizens of Minnesota would say, 'Release him and let him end his days in peace with those who love him as dearly as though he had never worn the degrading stripes.' I am not in the habit of slopping over on anyone, and I lost the key to my gush hose some years ago, but this is the way it looks to a man with only one eye and what brain you would notice if spread out on a two-cent stamp."[29]

That very day, Captain D. Cavanaugh of the Cavanaugh & Company Hardware and Farm Machinery Store wrote Governor Merriam. "I have recently visited the prison at Stillwater, and [by] what I have learned am of the opinion Robert Younger now confined there cannot survive many months.

"I, therefore, in the interest of humanity respectfully ask executive clemency in his behalf that he may pass his last hours among friends."[30]

Also, on June 22, G.W. Batchelder, an ex-state senator and one of the Youngers' attorneys after the raid, wrote Governor Merriam. Batchelder, an avid supporter of a Younger pardon wrote:

> Three gentlemen from the State of Missouri have called upon me in the interest of the Younger Brothers and have asked me to write you giving my opinion as to the propriety of granting them a pardon. I am willing to express myself upon that subject—as I have often done for the past two or three years.
>
> I know the crime they committed. That they were guilty of the crime of an attempt with others to rob the Northfield bank. I do not believe they were guilty of or intended to assist in the crime of murder.
>
> I know too that—they have been punished long and severely and believe that the ends of justice would be fully met if they should now be set at liberty. I believe

from my personal acquaintance with the men and things can change during their thirteen years of imprisonment, that no one can reasonably doubt [their right] to liberty. They would become good citizens. I cordially believe that their confinement has accomplished all which can be accomplished by a continuance of the same punishment—and so far as I can see is the opinion of a large majority in the community where I live.

But Batchelder's main concern was over the welfare of Bob Younger:

With regard to Robert Younger I want to say in particular. I understand he is afflicted with an incurable disease that is rapidly hastening toward death. This must be known to your Honor and the State in general. And I believe it would be as sinful in the highest degree to continue punishment down to death's door. I see nothing that the State can gain by prolonging his punishment and nothing that it can lose by allowing him to return to his home to die with friends, which is only a poor privilege at best.[31]

H.B. Wilson of Red Wing, former state superintendent of Public Instruction, also wrote Governor Merriam on the twenty-second, although he mistakenly addressed his letter to Governor William R. Marshall. Wilson wrote that some time earlier he had written Governor McGill requesting a Younger pardon, but since the executive was about to leave office, Wilson asked that his letter be passed on to his successor. Wilson said he had conversed with the Youngers in Stillwater on three occasions regarding the "mad and daredevil raid" on the Northfield bank and their lives in Missouri. He added, there were extenuating circumstances for the path they had taken, beginning with atrocities inflicted upon them and their family during the Civil War. According to Wilson, the Youngers would become good citizens if permitted to go free. His six-page letter concluded with:

"Still, I am fully aware that it is a delicate matter for the executive to handle. I am aware that there are those who would be

Jim Younger in 1889. (Courtesy of the National Archives)

ready to criticize and growl, should he exercise the Constitutional power of pardoning these men, but those who would have the most to say, are not among our best citizens. I trust our honored executive will give this subject his most careful thought, and that he will act wisely, and for the best interests of our State."[32]

But not everyone writing the governor was in favor of a Younger pardon as evidenced by a letter sent to Governor Merriam on June 23 by a Duluth roofer, H.P. Hynes.

> I see in the *St. Paul Globe* of today a petition for his [Bob Younger] pardon being largely signed by Bluff City people," wrote Hynes. "This is for Bob Younger's release, also his brothers Jim and Cole. 'In God's name' and in the name of one hundred and sixty-four (164) *poor sick soldiers* who Cole, Bob, and Jim Younger were the chief movers in taking out of a train on the old North Missouri R.R. at Centralia and murdering alongside of the track in 1864. Do not do it—do not let such a sin rest on your soul. Look at the records in the War Department concerning that event. Their [sic] you will find it—the most cold blooded uncalled for murders perpetrated in the last Civil War. There are many old soldiers who remember that event and if you do not want the implications of the whole grand A.R. brought down on your head do not— commit such an atrocity. I think it was in April or May 1864 General Clinton B. Fisk (Prohibition candidate in the last campaign) was at that time the commander of the Department of North Missouri with headquarters in the Paty [sic] House in St. Joseph. The hospitals in his department were over crowded. In order to better their condition, he order [sic] some of the patients to St. Louis. To some of them this was a leave of absence given to go home in the hope they would get well. The train proceeded on its way until it got to Centralia. Their [sic] it was stopped by Bill Anderson's gang of cut throat Gurillias [sic]. The Youngers were his lieutenants. They emptied the cars of all those who had a soldier's uniform on and drew them up in a line on the south side of the track. They (Youngers) had new Winchester rifles that had never been tested. They said they would test them on the 'yanks.' They did so the result of that test (using their own language) it sent a ball through *seven of them by god*. Then the work of slaughter began until the last man was killed. The government had them buried in a ditch where they were murdered and I think put a fence

around it later. The Youngers and James boys were born of viciousness, nursed in crime and wickedness followed it up until one got killed and the other three landed behind prison bars at Stillwater.[33]

Hyne's lengthy missive went on to discuss the attitude of the Youngers, how they had boasted they could never be conquered, and how they would continue to fight the war for the rest of their days. He called any requests for a Younger pardon "an insult to decency" and referred to the brothers as fiends.

The following day, G.M. Seymour of Stillwater wrote Governor Merriam in support of a pardon. According to Seymour, the Youngers had worked for him in prison and had done well. Seymour said the brothers were always reliable and he believed that if pardoned, they would lead honorable lives.[34]

Also on the twenty-fourth, E.W. Durant, Mayor of Stillwater, wrote Governor Merriam supporting a Younger pardon. Durant believed, because the brothers had been confined for thirteen years and had a good conduct record, plus won the friendship of officers, punishment should be salutary. By liberating the brothers on account of their good conduct, other convicts would be stimulated to conduct themselves in the same manner.[35]

D.M. Sabin, a United States Senator and Stillwater businessman, wrote Merriam supporting a pardon. According to Sabin, the brothers had exemplary records during their thirteen years of confinement, and he felt enough was enough.[36] Stillwater attorney, E.G. Butts, concurred with his letter, stating they had been punished long enough. By keeping them in Stillwater, he charged the government with vindictive punishment.[37] A.K. Doe, who had written the governor earlier, sent another letter in hopes of securing a Younger pardon. He felt that the crime for which they were persecuted was the result of circumstances rather than of confirmed criminals.[38]

As Bob's health deteriorated, more letters of support for his pardon were addressed to the governor. H.W. Pratt, a Minneapolis businessman, had recently toured the Stillwater prison and talked with Bob Younger. According to Pratt, all Bob had left was the hope of dying outside prison walls in the company of his friends. Bob had talked to Pratt about one of his sisters whom he wished to see before death took him.[39]

One of Bob's doctors at the prison, Dr. T.C. Clark, also took it upon himself to write the governor requesting a pardon for Bob. Dr. Clark informed Merriam that in his professional opinion, Bob was in the last stages of acute consumption and had only a few days to live. He could, wrote Clark, live as long as sixty days, but this he felt was unlikely. By sending Bob home, he admitted, his life would not be prolonged, but it would make his demise a more comfortable one.[40]

An editor of the *Kansas City Weekly Record*, Liberty Hall, also wrote the governor of Minnesota requesting Bob be sent home. "I read in yesterday's *Kansas City Times* a dispatch from Stillwater, Minn[esota], stating that a special effort was being made to secure the pardon of Robert Younger," wrote Mr. Hall. "I write simply to say from what I learned about Bob's personal character as a man and his record as a prisoner while acting as inspector of that state's prison, and also from what I have learned of his history as a boy since I came to this state, from his old neighbors and schoolmates. I sincerely believe that justice and humanity both demand his release. But you will hear all the arguments in his favor better than I can state them. If I held the pardoning power, I should consider, first, the fact that he was a good-sized infant at the time of the Northfield raid; second, that he has already served a life convict's life-time—nearly [thirteen] years—without a scratch to blot the record of his conduct; and third, the condition of his health and the almost absolute certainty that, if retained in prison, he cannot live but a few months. Together with the probability that, if liberated now, he will have but a little time to remain with his friends."[41]

J.H. Albert, Protestant chaplain at Stillwater Prison, wrote Governor Merriam, stating that he would soon see a petition for release of the Youngers. Albert, too, favored their release, but said he wanted to write a personal letter as well.[42]

Horace W. Pratt, who had written the governor two days earlier, requesting a pardon for Bob, wrote again on the twenty-sixth, this time asking a pardon for all three brothers. He asked Merriam to show mercy, but despite the hundreds of letters crossing his desk, the governor was not about to change his mind.[43]

M.E. Murphy, the Catholic chaplain at the prison, wrote Merriam on the twenty-ninth, saying he represented friends of the Younger boys.[44] He based his plea upon the brothers' "model prison" record. Samuel Mathus of Stillwater wrote the governor the following day, also in support of a Younger pardon.[45]

In July, one of the Youngers' staunchest crusaders wrote Merriam again. The author of "Justice" insisted the Youngers were good men and drew attention to their unblemished prison record in his six-page letter.

"I *know* that the ordinary stories about them are fiction," penned Harrington. Cole has never killed a man since the war; in service he did his duty. The only crime which Minnesota has to consider, it seems, is the Northfield robbery at which two men lost their lives. The Youngers were present and on being captured pleaded guilty to accessory to murder. For this they have already served four years longer than the term served by men sentenced for murder in the first degree."[46]

As in other letters, Harrington blamed the war for the Youngers' crimes and painted a pretty picture of their innocence. He concluded his epistle by saying, "To have these men for next door neighbors would be to enjoy the society of men of the highest social greatness and the incarnation of truth and honor."

On July 1, 1889, St. Paul attorney W.H. Grant cast his lot with those supporting a pardon. "I think the Younger Brothers have been punished enough, and ought to be pardoned," offered Grant in a letter to Governor Merriam. "Jesus Christ forgave his murderers on the spot. Let the State forgive the Youngers and give them the opportunity of becoming respectable people. I do not believe in everlasting punishment. I think they have fully resolved to lead an honest life and should be given the chance."[47]

Grant was not the only pardon enthusiast to write the governor that day. S.B. Lovejoy of Minneapolis also jumped on the bandwagon.[48]

The following day a petition signed by citizens of St. Paul was sent to the governor. Enclosed with the petition were nine letters, some with multiple signatures, all written on Merchants Hotel stationery and all favoring a Younger pardon. One five-page letter attempted to crack the heart of the governor with phrases such as, "A longer imprisonment cannot return the father to his child, but a pardon can give brothers to a lonely sister whose heart is bleeding with anguish for her unfortunate brothers."[49]

That same day, David Day of St. Paul wrote the governor a letter on Ramsey County Court House and City Hall Special Commission stationery. Day, a member of the commission and an officer at the prison at the time of the Youngers' incarceration, was quite adamant regarding a pardon for the brothers. He conveyed to Merriam his friendship with the brothers, summarizing with what good citizens they would become if freed. "Doubtless they have grievously sinned," expressed Day, "but doubtlessly they have grievously suffered for it." The letter was also signed by William Lee.[50]

W.M. Campbell, a United States marshal, also wrote Governor Merriam in support of a pardon. In his long letter, Campbell stressed that he was joining ex-Governor Marshall in his movement to secure a pardon. He was also concerned about Bob:

"That upon the theory that confinement in prison is for the punishment of crime, then these men have been sufficiently punished. They have been confined until they are utterly broken down, both in health and spirit, and one of them, Robert, whom I saw three weeks ago, is surely dying. He cannot possibly survive many months, probably not many weeks."[51]

While other letters supporting a pardon for Bob, such as that of St. Paul tobacconist Adam Fetsch, reached Governor Merriam, at least five letters attacking a would-be pardon were received over a two-day period.[52]

H.G. Finkle, judge of Probate Court of Clay County, Moorhead, stated he was against a pardon on legal grounds, not because it involved the Youngers. "The only complaint against your administration so far has been you have been using the pardoning power to [sic] much," wrote Finkle.[53]

St. Paul businessman Edward J. Hodgson wrote the governor on July 4 protesting a pardon. He enclosed a clipping from the *Red Wing Advance*, Sunday, July 3, with his letter.[54]

W.W. Griswold of Morris wrote Merriam a lengthy letter the same day attacking the reasoning behind considerations for a Younger pardon. He believed the boys should remain in jail for neither they nor anyone else could replace the life sacrificed. Said Griswold: "A hundred years of incarceration could not atone for the single life taken, and how many more they are guilty of, we can only conjecture."[55]

Thomas P. Ritchie of St. Louis also attacked a pardon in his letter to Governor Merriam. Ritchie criticized the boys' behavior practices and dismissed them as no means for a pardon. As to their suffering through thirteen years of confinement, he stated, "The jury of twelve good men and true have named 'life imprisonment' as the only means of satisfying the law. Is the decision by men thoroughly familiar with the case in all its details, to be put aside by the *opinions* of a few friends of the prisoners?"[56]

Still another critic, H.W. Brower of St. Charles, blasted those who had signed petitions to free the Youngers. Brower demanded that the laws of the land be adhered to and not allowed to be meddled with by friends of the Youngers.[57]

T.M. Newson of St. Paul wrote Cole Younger on July 6. In support of a pardon, he asked Cole to forward the letter to Governor Merriam. The letter to Cole read:

"A friend of yours asked me to write a letter to Governor Merriam in your favor and gave me his name, but in the excitement of the [Four]th, I have lost it. So I send the letter to you, and you can give it to your friend. I hope the effort will be successful, for I feel sure that if at liberty you would make good citizens."[58]

Newson's letter to Merriam read: "After thoroughly examining the case and facts of the Younger bros—that are in State Prison, I am satisfied that most of the stories depicting their careers are false—that they never committed murder—that they did not know that one of their company was to shoot Mr. Heywood, the cashier at Northfield—that they have been in prison for thirteen years for the crime of robbery—that during that time they have won the highest regards of the officers for their good behavior—that one of the brothers is nigh unto death—that it seems to me that they have been amply punished, and that if liberated they would make good citizens. I earnestly ask you to favorably consider their case and if possible grant them a pardon."[59]

Several prominent citizens wrote the governor the following week in favor of setting the boys free. B.G. Yates, former resident of Madelia and a participant in the capture of the Youngers, told the governor he had been in Madelia a week earlier, and sentiment there was pretty much in favor of a

Younger pardon. Julius A. Schmahl, editor of the *Redwood Gazette* in Redwood Falls, insisted his community was overwhelmingly in favor of a Younger pardon. S.A. Langum, editor and publisher of the *Preston Times,* stated his community was also in favor of a pardon. Langum added he had once served as an officer in the prison and was convinced the brothers were reformed. Writing, "I have never regarded them as ordinary criminals and think they were driven to criminal life by circumstances that might have driven good men to such a life," Dr. C.O. Cooley of Madelia spoke out in favor of a pardon. Dr. Cooley had been the Youngers' attending physician for about a week upon their capture. Captain W.W. Murphy, one of the seven brave men who had captured the Youngers, related to Merriam that the demands of justice had been satisfied. John C. Wise, editor of *The Review,* Mankato, agreed with Captain Murphy and told the governor that the Youngers could have killed their pursuers at several different sites during the chase. Another newspaperman, Harold I. Cleveland of the *St. Paul Pioneer Press,* asked the governor for a pardon. Cleveland had been present at the Younger capture and had stayed in contact with the boys since then. His long letter showed concern for Bob: "Especially do I ask you to consider the case of Robert Younger, who standing on the threshold of Death, deserves by every principal of mercy the clemency you can extend." Another petition reached the governor's office as well, this one signed by citizens of St. Paul and other cities. The supporters for a pardon included W.R. Gill and others.[60]

W.S. Culbertson of New Albany, Indiana, wrote the governor and denounced any idea of a pardon for "those vile red-handed murderers, the Youngers." Culbertson's main fear concerned the women of America and their progeny. Said Culbertson: "They are murders and thieves by nature and one serious objection to liberating them is that there are plenty of women that consider them heroes and [would] marry them and bring into the world a family of robbers."[61]

Elisha Taylor of Detroit and W.R. Estes of Madelia each wrote Merriam stating in no uncertain terms they were against a pardon. Both men expressed their desire that the three prisoners be hanged. Decorah, Iowa, banker, James H. Easton also wrote arguing against a pardon. Being in the banking business, he feared the prisoners would again turn to crime if released and prey upon banking establishments.[62]

An anonymous letter sent to Governor Merriam from Arkoe, Missouri, on July 12 insisted that nine out of ten Missourians were against a pardon. The letter, signed "A Citizen," promised, "The good people of Missouri would never forgive you if you would turn the Younger brothers loose to deprecate on us as they have in the past. We have too many of there [sic] kind here now."[63]

W.R. Estes wrote Governor Merriam on the fourteenth enclosing an unsigned copy of a petition being circulated in Madelia. Estes understood that the governor was making his decision on a pardon the following day, and he asked the executive to wait for the signed copy before deciding on a pardon. According to Estes, nineteen-twentieths of the people in Madelia were entering a solemn protest against a pardon of the "notorious criminals."[64]

The Board of Pardons, on July 16, received a letter from Fairmont attorney, H.M. Blaisdell thanking them for considering the cases of Cole and Jim Younger, and Lewis Kellihan. W.R. Estes sent his signed petition to the governor on the sixteenth, and the following day Merriam received a letter from M.D. Flower of St. Paul requesting a Younger pardon.[65]

On the twentieth, the governor's office filed an envelope labeled "Letters for Pardon of Younger brothers," containing letters from prominent Minnesotans. Among these letters was a three-page request for pardon from Ignatius Donnelly, one of Minnesota's most colorful figures. In the 1850s Donnelly charted his dream city of Nininger near Hastings, which many enthusiasts believed would blossom into a New York of the Midwest. During the congressional campaign of 1878, Donnelly, spokesman for the farmers, lost the election to W.D. Washburn. But Donnelly and the farmers were victorious later, when in 1885 a system of grading and inspection was established. Donnelly had always been a fighter, and he had now turned his attention to aiding the unfortunate Youngers.[66]

Donnelly's passionate letter may have convinced some persons, but it did not sway Governor Merriam. Donnelly penned:

Ignatius Donnelly. (Courtesy of the Rice County Historical Society)

I remember an incident which occurred when the Northfield robbers were seeking to escape from this state. In the woods, not far from Mankato, they were encountered by a citizen—a German, I think—who was looking for his cattle. The fugitives perceived that he recognized them. The two associates of the Youngers, who afterwards escaped from the state, proposed that, for their own safety, they should kill the man. To this the Youngers strenuously objected. It was their suggestion that he be gagged and tied to a tree in the depths of the forest, and left there. The Youngers replied that this would be more cruel than to kill him outright, as he might starve to death before he was discovered by those who might seek him. Upon this question the Youngers quarreled with their associates in crime, and separated. The Youngers gave the man his life, but swore him not to reveal the fact that he had met them. He did not keep his oath.

I always thought that there was something heroic in this action of these fugitives from justice, at a time when the woods swarmed with their pursuers. They were ready to risk their own lives rather than take the life of that stranger. It manifested a noble humanity when every circumstance of this desperate situation incited them to cruelty and bloodshed.

Now, I am told, the youngest of these brothers, then a mere boy in years, lies at the point of death. It seems to me that you can now justly remember that act of humanity, performed years ago in the woods of Blue Earth County, and permit this poor criminal to die outside the shadow of the penitentiary, and in the midst of those who love him.

I believe that such an exercise of your executive clemency will be justified by every humane heart in the state.[67]

Concurring with Donnelly were the other letter writers—Robert A. Smith, Mayor of St. Paul; John Clark, St. Paul Chief of Police; St. Paul Captain of Police John R. Bresett; and B.G. Yates, one of the 1876 posse members.[68]

B.G. Yates' second letter to Governor Merriam, written July 15, ended with a plea for Bob: "I am well aware of the unreasoning prejudice in some quarters against clemency for these men, but is it not a fact that they are now in prison because of crimes *rumour* [sic] has it they committed in other states and in other times of which they are probably innocent; at least these things have never been proved against them, and I envy not the man whose heart is so callioused [sic] to all the better instincts of humanity, who would begrudge Bob Younger the few days of life probably left. And believe, Mr. Governor, while I went out with horse, guns, and clerks (closing my place of business) after these men, none of us having the slightest intention of bringing them in alive, I would now rather take a pardon from your excellency to them, especially to Bob, than have a present of One Thousand Dollars."[69]

Willmar banker A.E. Rice was not of the same opinion. In a letter to Governor Merriam dated July 21, Rice argued, "If they are let out then, I say, open wide the prison doors that they may all walk out for if you open the door to the greatest why not to the lesser criminals?"[70]

On July 23, Cincinnati, Ohio, Chief Detective L.M. Hazen, who had pursued the Youngers in Missouri prior to the Northfield raid, wrote Governor Merriam. He commended the governor for his statement that he would do nothing at all in the case no matter how many petitions were sent him. Hazen included with his letter a newspaper clipping from that evening's *Cincinnati Commercial Gazette* entitled "Outlaw Dying of Consumption."[71] The article read:

"Bob Younger, the Missouri outlaw, must die in prison. He is in the last stages of consumption, and prominent men of Missouri have been trying to secure his pardon. Governor Merriam said to Colonel Bronaugh and ex-Governor Marshall last night, on their presentation of a large petition: 'I may as well say to you now, once for all, that I shall do nothing in this case—nothing at all. I have my own personal feeling and prejudice in the matter, and I should not be moved to interfere in the case of Bob, or any of them, even if Haywood's [sic] wife could come back from the grave and sign your petition, or if Haywood's [sic] surviving daughter should join in your appeal.'"[72]

Retta Younger arrived on September 2, and Cole and Jim were allowed to spend more time with their brother in his last days. Stillwater photographer J.M. Kuhn was brought into the prison to take a family portrait of Retta and her three brothers and separate shots of the boys. They were issued civilian clothing for the photo session, and despite the shadow of Bob's death hovering over them, all seemed to enjoy the shoot.[73]

Retta Younger with her brothers Bob, Jim, and Cole shortly before Bob's death. (Courtesy of the National Archives)

On Sunday evening, September 15, Bob Younger became suddenly ill. Unable to swallow, he could not take nourishment. His sister, Retta, as well as Cole and Jim, were at his side. The following evening, about six o'clock, Bob asked the trio not to leave because, he said, he had no more than four hours to live and wanted his family with him until the end. When Deputy Warden Jacob Westby entered the room three hours later, Bob asked him, since the official had been so kind to him, to also remain. Shortly after ten o'clock in the evening, on September 16, 1889, Bob passed away in the Stillwater Penitentiary.[74]

The *St. Paul Pioneer Press* carried the following: "Bob's account with the state is now fully settled, while his brothers Cole and Jim remain to drain the cup of expiation to the lees. A strenuous effort was made a few months ago by prominent

Missourians, backed by ex-Governor Marshall and a few other sympathetic gentlemen of Minnesota, to secure the pardon of the Youngers, but Governor Merriam refused to exercise clemency, in which decision the popular sentiment of the state supported him."[75]

The *Stillwater Daily Gazette* reported: "Bob Younger, the Missouri outlaw, died of consumption at 10:20 P.M., at the age of [thirty-four] years after imprisonment of thirteen years. Death at last came suddenly and hardly expected under two or three weeks. He began to feel the end approach at [six] o'clock and told Jim and Cole, his brothers, also serving life sentences, to remain, as he had but two or three hours to live. He sank gradually, kept his mental faculties up to the last breath, and bade his brothers and sister goodbye. His remains will probably be taken to his native county of Jackson, Missouri, for interment. All the Youngers always claimed that Bob never participated in any lawless act or excursion except the Northfield affair."[76]

In an article entitled, "Freed by Death," the *Stillwater Democrat* described Bob's failing health, which led to his death and "at last his eyes closed forever, and the most picturesque figure in modern outlawry closed his career on earth." The *Democrat* gave a brief history of Bob's life beginning with his birth in Jackson County, Missouri, on October 20, 1854. He was one of fourteen children, six of them boys. His father was a Union man, although a slaveholder, and was killed in the troubled times of the border war and Civil War. His older brothers rode with Quantrill during the war and returned to work the farm after hostilities ceased. Returning to outlawry to avenge their father's death, the article stated the brothers robbed a Rock Island train near Casey, Iowa, with the James boys, followed by stage robberies in Nevada and Arkansas, the Iron Mountain train robbery, a gun battle and killing of Captain Lull near Osceola, Missouri, and the Gad's Hill train robbery. The Northfield, Minnesota, robbery attempt of the First National Bank in Northfield proved their downfall.[77]

On the eighteenth, last rites were held over the remains of Bob Younger in the prison chapel at 1:30. Reverend J.H. Albert, prison chaplain, conducted the services with all the prisoners and a number of visitors present. Retta Younger was accompanied by Mrs. Samuel McClure of Kansas City and several friends she had met in St. Paul during her visits to the prison. Ex-Governor Marshall was also in attendance.[78]

The chapel was draped in black along the walls, the sable drapery caught up at each window by a bow of white, and the pillars down the center were similarly entwined as was the desk upon the platform. All the inmates of Stillwater Prison were in attendance, six with badges of mourning on their arms acting as pallbearers. Sitting on the platform with the prison chaplain were Ex-Governor William R. Marshall, Warden Randall, Dr. T.C. Clark, and others.[79]

The fancy coffin was covered with cloth and finely mounted and was situated at the front of the platform. At the head, facing the south, sat Bob's sister, Henrietta Younger, supported on either side by Cole and Jim. Retta shed no visual tears, but her face was set, and she continually swayed her body and could not repress audible sighs of anguish.

The prison choir opened the services with the song, "Jesus, Lover of my Soul," and the chaplain offered a prayer and read the verses of the fourteenth chapter of St. John's gospel. George Elliott, of the prison choir, sang a solo, "Asleep in Jesus, Blessed Sleep." The chaplain's remarks were brief but fitting as he pointed out the noble traits of Bob's character, his firmness of purpose, and his energy in carrying through whatever he had set his mind to doing. Chaplain Albert summed up his career by speaking of him as possessing "a will, fearless and determined; a heart honest and sincere; a tender affection for others; a mind full of the higher truths of life; a soul resting upon God."

Following the hymn, "Shall We Meet Beyond the River," the prisoners were allowed to walk forth and gaze upon the still face of their departed friend. As Retta and the brothers left the chapel, many persons broke into tears.

The *Prison Mirror*, of which he was a cofounder, eulogized: "Quiet, good-natured Bob Younger has gone down to his grave. He is gone to meet the parents whom violence sent to an untimely death. They left him, a child; he goes to them, a man. Let those who demanded his life be content—they have it."

The article stressed the good side of Bob's nature, and like many others, dealt with the circumstances, which may have driven him to a life of outlawry. The article concluded:

"He suffered with patience and when the hour of going came he was the first to recognize it, and when grim death grew nigh, he looked it full in the face; and then, casting a last loving look at his faithful sister, Bob Younger died without a moan or quaver. Let us hope that ere the light of this world faded into darkness his eyes were greeted by the dawn of eternal day."[80]

A few days later, accompanied by Retta, Bob's casket was placed on a train and taken to its final resting place in Lee's Summit, Missouri.

Warren Carter Bronaugh learned of Bob's death quite by accident. Performing on stage, while playing in *La Belle Marie*, he had to pretend to be reading a newspaper. When the prop man placed one on the desk used in the office scene of the second act, he read the headline, "Bob Younger Dead." The lines Bronaugh was speaking as the villain died upon his lips, but he had to proceed with his performance.[81]

Shortly after Bob's demise, Bronaugh went to see the governor of Minnesota and asked him to recommend a pardon for the two remaining brothers. The governor told him that such a move would be political suicide as everyone concerned with Minnesota politics had agreed that no candidate would be endorsed for governor if he advocated the freedom of the Youngers.[82]

In August of that same year, John J. Randall, a sixty-year-old coal merchant from Winona, replaced Stordock as warden. He was highly regarded by a Stillwater newspaper, which announced, "Randall has a good record and will doubtless make a good warden."[83] Still, the Stillwater newspaper insinuated that Randall had been appointed via the influence of Senator Sabin of the prison-contracting firm.

Although Randall served a brief term of only eighteen months, he took the first steps toward establishing a school in the prison. He also organized a Chautauqua reading circle. Still, accusations were made against him from discharged prison officials claiming he was too lenient toward the inmates. Randall was removed from office.[84]

The *Stillwater Gazette* concluded, "Until the position is removed from politics, the life of a warden in Minnesota will continue to be an unhappy one."[85] The *Messenger* asserted, "If he [Randall] erred, it was in placing too much confidence in convicts and subordinate officers who were unworthy."[86]

The year 1889 was one of significant change regarding the prison system in Minnesota. A board of managers, which consisted of five members appointed by the governor to staggered five-year terms, and which, was empowered to appoint the warden for an indefinite term, replaced the board of inspectors. Two members of the last Board of Inspectors were appointed to the Board of Managers. These changes in policy were made by the legislature, which at the time codified the duties of the deputy warden, physician, chaplain, principal teacher, clerk, treasurer, matron, and steward.[87]

Some of these changes may have been inspired by prisoner complaints addressed via articles in the *Mirror*. A lengthy article in the October 10 installment, "A Useful Fiction," began, "One of the greatest evils of the present day in the management of penal institutions is the utter dumbness to which the men are reduced; and I do not wish anything I may now advance to be construed in favor of it. I think it is unjust, inhuman, and like many other relics of the ancient prison regime, will surely pass away."[88]

There were changes, too, in the life of Warren Carter Bronaugh. The Youngers' most enthusiastic crusader had run out of money, and he was forced to become manager of the Confederate Home in Missouri. At night, he sat at his desk writing letters to important people at his own expense, all the while hoping some of these men would aid his cause to free the Youngers.[89]

He did secure help from Denman Thompson, a renowned actor who was performing in the successful play, *The Old Homestead*. In a visit to Thompson, the actor handed him one hundred dollars to assist in the efforts of securing a Younger pardon.

On Wednesday evening, October 16, Cole and Jim Younger and the other prisoners of the institution were treated to a temperance lecture by the Reverend Father Nugent of Liverpool, England. The ceremony opened with a musical selection by the prison choir and was followed by Father Murphy's introduction of the guest speaker. Reverend Nugent gave a brief history of his years as a prison chaplain before discussing his mission of temperance. According to the *Mirror*, "and though there is but little chance of any of us indulging too freely in the flowing bowl at present, the speaker could not have found an audience more in need of, or that more highly appreciated his words."[90]

Christmas in prison that year was well received and, according to many, eclipsed Thanksgiving and all other holidays combined. The morning opened bright and clear and just before 8:00 A.M. a rustle of expectancy was noticeable throughout the cell room. When the doors were unlocked and the bars thrown, the boys began looking for their personal acquaintances. Groups formed in all parts of the building as prisoners chatted and engaged in holiday handshaking. Sounds of musical instruments were heard and coteries were formed for "stag" waltzes in different corners of the cell building. A rumor circulated that the prisoners were to receive entertainment out of the ordinary but few knew the meaning of the statement.[91]

The dinner bell sounded at noon, and the men took their well-stocked platters to a friend's cell or their own to eat and drink. Christmas dinner included a roast turkey with dressing and cranberry sauce, oyster stew, mashed potatoes and gravy, sweet buns, pumpkin pie, coffee, and milk.

Following dinner, several visitors mingled with prisoners, and about three o'clock, someone noticed musical instruments being brought into the chapel hall. An hour later, the doors of the chapel were thrown open, and the room was filled to capacity. The stage was arranged in theatrical style, with curtains and dressing rooms. Inmate C.M. Morton walked on stage and delivered a humorous impersonation of the typical clergyman, interspersing his sermon and readings with local witticisms.

Mr. Young's orchestra of four pieces began playing and then the show began—"Christmas 1889, Program of a Minstrel and Specialty performed by black minstrels." The show lasted three hours and was a great success, even more so because the minstrels had had but four rehearsals. The program had been conceived only two weeks before Christmas.

When the curtain fell, Warden Randall stepped on stage and thanked the inmates for their gentlemanly conduct. One of the prisoners stood up and proposed three cheers for the warden, and everyone, including the Youngers, stood and cheered. Then the satisfied men returned to their cells, thus closing, what the *Mirror* called, "the most enjoyable holiday ever spent within the walls of Minnesota's state prison."

Notes

[1]*Minneapolis Tribune,* September 23, 1876.

[2]Homer Croy, *Last of the Great Outlaws,* pp. 122-123.

[3]W.C. Bronaugh, *The Youngers' Fight For Freedom,* pp. 308-309.

[4]*Cincinnati Enquirer,* April 17, 1889.

[5]W.C. Bronaugh, *The Youngers' Fight for Freedom,* pp. 309-310.

[6]June D. Holmquist and Sue E. Holbert, A *History Tour of 50 Twin City Landmarks,* pp. 54-56.

[7]Dallas Cantrell, *Northfield, Minnesota: Youngers' Fatal Blunder,* pp. 114-115.

[8]Ibid., pp. 243-244.

[9]J.A. Reed letter circa 1889 to Governor William R$. Merriam. Northfield, Minnesota, Bank Robbery of 1876. Selected Manuscripts and Government Records, Microfilm Edition, Roll 3, Minnesota Historical Society.

[10]Petitions from State of Missouri Officers to Governor William R. Merriam, 1889. Northfield, Minnesota, Bank Robbery of 1876. Selected Manuscripts and Government Records, Microfilm Edition, Roll 3, Minnesota Historical Society.

[11]Dallas Cantrell, *Northfield, Minnesota: Youngers' Fatal Blunder,* p. 118.

[12]Ibid.

[13]R.A. Mott letter to Governor Marshall (notation on letter—"Respectfully referred to Gov. Merriam"), dated June 22, 1889. Northfield, Minnesota, Bank Robbery of 1876. Selected Manuscripts Collections and Government Records, Microfilm Edition, Roll 3, Minnesota Historical Society.

[14]Homer Croy, *Cole Younger: Last of the Great Outlaws,* Lincoln, University of Nebraska Press, 1999, p. 168; Dallas Cantrell, *Northfield, Minnesota: Youngers' Fatal Blunder,* pp. 120-121.

[15]*The Mirror,* August 11, 1989.

[16]A.K. Doe letter to Hon. W.R. Merriam dated May 27, 1889. Northfield, Minnesota, Bank Robbery of 1876. Selected Manuscripts Collections and Government Records, Microfilm Edition, Roll 3, Minnesota Historical Society.

[17]W.H. Harrington letter to W.R. Merriam dated June 1889. Northfield, Minnesota, Bank Robbery of 1876. Selected Manuscripts Collections and Government Records, Microfilm

Edition, Roll 3. Minnesota Historical Society.

[18]Colonel A.W. Edwards, editor *The Argus*, Fargo, North Dakota, letter to W.R. Merriam dated June 12, 1889. Northfield, Minnesota, Bank Robbery of 1876. Selected Manuscripts Collections and Government Records, Microfilm Edition, Roll 3, Minnesota Historical Society.

[19]*The Mirror*, August 11, 1989.

[20]Dallas Cantrell, *Northfield, Minnesota: Youngers' Fatal Blunder*, San Antonio, The Naylor Company, 1973, p. 122; H. F. Koeper, *Historic St. Paul Buildings*, St. Paul, St. Paul City Planning Board, 1964, p. 37.

[21]Marley Brant, *Outlaws: The Illustrated History of the James-Younger Gang*, pp. 106, 186.

[22]*Stillwater Messenger*, Saturday, May 25, 1889.

[23]W.H. Pratt letter to Board of Pardons dated July 3, 1897. Northfield, Minnesota, Bank Robbery of 1876. Selected Manuscripts Collections and Government Records, Microfilm Edition, Roll 3, Minnesota Historical Society.

[24]Petition for pardon of Robert Younger sent to Governor William R. Merriam 1889. Northfield, Minnesota, Bank Robbery of 1876. Selected Manuscripts Collections and Government Records, Microfilm Edition, Roll 3, Minnesota Historical Society.

[25]Captain Ara Barton letter to Governor W.R. Merriam dated June 21, 1889. Northfield, Minnesota, Bank Robbery of 1876. Selected Manuscripts Collections and Government Records, Microfilm Edition, Roll 3, Minnesota Historical Society.

[26]"The Enos Murders," Enos Family Records.

[27]*Butler* (Missouri) *Times*, Thursday, June 12, 1889.

[28]*Stillwater Messenger*, Saturday, June 22, 1889.

[29]Ibid.

[30]Captain D. Cavanaugh letter to Governor W.R. Merriam dated June 22, 1889. Northfield, Minnesota, Bank Robbery of 1876. Selected Manuscript Collections and Government Records, Microfilm Edition, Roll 3, Minnesota Historical Society.

[31]G.W. Batchelder, Attorney, Faribault, letter to Governor William R. Merriam dated June 22, 1889. Northfield, Minnesota, Bank Robbery of 1876. Selected Manuscripts Collections and Government Records, Microfilm Edition, Roll 3, Minnesota Historical Society.

[32]H.B. Wilson letter to Governor Marshall (i.e. Merriam)

dated June 22, 1889. Northfield, Minnesota, Bank Robbery of 1876. Selected Manuscripts Collections and Government Records, Microfilm Edition, Roll 3, Minnesota Historical Society.

[33]H.P. Hynes letter to Governor Merriam dated June 24, 1889. Northfield, Minnesota, Bank Robbery of 1876. Selected Manuscripts Collections and Government Records, Microfilm Edition, Roll 3, Minnesota Historical Society.

[34]G.M. Seymour letter to Governor William R. Merriam dated June 24, 1889. Northfield, Minnesota, Bank Robbery of 1876. Selected Manuscripts Collections and Government Records, Microfilm Edition, Roll 3, Minnesota Historical Society.

[35]Mayor E.E. Durant of Stillwater letter to Governor William R. Merriam dated June 24, 1889. Northfield, Minnesota, Bank Robbery of 1876. Selected Manuscripts Collections and Government Records, Microfilm Edition, Roll 3, Minnesota Historical Society.

[36]D.M. Sabin letter to Governor Merriam dated June 24, 1889. Northfield, Minnesota, Bank Robbery of 1876. Selected Manuscripts Collections and Government Records, Microfilm Edition, Roll 3, Minnesota Historical Society.

[37]E.G. Butts letter to Governor Merriam dated June 24, 1889. Northfield, Minnesota, Bank Robbery of 1876. Selected Manuscripts Collections and Government Records, Microfilm Edition, Roll 3, Minnesota Historical Society.

[38]A.K. Doe letter to Governor Merriam dated June 24, 1889. Northfield, Minnesota, Bank Robbery of 1876. Selected Manuscripts Collections and Government Records, Microfilm Edition, Roll 3, Minnesota Historical Society.

[39]W.H. Pratt letter to Governor Merriam dated June 24, 1889. Northfield, Minnesota, Bank Robbery of 1876. Selected Manuscripts Collections and Government Records, Microfilm Edition, Roll 3, Minnesota Historical Society.

[40]Dr. T.C. Clark letter to Governor Merriam dated June 24, 1889. Northfield, Minnesota, Bank Robbery of 1876. Selected manuscripts Collections and Government Records, Microfilm Edition, Roll 3, Minnesota Historical Society.

[41]Liberty Hall letter to Governor Merriam dated June 24, 1889. Northfield Bank Robbery of 1876. Selected Manuscripts Collections and Government Records, Microfilm Edition, Roll 3, Minnesota Historical Society.

[42]J.H. Albert letter to Governor Merriam dated June 24, 1889. Northfield, Minnesota, Bank Robbery of 1876. Selected manuscripts Collections and Government Records, Microfilm Edition, Roll 3, Minnesota Historical Society.

[43]Horace W. Pratt letter to Governor Merriam dated June 26, 1889. Northfield, Minnesota, Bank Robbery of 1876. Selected Manuscripts Collections and Government Records, Microfilm Edition, Roll 3, Minnesota Historical Society.

[44]M.E. Murphy letter to Governor Merriam dated June 29, 1889. Northfield, Minnesota, Bank Robbery of 1876. Selected Manuscripts Collections and Government Records, Microfilm Edition, Roll 3, Minnesota Historical Society.

[45]Samuel Mathus letter to Governor Merriam dated June 30, 1899. Northfield Bank Robbery of 1876. Selected Manuscripts Collections and Government Records, Microfilm Edition, Roll 3, Minnesota Historical Society.

[46]W.H. Harrington letter to Governor Merriam dated July 1889. Northfield, Minnesota, Bank Robbery of 1876. Selected Manuscripts Collections and Government Records, Microfilm Edition, Roll 3, Minnesota Historical Society.

[47]W.H. Grant letter to Governor Merriam dated July 1, 1889. Northfield, Minnesota, Bank Robbery of 1876. Selected Manuscripts Collections and Government Records, Microfilm Edition, Roll 3, Minnesota Historical Society.

[48]S.B. Lovejoy letter to Governor Merriam dated July 1, 1889. Northfield, Minnesota, Bank Robbery of 1876. Selected Manuscripts Collections and Government Records, microfilm Edition, Roll 3, Minnesota Historical Society.

[49]Petition by Citizens of St. Paul and nine letters written between June 28 and 30 on Merchants Hotel stationery, mailed July 2, 1889 to Governor Merriam. Northfield, Minnesota, Bank Robbery of 1876. Selected Manuscripts and Government Records, Microfilm Edition, Roll 3, Minnesota Historical Society.

[50]David Day letter to Governor Merriam dated July 2, 1889. Northfield, Minnesota, Bank Robbery of 1876. Selected Manuscripts Collections and Government Records, Microfilm Edition, Roll 3, Minnesota Historical Society.

[51]U.S. Marshal W.M. Campbell letter to Governor Merriam dated July 3, 1889. Northfield, Minnesota, Bank Robbery of 1876. Selected Manuscripts Collections and Government Records, Microfilm Edition, Roll 3, Minnesota Historical Society.

[52]Adam Fetsch letter to Governor Merriam dated July 2, 1889. Northfield, Minnesota, Bank Robbery of 1876. Selected Manuscripts Collections and Government Records, Microfilm Edition, Roll 3, Minnesota Historical Society.

[53]H.G. Finkle letter to Governor Merriam dated July 4, 1889. Northfield, Minnesota, Bank Robbery of 1876. Selected Manuscripts Collections and Government Records, Microfilm Edition, Roll 3, Minnesota Historical Society.

[54]Edward J. Hodgson letter to Governor Merriam dated July 4, 1889. Northfield, Minnesota, Bank Robbery of 1876. Selected Manuscripts Collections and Government Records, Microfilm Edition, Roll 3, Minnesota Historical Society.

[55]W.W. Griswold letter to Governor Merriam dated July 4, 1889. Northfield, Minnesota, Bank Robbery of 1876. Selected Manuscripts Collections and Government Records, Microfilm Editions, Roll 3, Minnesota Historical Society.

[56]Thomas P. Ritchie letter to Governor Merriam dated July 4, 1889. Northfield, Minnesota, Bank Robbery of 1876. Selected Manuscripts Collections and Government Records, Microfilm Edition, Roll 3, Minnesota Historical Society.

[57]H.W. Brower letter to Governor Merriam dated July 5, 1889. Northfield, Minnesota, Bank Robbery of 1876. Selected Manuscripts Collections and Government Records, Microfilm Edition, Roll 3, Minnesota Historical Society.

[58]T.M. Newson letter to Cole Younger dated July 6, 1889. Northfield, Minnesota, Bank Robbery of 1876. Selected Manuscripts Collections and Government Records, Microfilm Edition, Roll 3, Minnesota Historical Society.

[59]T.M. Newson letter to Governor Merriam dated July 6, 1889. Northfield, Minnesota, Bank Robbery of 1876. Selected Manuscripts Collections and Government Records, Microfilm Edition, Roll 3, Minnesota Historical Society.

[60]B.G. Yates letter to Governor Merriam dated July 8, 1889; Julius A. Schmahl letter to Governor Merriam dated July 9, 1889; S.A. Langum letter to Governor Merriam dated July 9, 1889; Dr. C.O. Cooley letter to Governor Merriam dated July 10, 1889; W.W. Murphy letter to Governor Merriam dated July 11, 1889; John C. Wise letter to Governor Merriam dated July 12, 1889; Harold I. Cleveland letter to Governor Merriam dated July 13, 1889; Petition by citizens of St. Paul to Governor Merriam dated July 13, 1889. Northfield, Minnesota, Bank Robbery of 1876. Selected Manuscripts Collections

and Government Records, Microfilm Edition, Roll 3, Minnesota Historical Society.

[61]W.S. Culbertson letter to Governor Merriam dated July 8, 1889. Northfield, Minnesota, Bank Robbery of 1876. Selected Manuscript Collections and Government Records, Microfilm Edition, Roll 3, Minnesota Historical Society.

[62]Elisha Taylor letter to Governor Merriam dated July 9, 1889; W.R. Estes letter to Governor Merriam dated July 11, 1889; James H. Easton letter to Governor Merriam dated July 11, 1889. Northfield, Minnesota, Bank Robbery of 1876. Selected Manuscripts Collections and Government Records, Microfilm Edition, Roll 3, Minnesota Historical Society.

[63]"A Citizen" letter to Governor Merriam dated July 12, 1889. Northfield, Minnesota, Bank Robbery of 1876. Selected Manuscripts Collections and Government Records, Microfilm Edition, Roll 3, Minnesota Historical Society.

[64]W.R. Estes letter and unsigned petition to Governor Merriam dated July 14, 1889. Northfield, Minnesota, Bank Robbery of 1876. Selected Manuscripts Collections and Government Records, Microfilm Edition, Roll 3, Minnesota Historical Society.

[65]H.M. Blaisdell letter to Board of Pardons dated July 15, 1889; W.R. Estes letter to Governor Merriam dated July 16, 1889; M.D. Flower letter to Governor Merriam dated July 17, 1889. Northfield, Minnesota, Bank Robbery of 1876. Selected Manuscripts Collections and Government Records, Microfilm Edition, Roll 3, Minnesota Historical Society.

[66]Theodore C. Blegen, *Minnesota: A History of the State*, Minneapolis, University of Minnesota Press, 1963, pp. 177, 355.

[67]Ignatius Donnelly letter to Governor Merriam dated July 18, 1889. Northfield, Minnesota, Bank Robbery of 1876. Selected Manuscripts Collections and Government Records, Microfilm Edition, Roll 3, Minnesota Historical Society.

[68]Robert A. Smith letter to Governor Merriam dated July 18, 1889; John Clark letter to Governor Merriam dated July 18, 1889; John R. Bresett letter to Governor Merriam dated July 18, 1889. Northfield, Minnesota, Bank Robbery of 1876. Selected Manuscripts Collections and Government Records, Microfilm Edition, Roll 3, Minnesota Historical Society.

[69]B.G. Yates letter to Governor Merriam dated July 15, 1889. Northfield, Minnesota, Bank Robbery of 1876. Selected

Manuscripts Collections and Government Records, Microfilm Edition, Roll 3, Minnesota Historical Society.

[70]A.E. Rice letter to Governor Merriam dated July 21, 1889. Northfield, Minnesota, Bank Robbery of 1876. Selected manuscripts Collections and Government Records, Microfilm Edition, Roll 3, Minnesota Historical Society.

[71]L.M. Hazen letter to Governor Merriam dated July 23, 1889. Northfield, Minnesota, Bank Robbery of 1876. Selected Manuscripts Collections and Government Records, Microfilm Edition, Roll 3, Minnesota Historical Society.

[72]*Cincinnati Commercial Gazette*, July 23, 1889, "Outlaw Dying of Consumption."

[73]Dallas Cantrell, *Northfield, Minnesota: Youngers' Fatal Blunder*, pp. 122-123.

[74]Carl W. Breihan, *Younger Brothers*, pp. 183-184; *St. Paul Pioneer Press*, Tuesday, September 17, 1889, "Bob Younger Free."

[75]*St. Paul Pioneer Press*, Tuesday, September 17, 1889.

[76]*Stillwater Daily Gazette*, Tuesday, September 17, 1889.

[77]*Stillwater Democrat*, Thursday, September 19, 1889.

[78]*St. Paul Pioneer Press*, Thursday, September 19, 1889, "Stillwater Old Settlers of the St. Croix Valley Meet—Bob Younger's Funeral."

[79]*Stillwater Daily Gazette*, Wednesday, September 18, 1889.

[80]*Prison Mirror*, Thursday, September 19, 1889, "Bob Younger."

[81]W.C. Bronaugh, *The Youngers' Fight For Freedom*, p. 156.

[82]Carl W. Breihan, *Ride the Razor's Edge: The Younger Brothers Story*, p. 245.

[83]*Stillwater Messenger*, August 3, 1889.

[84]James Taylor Dunn, "The Minnesota State Prison during the Stillwater Era, 1853-1914," *Minnesota History*, December 1960.

[85]*Stillwater Gazette*, December 4, 1890.

[86]*Stillwater Messenger*, March 28, 1891.

[87]"Stillwater State Prison," Agency Record Group Administrative History, Minnesota Historical Society.

[88]*Prison Mirror*, October 10, 1889.

[89]Homer Croy, *Last of the Great Outlaws*, p. 125.

[90]*Prison Mirror*, October 17, 1889; October 24, 1889.

[91]*Prison Mirror*, December 26, 1889.

VI

1890 to 1897

---

*"The man who chooses the career of outlawry is either a
natural fool or an innocent madman."*

—Cole Younger[1]

etta Younger visited Warren Carter Bronaugh,
coming all the way from Stillwater in 1890 deliver-
ing a message from her brothers Cole and Jim that
he should come to Minnesota immediately.
Governor Marshall wrote Bronaugh about this same time with
the same message. Bronaugh left for St. Paul and met with several Democrats and Republicans—all supportive of a Younger
pardon—just prior to Merriam's second election. When
Merriam was reelected, Bronaugh and Marshall had to aban-
don their push to free the Youngers. Merriam had earlier conveyed to them that to carry on would be "a needless expense
and waste of time."[2] The Youngers, too, realized their plight
with another two years of the Merriam administration.

Anyone entering the front portion of the prison in
1890 would think he or she had stepped into just another
business building. The warden's office and manager's meeting room were situated on the left of the entrance, but
beyond that, "the iron-grated door and occasional click of
the heavy keys," plainly indicated the purpose the institution.

The reception room where incoming prisoners were received was between two iron doors—one leading to freedom, the other to the interior of the prison, and the space between these two doors was known to prisoners as "the bridge of sighs." A portion of the second and third story of the front part of the building was divided into comfortable sleeping apartments for those officers who resided within the prison. The female prisoners were kept on the south side of the second story of the front part of the building.[3]

Albert Garvin, the first professional penologist to head the prison, became warden in February 1891. Garvin had undergone extensive training at the Illinois State Prison in Joliet and was quick to bring back discipline into Stillwater prison life. The prisoners called him "fearlessly progressive." To the joy of some inmates, Garvin left his position after only a year and a half to become St. Paul's chief of police.[4]

Cole and Jim were probably amused by the following article, which appeared in a Missouri newspaper in July of 1891. "There is a movement on foot we understand for taking the Jesse James house of this county to Chicago for the benefit of the world's fair," read the astonishing piece. "It should not succeed. The home is one of the attractions of the county—a sort of historical spot—and should remain here. People, mainly strangers, go from all parts of the country to see the place where Jesse lived, and if the house should be taken away

The hospital at the old state prison in Stillwater, ca. 1890. (Courtesy of the Minnesota Historical Society)

we feel that one of the attractions of the county would be gone. 'In these piping times of peace,' we would not do as Jesse James did, but let us keep the historic house."[5]

Henry Wolfer, with twenty years' experience at Joliet, became the new warden in June 1892, introducing a new era in prison management. Wolfer's reformation policy included the granting of conditional pardons to deserving men. Prior to 1897, the governor extended pardons, but new reforms placed the powers in the hands of a board, consisting of the governor, chief justice of the supreme court, and the attorney general. Wolfer established a grading system for prisoners in 1893 and established a prison school under Carlton C. Aylard, principal of the Stillwater High School.

When Warden Wolfer took over as warden, he placed Jim Younger in charge of the mail and the library, and Cole was sent to work temporarily in the laundry until the new hospital building was completed. Cole quickly became head nurse in the hospital, a position he held until his release. He later referred to the wardens, deputy wardens, and doctors as his friends, in particular Abe Hall, Will Reed, A.D. Westby, Sam A. Langum, T.W. Alexander, Jack Glennon, Dr. Pratt, Dr. T.C. Clark, Dr. B.J. Merrill, Dr. Sidney Boleyn, Gustavus A Newman, Dan Beebe, A.E. Hedback, Morrill Withrow, and Jenner Chance. He also was partial to the stewards, Benner and Smithton, and recalled the former, with a twinkle in his eye, exclaiming, "Cole, I believe you come and get peaches for your patients up there long after they are dead."[6]

Henry Wolfer. Photo by John M. Kuhn. (Courtesy of the Minnesota Historical Society)

Late in the morning of June 8, Ed O'Kelly roamed the streets of Creede, Colorado, searching for Jesse's killer, Bob Ford. Creede in 1892 was a rough, tough mining town with an estimated thirty thousand fortune hunters filtering in and out of town from the diggings. Many triggermen, including Bat Masterson, called Creede home at the time. Masterson sold his saloon holdings in Denver and, during the rush to the new silver camp at Creede, moved there as a gambling manager of a combination restaurant, saloon, and gambling house. It was

Robert Ford. (Courtesy of the Armand DeGregoris Collection)

said of Creede that, "It is day all day in the daytime, and there is no night in Creede."[7]

According to the *Creede Candle,* Ford and his friend, Joe Palmer, went on a rampage, only two months before O'Kelly came in town. They "shot Jimtown (a portion of Creede) full of holes. Buildings were perforated, window panes broken, and the air badly cracked up with pistol balls. Not an officer was to be seen. One of them had a sudden attack of nausea and went home to bed. Another had forgotten his buttonhole bouquet and was ashamed to appear on the streets without it. So with one excuse and another, the hired supporters of the law kept out of the way and let the fun go on. It lasted from [nine to twelve] o'clock, when the ammunition ran out and the jags got too big to carry, when it died out of its own volition."[8]

Ford had murdered Jesse James on the Saturday before Easter in 1882. Exactly ten Easter Saturdays later, he nearly tore apart the silver mining town of Creede. Bob may have been seeking to reestablish the "tough guy" image he felt he once had or he may have been unconsciously afraid of the anniversary.[9]

Bob Ford had gained national attention after taking to the stage with his one-man show, *The Outlaws of Missouri.* Between curtain drops during shows, he would step out onto the stage and tell "how it really was"—how he had shot down Jesse James. The crowds nearly always responded with boos and jeers, and Ford was haunted by the memory of the outlaw. This lack of respect transformed Ford into a heavy drinker and gambler.[10]

"Ford was a tall, slim young man, with a pale face, small blue-ish eyes, and a thin blonde moustache," reported the *Denver Republican.* "He would weigh perhaps 135 pounds. His life as a desperado has entirely been assumed. He was cunning, looked upon as a coward in the face of danger, and the laughing stock of the men whom he sought for friends."[11]

Bob Ford first learned of the stranger's presence in town when he allegedly heard him singing in a lugubrious voice:

"Jesse leaves a wife to mourn all her life,
  His children they were three.
  But the dirty little coward who shot Mr. Howard,
  Has laid Jesse James in his grave."[12]

As far as Ford was concerned, the song was taboo in the town of Creede, but O'Kelly meant for him to hear it. O'Kelly entered Ford's Exchange and asked to see Bob. When he refused to say why he wanted to see him, he was immediately ejected. O'Kelly moved to the Orleans Club where he ended up in a fight over a poker game. By this time, however, he had talked his way into an appointment as marshal of the Bachelor Camp, one of six towns in the mining district. Playing in the game with him were two other marshals—Jeff "Soapy" Smith and Bat Masterson. Following the quarrel, Bat and Soapy ordered O'Kelly out of town; instead, he went looking for Ford.

Bob Ford. (Courtesy of the Armand DeGregoris Collection)

O'Kelly stopped at the Holy Moses Saloon, the Leadville Club, and other barrooms but came up empty-handed. He found Ford at the Exchange Saloon ascending the stairs to a raised platform that served as a combination office and living quarters. O'Kelly called out to his quarry, "Hello, Bob!" Ford spun and drew his gun. O'Kelly fired two barrels of duck shot, hitting Ford in the throat, and severing two-thirds of its tissues. Ford had been a braggart and nobody liked him except his live-in girlfriend, Ella Mae Watterson, who held his almost headless body in her lap. The murderer of Jesse James was dead. The Youngers were informed of the killing but neither of the brothers had anything significant to say to the press.[13]

Horace Greeley Perry, the little girl who had ridden with Cole on his horse at St. Peter in 1876, was a surprise visitor in 1892. When she became editor of the *St. Peter Journal* two years later, she joined in the fight for a Younger pardon. She and Cole exchanged numerous letters, and their casual friendship was interpreted as being more than that by many of the curious.

Horace Greeley Perry wrote Warren Carter Bronaugh on January 26, 1894, discussing the correspondence situation between herself and Cole. She insisted that she thought very highly of Cole and had even offered him a business partnership should he be released from prison. She believed, that because of this proposal, the warden had cut off communications between Cole and her. Miss Perry thanked Bronaugh for his understanding of the Cole Younger situation—friendship, but nothing more. She intimated that the warden had spread rumors that there was more to their friendship than there was, and her own father had drawn the line when he believed Cole had another idea of their relationship. Mr. Perry felt it was fine to correspond while Cole was incarcerated, but if released, it must end.[14]

"I do love Cole very much, but in friendship only, and it is very wrong for the Warden to misconstrue my motives," wrote Miss Perry. "He might be a good deal more favorable if he wanted to, but since I have editorially denounced him as an unfit man for the care of God's most unfortunate creatures, he has ceased to favor anyone whom I like up there."[15]

She informed Bronaugh that she was also at work trying to free a young man serving fifteen years for murder. The man was of one of the wealthiest families in Minneapolis, and she was fighting for a pardon, not a parole.

Cole wrote W.C. Bronaugh on January 15, 1893, stating that he was not feeling very good and was a little nervous. He said he was writing on his forty-ninth birthday and felt he did not have much longer to live. After serving sixteen years in prison, he believed that if he began to fail, he would go very quickly.[16]

Writing again on March 26, Cole called Bronaugh his best friend in the world and discussed an upcoming trip his friend was taking to Kansas City in his behalf. On May 21, he wrote that he was as "fleshy as he ever was" and must weigh well over 200 pounds. He said he was disappointed that the legislature had convened and done nothing for "life men" but that he hoped the inspectors from the parole board would act favorably for prisoners in Stillwater and in the reformatory at St. Cloud. He again stressed his nervousness and said he was like a boy in a graveyard.

Cole wrote again on July 2, saying he had not heard from Bronaugh in a long time. He had heard Bronaugh had passed through Denison, Texas, but supposed he had returned to Missouri. He informed Bronaugh his sister Retta would be in Missouri later that month and would be stopping to visit his wife. Cole said he felt state banks would be a farce in their age with the rapid transit of commerce going by rail from the Pacific to the Atlantic, and from the Gulf of Mexico to the Great Lakes. He recalled that in antebellum days if a man left Missouri, he had to exchange his Missouri money for that of the state he was entering, and always at a discount. To straighten out the financial disparities, he felt the country needed a Jefferson, Jackson, or a Lincoln with a few Websters, Clays, Calhouns, and Bentons in the Senate.

Cole wrote Bronaugh on July 16 to say he and Jim were feeling better. He told of a cyclone that had hit the city of Stillwater, and since he could see it forming plainly, he considered it beautiful. The funnel stretched the lower end down two to three hundred feet and he said it would "go like a pile driver, and then rebound like a piece of rubber that had been stretched full length and let go." He said he didn't know the extent of damage caused by the cyclone but that two men in the city had been killed.[17]

In still another letter, this one penned September 8, Cole insisted he and Jim were both in good health. He felt regret that he had missed the World's Fair but said he hoped he might someday catch another. He was disappointed that Retta, due to rheumatism in her right arm and shoulder, had not made the visit to the Bronaughs while in Missouri. Despite many setbacks, Cole seemed to be in a positive state of mind and the many new friends who had joined his cause helped make his plight a bit easier.

According to Cole Younger, "As the years went by the popular feeling against us not only subsided, but our absolute obedience to the minutest detail of the prison discipline won us the consideration, and I might even say, the esteem of the prison officials."[18]

On October 4, 1893, the Reverend J.H. Albert wrote Warren Carter Bronaugh explaining that he was anxious "to see the Youngers out." Albert, Protestant chaplain of the prison, urged Bronaugh to accomplish some of his goals as the strain of waiting and expectancy was wearing on the Youngers. He asked that his message to Bronaugh be kept from the Youngers as he did not wish to do anything that might diminish their hope.[19]

A *Stillwater Messenger* reporter who visited Cole and Jim in 1894 was moved to write: "I met Cole Younger and his brother Jim. They stand out distinctly from all around them.

They are not criminals, in the narrow sense of the word. They are the out-crop of the great Civil War; wrecks of a brutal era, cast up on the flower-decked shores of peace. If there had been no rebellion, they would have lived and died peaceful, honored farmers, on their 3,500 acres of ancestral land. But they were sucked into the awful and blood-stained vortex of the maelstrom, and cast up at Northfield."[20]

The reporter, touched by the kind dispositions of the two brothers, reflected: "There is one thing makes me feel kindly toward the Youngers. When they were escaping, after the robbery of the Northfield bank, and the murder of the cashier by the James brothers, they made their way into the woods back of Mankato. No one knew they were in that vicinity, but a farmer, hunting his cattle, stumbled onto them, and [was] made prisoner. The question then arose what to do with them. The James boys proposed to kill him, for if they let him go he would bring the whole country upon them. Cole objected. He refused to take the life of a man who had done them no harm, even for his own safety. The other then proposed to tie him to a tree and gag him. Cole said this would be worse than killing him outright, for he might starve to death. Over this issue the gang quarreled and separated. The James boys pushed west and escaped, the Youngers and their party moved south and were finally killed or captured. Before releasing his prisoner Cole swore him not to tell of their presence—the ungrateful fellow, whose life had been spared, hurried back to town and roused the whole country.

"Now, when you remember that the Youngers were at that time outlaws—Ishmaelites—with every man's hand against them; and were fresh from terrible scenes of bloodshed and Civil War, it showed a certain nobility of nature to save the life of a stranger at the risk of their own. And this generosity should be remembered to their credit now; for there is not one man in 10,000 who, under the same circumstances, would have been equally magnanimous and generous."[21]

Cole wrote Bronaugh on October 28, 1894, calling him "God's Nobleman." He conveyed the news that many of the officials who had worked in the prison during Bronaugh's last visit were no longer engaged there. Cole said he had been working in the prison hospital aiding the steward since July.[22]

On October 30, Kansas City businessman, E.F. Rogers, wrote the governor of Minnesota requesting a Younger pardon. The two brothers had been in prison for eighteen years, and according to Rogers in his two-page letter, it was time to release them.

"From what I learn of your good will to men, I feel justified in calling your attention to the Younger Brothers, now convicts in your State Prison," wrote Rogers. "I am no advocate for them as men whose hands are clean and without the stain of blood.

"I knew the eldest one [Cole] before the war, and during the war fought him. I was an officer in the federal army. The Younger family was well thought of, and stood well." Rogers quoted the Bible several times in an effort to move the governor.[23]

Rogers wrote again on November 21, this time directing his letter to incoming Governor Knute Nelson. He offered his congratulations to the new governor and asked him to read his October 30th letter requesting a Younger pardon.[24]

Governor Nelson, born in Alexandria in the western part of the state, was a veteran of rough and tumble political battles in the Senate and those of combat during the Civil War. A farmer, Nelson was supported by Minnesota Scandinavians and more concerned with bringing local elevators under state inspection than he was in supporting a pardon for Missouri outlaws.[25]

But like Rogers and so many others, B.G. Yates also addressed the new governor. In a December 14 letter, Yates informed the executive that he was working with ex-Governor Marshall in an effort to free the Youngers. He mentioned that he was enclosing letters from other individuals, but none were listed, and none were with his letter.[26]

In 1895, Honorable W.C. Masterman, chairman of the Senate Committee on State Prisons, accompanied his committee to Stillwater for its annual inspection of the prison. George T. Barr, state senator for Blue Earth County, recalled that when he and his cohorts entered the prison library, they found Cole and Jim Younger in charge. The committee members passed quickly through the library, but Barr remained hoping to ask the brothers a few questions.

"I recognized the larger of the two men as being the one who had asked me for change back in 1876 in the bank at Mankato, and so [I] lingered," remembered Barr. "He said he was the man when I asked and then volunteered the information that the original plan of the raiders had fixed on Mankato as the point they would strike and that the call on the Mankato banks, for they did visit both, was a survey upon which to determine which of them to choose."[27]

Cole wrote Bronaugh on October 4, 1896, writing that the state was ablaze with politics over the upcoming election. He said John Lind, running for governor, had spoken in Stillwater the night before, and from his cell, he could hear the band playing and the people shouting. The loud voices he heard undoubtedly came from those in the street, wrote Cole, since the hall was packed with spectators. Cole called Lind one of the ablest and most powerful men in the state.

Cole wrote Bronaugh one week later, shifting gears to William Jennings Bryan who had addressed a large crowd in St. Paul, and was about to speak in Minneapolis and Duluth before moving through Wisconsin and Michigan. He also mentioned a bank robbery in the state where two or three men were killed. Cole believed that he and his brother, despite their prison status, would somehow have their names linked with the robbery.

Regardless of the excitement in Stillwater over the candidacy of John Lind, David M. Clough became governor of Minnesota. Clough, a staunch Republican, defeated "Honest John Lind," who had the triple endorsement of Democrats, Silver Republicans, and Populists. He succeeded Knute Nelson as governor. Bryan, in his presidential bid, fared no better.

Bronaugh produced an updated group of letters requesting a Younger pardon, which he mailed to the new governor. In October 1896, Bronaugh, Pleasant Hill, Missouri, lawyer Harry A. Jones, State Senator James O'Brien, State Auditor R.C. Dunn, and Warden Henry Wolfer, met with Clough in St. Paul. Bronaugh and his party were quite confident that they would attain their objective. Governor Clough was cordial and listened intently to the pleas entered by Wolfer, Dunn, and O'Brien.[28]

Following their presentations, the delegation remained seated in the office while Clough rose from his chair and began pacing. During his deliberation, he was silent, and Auditor Dunn, who could keep silent no longer, told the governor to sit down and write out the pardon for the Youngers. But Clough continued walking and did not answer. The governor, unable to make up his mind, decided the matter should be left up to the Board of Pardons. He told the delegation to go home and get another petition and then address it to the Minnesota State Board of Pardons.[29]

Bronaugh returned to Missouri and collected a third petition from the Missouri General Assembly. He also procured several letters of recommendation for a Younger pardon from influential citizens.

Cole wrote him again saying he had enjoyed a pleasant Thanksgiving of turkey and cranberry sauce. The prisoners had been entertained by a brass band and several recitations from Miss Dixie Smith of Minneapolis. Ex-Mayor Eustis delivered a lecture on a medical cure. Introduced to Eustis by Warden Wolfer, the former mayor told Cole that he should have been in Congress or in the U.S. Senate rather than in prison.[30]

Miss Horace Greeley Perry, still sympathetic towards a Younger pardon, wrote Bronaugh again on December 7. "I was going to work this morning and saw the birds so free and happy," wrote Miss Perry. "My thoughts flew right to a couple of prison cells up at Stillwater, and you may believe me or not, I could not hold back the unhidden tears. I tell you why I can sympathize with the boys so much. I myself am just like the wild things on the hills, and I can enjoy myself more in the woods alone than anywhere else. To be shut up in a parlor is like caging a wild bird, and I tell you, my friend, when you stop to think seriously of the awfulness of confinement it is a sad thing."[31]

On December 8, Nicholas A. Nelson, publisher of the *Washington County Journal*, Stillwater, wrote Governor David M. Clough requesting a pardon. His two-page missive began: "While it may be presuming a great deal on my part, I desire to appeal to you in behalf of Coleman and James Younger, who are now confined in the state prison in this city, and for whom an effort is now being made to secure a pardon. During my experience as a newspaperman in this city, dating back over a period of some eight or nine years, I have had the pleasure of becoming intimately acquainted with the Youngers, and naturally feeling an interest in them I have watched their life in the prison. My observation has been that they have in every way endeavored to conform with the rules and regulations of that institution and their conduct has been such as to justify some consideration upon the part of the citizens of Minnesota."[32]

In 1897, Cole was assigned to help prison physician A.E. Hedback in his office. Cole occupied a cell in the hospital, recalled the physician. "At that time, the first effort to secure a pardon for the Younger brothers was made," remembered Dr. Hedback. "Warden Henry Wolfer, who I believe started, and certainly favored this action, advised Cole to break his silence of twenty-one years relative to the raid at Northfield and tell his own story of what took place. This he did, and later when he was about to throw the original into the waste basket, I asked for it and have kept it in my possession up to the present."[32]

According to Dr. Hedback, "Cole Younger had a charming personality, was a giant intellectually as well as physically and had a good command of the English language, frequently using quotations from Shakespeare in conversation. I shall never forget his admonition: 'You can run away from everybody else but you can never run away from yourself.'"[34]

Meanwhile, Captain Bronaugh waged war on the legal system, soliciting support from those individuals sympathetic to a Youngers' parole. Peter Brennan, a St. Paul railway contractor and supporter of Bronaugh's efforts, penned a letter to Retta Younger. In the letter he discussed a Bronaugh financial endeavor and the brothers' work. "I visited the boys on the 19th and saw Cole. They are well as usual. Jim did not come down. They are very busy just now covering the books over. Cole cuts the covers, Jim pastes and numbers them. All things are running smoothly just at present."[35]

Minnesota State Prison, Stillwater, Minnesota. (Author's Collection)

Cole wrote Bronaugh again on January 3, 1897, discussing the holidays in prison. On Christmas and New Year's Day, they were again entertained by musicians, and a good-looking lady, according to Cole, did a reading for the prisoners. Wednesday before Christmas, the governor, his daughter and her husband, and his mother, visited the prison. Much of their day was spent with Jim in the library. Cole claimed to have received a Catholic prayer book from Horace Greeley. Dr. Beebe played Santa Claus in the prison and slipped Cole a meerschaum pipe and tobacco, much to his delight. Among the several letters from friends, he said he was partial to one from a beautiful lady in Minneapolis.[36]

The following month, Cole wrote that he and Jim were in good health, despite a bit of rheumatism in his breast, in another letter to Bronaugh. He felt genuine sadness upon learning of the death of his old friend, former Confederate General Jo Shelby. Cole said he had read all the tributes to Shelby in the *Republic*, *Globe-Democrat*, *Kansas City Times*, *Kansas City Star*, *St. Joseph Gazette*, and the *Appleton City Herald*.

Prominent persons in both Missouri and Minnesota continued to write letters to the governor of Minnesota requesting a Younger pardon. In a letter dated February 10, 1897, Missouri State Treasurer L.L. Pitts wrote Minnesota Governor David M. Clough, Chief Justice Charles M. Start, and Attorney General H.W. Childs, stating:

"I am informed that the pardon of James and Cole Younger is being sought by some of our best and most loyal citizens.

"Without justifying any of the acts which led to their incarceration; by reason of their environments at the time they entered upon their life of crime, their long imprisonment, their reputation as model prisoners and the state of their health, I most cheerfully and earnestly join in the request for clemency at your hands.

"In asking this, I feel that they have fully expiated their crime and, if released, will become law-abiding and peaceable citizens."

Pitts signed his name "With the hope that you may look with favor upon their petition for pardon."[37]

The law governing the granting of pardons stated: "Such board may grant an absolute or a conditional pardon, but every conditional pardon shall state the terms and conditions on which it was granted. A reprieve in a case where capital punishment has been imposed may be granted by any member of the board, but for such time only as may be reasonably necessary to secure a meeting for the consideration of an application for pardon or commutation of sentence. Every pardon or commutation of sentence shall be in writing and shall have no force or effect unless granted by a unanimous vote of the board duly convened."[38]

Following the creation of the Board of Pardons by a Constitutional amendment in November 1896, Cole and Jim applied for a pardon or commutation of their sentences on June 16, 1897. The brothers applied on the grounds that they had been imprisoned nearly twenty-one years, more than double the average time served by life prisoners; that during their entire confinement they demeaned themselves in perfect conformity to all prison regulations; and the main object of the imprisonment had been accomplished, the reformation of the prisoners.

State Auditor Dunn wrote W.C. Bronaugh promising his support: "Rest assured you have my heartfelt sympathy and I will do everything in my power to assist you, and I sincerely hope that ere many weeks roll around, the boys will again breath the air of freedom in old Missouri."[39]

Henry Wolfer wrote Bronaugh on June 9 and stated he had requested some official action on the part of the board of pardons in behalf of the Youngers. He reported that the board had assured him they would visit the governor in an official body and say all they could in support of a Younger pardon. He added he planned to have Judge Start over on the fourth of July to deliver the July oration, and he planned to urge him to interview Cole and Jim so he would come away with a favorable impression of them.[40]

On June 27, the Youngers' aunt, Fanny Twyman, wrote Bronaugh thanking him for his crusade to free her nephews. She referred to him as the boys' best friend and called him a brother to them. She said she prayed that God would spare her life until she could see her nephews free men.

George Wilson, too, wrote Bronaugh, in hopes of finding the name of the Sedalia lawyer who had written against a Younger pardon. He suggested Bronaugh gather letters of support from bankers in that state to counteract the Sedalia let-

ter. The governor of Minnesota, he said, was in Buffalo to cel-
ebrate Minnesota Day, giving Bronaugh additional time to
accumulate more letters of support.

Scores of letters were sent to Governor Clough by persons supporting a Younger pardon. Arthur Pomeroy of New
York wrote on June 24, concluding his letter with: "I know the
character of these men now, and have known it for seven
years, and I can say most emphatically, that whoever opposes
the granting of a pardon to the Younger Brothers now, if there
are such, which I doubt, he or she does not understand the situation in its true light. It has reached a point, where in my
opinion; it is simply a matter of justice, and I hope and pray for
their relief through your prompt and just consideration."[41]

Dr. G.A. Newman, who had served as hospital steward at the prison from July 1, 1895, to August 1, 1896, also
approached the Board of Pardons through the mail. He
informed the executive that he had known the boys well and
they had always been true gentlemen who deserved to be given
their liberty.[42]

W.H. Harrington sent yet another letter to the Board
of Pardons. His rambling six-page treatise was a recapitulation
of his earlier correspondence, closing with the statement:
"Gentlemen, I have had a wide experience with men, and I
now say that if I could form a picked colony of nature's noble-
men with whom to spend the remaining time of my life, men
of truth, men of soul and brains and honor, if I were to have
just twenty such men, Cole and James Younger would be
among them."[43]

Attorney A.T. Cole of Fargo, North Dakota, dedicat-
ed five pages to his reasons why the Younger should be pardoned. His letter, written July 6, to Warden Henry Wolfer of
Stillwater Prison, discussed the upcoming July 12 appearance
of the Youngers before the Minnesota Board of Pardons.[44]

That same day, Warren Carter Bronaugh left Kansas
City with a large leather valise containing important documents, including a third petition from the General Assembly
of Missouri, for St. Paul. He was again accompanied by the
Youngers' nephew, H.A. Jones. They arrived on the eve of July
7 at the Minnesota State Capitol, too late to file papers that
day with the Board of Pardons. Hoping to keep their arrival in
the city secret, they stayed away from newspaper reporters and
took extra precautions to maintain their privacy.[45]

Like so many others that month, Kansas City attorney William H. Wallace also addressed the Board of Pardons requesting a pardon. Wallace had grown up in the same area as the Younger boys but was too young to take part in the war. He remembered Cole Younger very distinctly. He also knew Bob, who worked after the war in the blacksmith shop of Dick Hall, his brother-in-law, where Wallace's father, a minister and farmer, had his blacksmithing done. Wallace said he was raised in the same neighborhood as Charlie Pitts, also known as Sam Wells and son of Wash Wells, who was killed during the capture of the Youngers. Having lived forty years in Jackson County, Wallace claimed he knew the lineage relatives and friends of the Youngers about as well as any man in Missouri. Most of the relatives, said Wallace, were law-abiding and most never sympathized with the boys' post-bellum exploits. Upon the capture of the Youngers, these same relatives believed the boys innocent of all charges. Wallace was practicing law in Independence at the time of the Northfield tragedy.[46]

According to Wallace, a most reputable lady, an aunt of the Youngers, whom he knew well, came to his office upset because another crime had been attributed to her nephews. When Wallace stated the stories were true, the lady was shocked to learn the truth.

Wallace left his position as public prosecutor to study the exploits of the James-Younger Gang. He claimed there were twenty-one men who belonged to the gang from its inception in 1866 to its overthrow in 1882 and that Cole Younger "possessed more good qualities and less bad ones that any man that ever belonged to it." He was the only man in the band who could control Jesse James, and many times he prevented Jesse from taking lives. Wallace added that since thirty years was the average lifespan of man, a generation had passed since their imprisonment, and it was time to send them home as free men.

The following day, E.D. Wheelock of South Dakota wrote Warden Wolfer in favor of a pardon. He asked the warden to add the approval of an old Union soldier to his effort in behalf of the Youngers. Wheelock had served in an Illinois cavalry regiment during the war and had seen action in 1864 Missouri. With the chaos on the Kansas-Missouri border, he claimed to have learned that men like the Youngers had no real chance of becoming peaceful farmers.[47]

On July 8, W.C. Bronaugh filed his papers with the Board of Pardons in the governor's office. News of the meeting had leaked out in the newspapers, and the date of July 12 was set for the Younger hearing before the board.

Citizens of Preston, Minnesota, sent a petition to the Board of Pardons on July 8. The signers felt the Youngers had been incarcerated for a sufficient amount of time. They also stated that the Youngers did not directly participate in the killing that occurred at Northfield on September 7, 1876. The petition was filed on July 10.[48]

E.B. Ellison wrote Governor Clough on July 9 that he should pardon the Youngers "for the reason that they were manly enough to stay with their brother when he was almost dead [during their flight from Northfield]." Had they not been responsible for their brother, according to Ellison, they could have escaped with the James boys. Clough, however, was probably not impressed.[49]

Letters continued to pour into state offices requesting a pardon for the Youngers. Chaplain Robert Forbes of the State Senate in Duluth wrote Governor Clough on July 9. That same day, W.W. Snow of St. Paul wrote the Board of Pardons. On the 10th, Burr Duell of Red Wing wrote the Board suggesting an exchange of James stock from Missouri for the Youngers. Thomas H. Loyhed, Faribault, a member of the capture party, also wrote the board on the same day, as did Faribault Attorney Robert Mee; H.M. Barton, Deputy Sheriff of Rice County at the time of the robbery; Judge Mott of Faribault. In addition to Mott's letter to the Board of Pardons was another sent to Governor Clough dated the same day.[50]

George P. Wilson, Attorney General at the time of the raid, wrote Warden Wolfer on the 10th, his letter passed on to the Board of Pardons. Wilson agreed that it was just sending the brothers to Stillwater for their crimes. But, he penned:

"Embittered as I was at that time against the accused I felt chagrined that by pleading guilty they could avoid a trial, and in the state—feeling then existing, avoid conviction and hanging by the neck until dead. They are now old men, have endured more than twenty years of confinement and during all that time have behaved like gentlemen. The state has nothing to fear from giving them their liberty for the few remaining years they will have on earth. To refuse them a pardon would savor strongly of vindictiveness. To release them would not establish a bad precedent—on the contrary, it would be a generous and just thing to do."[51]

Several others wrote on the 10th: George W. Newell addressed the Board of Pardons; George W. Batchelder wrote Charles W. Start, Chief Justice and member of the Board of Pardons; D. Cavanaugh penned a letter to the board; and C.O. Cooley wrote Governor Clough enclosing a petition asking for a Younger release. Three of the seven posse members that captured the Youngers signed the petition.[52]

Governor Clough received an interesting letter that day from George W. Tressler, a former inmate at Stillwater Prison, requesting a pardon for Cole and Jim. After providing a history of his own case, Tressler wrote:

"I feel friendly towards the Younger Brothers and during my [twelve] years servitude in prison I found them gentlemen, and I expect they will have quite a little money coming to them and to put you and your guard to watch Wolfer from another successful robbery. I have taken this opportunity—money will be the chief object for anyone released from such a place as it is a very difficult matter to fly without wings and to live without eating."[53]

Over the 11th and 12th, more letters were sent to Minnesota officials requesting a Younger pardon. Hector McLean of Minneapolis wrote Judge Start; W.N. Cosgrove of Faribault penned a missive to the Board of Pardons; William R. Estes sent a petition with signatures of business and professional men to the board; D.M. Sabin of Bayfield, Wisconsin, wrote the board, in care of Warden Wolfer; T.T. Crittenden, Jackson, Missouri, sent a telegram to Governor Clough and the chairman, State Board of Pardons, that included signatures of prominent Missourians in favor of a Younger pardon; and John Q. Crisp of Missouri also addressed the board.[54]

George M. Bennett, attorney for James J. Hill and the Great Northern Railroad, sent a seven-page signed affidavit to the Board of Pardons in favor of the Youngers' freedom. In his lengthy endeavor, Bennett stated, "If the statements of Cole Younger, now for the first time probably made over his own signature, are true, it is certain the neither he nor Jim had any hand in the killing of Cashier Heywood. That neither were in the bank at any time during the fracas, and that instead of trying to shed blood, their shots were intended only to frighten people off the street and enable them to get away safely with their party, and booty if any had been secured; that it was part of the pre-arranged program that nobody was to be harmed except in the case of dire necessity in order to save their own lives. . . ."[55]

Bennett went on to cite several incidences when Cole and Jim Younger performed noble deeds. He even included a quote from an old friend of Cole's, who had lived at Monegaw Springs near Kansas City. Said the associate: "He [Cole] was a quiet gentlemanly fellow, and considerate in his way; one could talk with, argue and disagree with him without there being a row or anybody getting hurt, which is saying a good deal for him considering the condition of affairs here after the close of the war."

Bennett made much of the Kansas-Missouri border conflict before and during the Civil War. "It must be admitted that the border counties of Missouri and sometimes of Kansas were the scenes of bloodshed and violence, and common honesty compels us to concede on the side of the North, that none can tell on which side the greatest brutality was practiced," argued Bennett. "Missouri guerrillas understood it to be their duty to kill Yankees. Kansas Jayhawkers understood it to be their duty to kill Rebels. If we are to hold the Youngers in prison for what it is reported they then were guilty of, what are we to do with those among us who were as deep in that game as they. I can walk into churches here on Sunday morning and point my bony finger at more than one who was engaged in that unholy business, on our side of the cause."[56]

Bennett, a widower, had become interested in the plight of the Younger brothers after meeting Jim's former sweetheart, Cora Lee McNeill. Shortly after making Cora's acquaintance, he accompanied her to Stillwater to see the brothers. Cora was a strong crusader for a Younger pardon, and the smitten Bennett, offered her his legal counsel gratis. Cole greeted Bennett cordially, but Jim was distant, having sensed that the attorney was giving aid only because of a personal interest in Cora. Bennett soon managed Cora's crusade to free the brothers. Jim was right about George Bennett. On Friday, October 18, 1901, he married Cora Lee, and they moved to South Dakota.[57]

Governor Clough received an anonymous telegram from a friend of the Youngers in Hannibal, Missouri. It read simply: "A friend in need is a friend indeed. Please pardon those boys[. Y]ou will do a righteous act.—A Friend."[58]

J.N. Rogers of Princeton sent a letter to Governor Clough as well, and like the many others, he requested a pardon for the Youngers. Warden Henry Wolfer gave Roland H. Hartley, Secretary of the Board of Pardons, an envelope of letters requesting a pardon for the boys. Included was a letter from Nicholas A. Nelson; another from Dr. W.H. Pratt of Stillwater, who described the exemplary conduct of Cole during the January 25, 1884, prison fire; and another from H.A. Jones of Pleasant Hill, Missouri, with an enclosed petition from the Thirty-seventh General Assembly of Missouri addressed to Governor Nelson.[59]

Frank J. Wilcox. (Author's Collection)

But not all the letters were in favor of a Younger pardon. At least as many protesting a pardon, were received by the governor and the Board of Pardons this same week. Frank J. Wilcox, clerk of the Northfield bank during the robbery, sent a signed affidavit on June 10 entitled, "In the Matter of the Application for the Pardon of Coleman Younger." Wilcox described the shooting of Heywood, but his affidavit carried little weight, because he did not say who shot him.

Wilcox began his writing with a short history of his twenty-one years in Northfield. He said three men entered the bank on September 7, 1876, and one of them struck J.L. Heywood on the head with a large revolver. The blow was a very severe one and caused Heywood to drop to the floor, partially stunned. He was abruptly seized by one of the robbers and dragged to the vault door. They were unsuccessful in opening the vault door. One of their confederates out in the street called for them to come out, and in dropping Heywood, they dashed toward the door.

"After they let go of Heywood, he staggered a few steps about the room, but made no attempt whatever to secure any weapon of any kind or in any way to prevent the escape of said robbers or any of them, that he had not recovered from the blow which one of the robbers had struck him on the head with a revolver and was hardly able to stand without support."[60]

Wilcox added that the last robber leaving the bank, "leaped upon the cashier's desk as he was leaving, and while he stood there, turned and shot Heywood as Heywood was staggering about the room in an effort to prevent himself from falling, but the shot so fired killed Heywood, that the robber who did the firing did not order Heywood to stop or give him any other order whatever at the time, nor did either of the other robbers give him or anyone else any order as they were leaving the bank or about to leave it, that Heywood never spoke after he was struck on the head with the revolver and was from that time until he was shot in a dazed and particularly unconscious condition and wholly unable to make any active resistance, and that when he was shot he was simply staggering about the room in an effort to prevent himself from falling to the floor."

Dr. D.J. Whiting, Northfield dentist, sent an affidavit saying that he had witnessed Cole Younger giving orders in the street during the raid and saw men he thought were Bob and Jim Younger shooting on Anselm R. Manning, Northfield hardware merchant. Whiting's office was located in the second story of the building in which the First National Bank was located. Some time in the forenoon of that day [his time was off by more than two hours], he saw two men sitting on a

Anselm R. Manning. (Author Collection)

157

box on the street, conversing in such manner that his attention was drawn to them. One of the men was apparently
describing something to the other and making marks on the
box upon which they sat.[61]

Shortly thereafter, Whiting noticed two more men
riding across the public square. When the robbers commenced
their attack on the bank, Whiting was attracted by the sound
of gunfire. He went to his door and walked to the head of an
outside stairway. He noticed one man in particular in the
street [Cole Younger], who appeared to be in command and
giving orders to the other men. The outlaws rode up and down
the street ordering everyone they saw to get in out of sight of
the fracas. According to Whiting, their shouts were filled with
the "most blasphemous profanity and foul obscenity, and firing
of their revolvers all the time."

Then Whiting observed a man running down the side-
walk, "with bullets raining about him," and the robbers screaming at him to get out of sight. Whiting said he did not hear Cole
Younger tell the others not to shoot anyone. One of the robbers
discovered him, "and with oaths and obscene epithets," ordered
him to get back inside. One of the men fired at him, the bullet
striking the wall of the building near him. He went inside for a
moment or two but came back outside and resumed his position.

Whiting said, at this point, the fighting was becoming
hot, but Cole Younger "was still in the street directing the
affair." Bob Younger, and a man he believed to be his brother
Jim, were attacking A.R. Manning, who had appeared at the
corner of the building brandishing a gun. Manning sheltered
himself behind the foot of the stairs and the corner of the
building, while Bob used a stairway as shelter. The brothers
were shooting at Manning as the merchant took deliberate
aim and fired back. Whiting heard Cole shout for his men to
"charge up on him [Manning]," and directed his brother Bob
to shoot through the stairs. When Cole noticed Whiting
again, he bellowed, "Shoot that man up in the window."

Other affidavits were filed from Northfield citizens on
July 8. Northfield jeweler, John Morton, stated that he saw
Cole Younger shoot Nicolaus Gustavson in the street. His
store was situated only five doors away from the bank, and
during the latter part of the fight, Morton stood in a nook
beside the door of his store and plainly saw all that transpired
in the street.[62]

Morton said he saw Gustavson come up to the corner of the block and noticed one of the robbers approach him yelling, "Get back, you son of a bitch." The robber then whirled his pistol and fired at Gustavson, who fell after being hit. This same robber, in seeing one of his own men killed, went over to him, removed his pistol, and rode out of town with the others. Morton said he later visited the robbers in jail and identified Cole Younger as the man who shot Gustavson.

The same day, P.S. Dougherty of Northfield, filed an affidavit. While Dougherty says he saw the man who killed Gustavson, he does not name the man. When the attack broke out, Dougherty was partially sheltered behind an outside stairway on the corner of Division and Fourth Streets. He related that the man in the street who was in command called for his men inside the bank to come out because the "game was up." This same man, stated Dougherty, shot Gustavson, who had come up from a basement saloon on the corner south of the bank.[63]

Northfield storekeeper, W.H. Riddell, offered his affidavit on the same day. A customer in his store had called his attention that "something unusual was transpiring at the bank" the day of the raid. Riddell and his companion began crossing the street to the bank where they saw a man [outlaw Clell Miller], leaning against a hitching post in front of the bank. Citizen J.S. Allen approached the bank when the stranger grabbed him by the shoulders, whirled him around, and commanded him to, "Get out of here, you son of a bitch."[64]

Riddell said there was no attempt on the part of the robber to shoot at Allen and none ordering him to stop. On the other hand, Riddell said he heard none of the outlaws order their confederates not to shoot either. Another rider came galloping down the street screaming at Riddell to, "Get in there, you Goddamn son of a bitch!" At the same time, the man fired his pistol into the air, and according to Riddell, these were the first shots fired in the Northfield raid.

Others sent letters on July 7, 8, and 9 denouncing a pardon. D.B. Thurston of Kansas City addressed the governor; District Court Judge, H.A. Brill of St. Paul wrote Charles M. Start; County Attorney Anson L. Keyes wrote the Board of Pardons; Minneapolis cashier, F.A. Smith, contacted the board; John McKinley of Duluth penned a letter to Attorney

General Henry W. Childs (a member of the Board of Pardons); Charles C. Otis, District Court, St. Paul, wrote Charles M. Start; William B. Dean and J. Ross Nichols, St. Paul businessmen, also wrote Justice Start.[65]

Dr. Ed A. Paradis, editor of St. Paul's, *The Midway News*, sent an editorial he had written in his newspaper to Henry A. Childs. He stated that Cole Younger was a manipulator and was luring the press, the people of Minnesota, and the officials of state government into his lair in order to secure a pardon for him and his brother.[66] In his lengthy narrative, Paradis stated, "The Younger gang misjudged our people when they made their raid on Northfield. We hope they are doomed to another disappointment."[67]

That same day, Governor Clough received a letter protesting a pardon from, "Not Safe to Give My name;" the Board of Pardons received a petition from the citizens of Howard Lake; Attorney General Childs another from Fergus Falls Attorney J.W. Mason; Charles M. Start still another from District Judge William Louis Kelley of St. Paul; and Henry W. Childs another from C.R. Barns, editorial writer for the *St. Paul Pioneer Press*. Barns called the pardon movement in Missouri a "political one," and stated that the boys were popular with Southerners because of their Civil War experience, which earned them the title, "Champions of the Lost Cause."[68]

Ellen M. Ames, a witness to the Northfield raid, sent a signed affidavit to the Board of Pardons on the 10th. She stated she was driving her carriage between Water and Division Streets when she heard firing. Reaching the middle of the block, she encountered Alonzo E. Bunker, holding a hand on his shoulder. Bunker yelled he had been shot at the bank and continued down the street. Right behind him came Mr. Beneke, who told her to get out of the carriage "or you'll be killed." Beneke lifted her from the carriage, and another man led the horses away.

"In the basement of Thorson's block between me and the corner was a saloon and several men were coming out of it, evidently to see what was the matter," wrote Ellen Ames. "At the same time, men on horseback on Division Street, crossed Fifth Street, firing right and left, with a revolver in each hand. The last man coming out of the cellar seemed to be intoxicated. I was within a few feet of him and as the robbers passed the corner, the one nearest me wheeled and said,

'Lady, get out of the street or you will be killed,' at the same time discharging his revolvers. Just as he fired, the man who had come out of the saloon fell wounded. His command accompanied by the shot fixed my attention upon him, and as soon as their photographs appeared I at once confidently recognized Coleman Younger as the man who had accosted me and shot the citizen . . ."[69]

On July 12, the Board of Pardons received a packet of protests against the Youngers (Numbers 85 and 86). St. Louis banker Charles Parsons commenced his letter with, "I see there is an effort to get the Younger party pardoned. Now it seems to me the deliberate preparation of a scheme to rob a bank, commencing it with a threat to murder, and finally ending with murder, should have met, as its punishment death."[70]

Fred Bloom of Woodstock, Minnesota, wrote Governor Clough protesting a pardon. According to Bloom, he resembled the governor so much, people mistook him for the politician. He added, "I think I am the best looking man of the lot," before entering his protest.[71]

Governor Clough also received a letter from Marian B. Lull, Brooklyn, New York, stating that her husband, Captain Louis J. Lull, had been killed in a fight with the Youngers following an 1874 Missouri train robbery. Her husband, she said, was in the company of W.J. Whicher and a man named James Wright, and the trio left Chicago to pursue the James-Younger Gang. One week after they left, Whicher was murdered by the gang near Independence, Missouri, and a week later, Lull and Sheriff Edwin Daniels of Osceola were surprised by the Youngers. In the battle that followed, John Younger and Sheriff Daniels were killed, and Jim Younger wounded. According to Mrs. Lull, Jim still bore the scar in 1897. Mrs. Lull's own husband was shot through the body. He passed away in Roscoe, Missouri, May 6, 1874, from the gunshot wound.[72]

The same packet included letters from Fanny Lull Henderson, Minerva Lull, and Julia Lull Royce, Boston, Massachusetts, commenting upon the death of their relative, Captain Lull.[73]

The Board of Pardons received six separate petitions on July 12, all denouncing a pardon or parole for the Youngers. The citizens of Madelia sent two separate positions, and one each was received from the citizens of Dassel, Faribault, Northfield, and the Rice County Board of Commissioners.[74]

That same day, Charles M. Start received a letter from Attorney Samuel M. Davis, Minneapolis, blasting the idea of any pardon; Governor Clough received a missive from Minneapolis architect, C.A. Patterson and another from G.W. Plank of Laird, Minnesota; and the Board of Pardons got still another from F.E. Dudley of Minneapolis. The board, however, received the most interesting letter of the batch, a lively piece from Dr. Martha G. Ripley of Minneapolis. According to Dr. Ripley, the men should remain in prison for the reason, that by doing so, they could not reproduce.[75]

After several letters, all denouncing a Younger pardon, reached Governor Clough and the Board of Pardons, a reporter approached W.C. Bronaugh and asked him whether he had given up all hope for accomplishing his purpose.

"Very far from it," replied the genial and popular Henry County gentleman. "The prospects of the early release of the boys was never better, not withstanding Gov[ernor] Clough is an extremely strong Republican, and the boys seek freedom again to show that, thru good citizenship, they can make some atonement for the past." Bronaugh added that there were several ex-Confederates and G.A.R. men in sympathy with his cause.[76]

The Minnesota State Board of Pardons traditionally met quarterly in the state capitol building on the second Monday in January, April, July, and October. This board consisted of the governor, chief justice of the Supreme Court, and the attorney general.

On Monday, July 12, 1897, the Minnesota Board of Pardons went into session to consider pardons for six inmates, two of which were Cole and Jim Younger. Farmers packed the town and local businessmen closed their offices and swarmed the governor's office.

Cole prepared a written statement of the Northfield bank robbery, concluding the piece with:

"I will leave it to Sheriff [Ara] Barton and the wardens of this institutions to speak of us during the last twenty years. I have often met Captain Yates, and most of the men several times that were directly concerned in our capture. They have been most kind in word and feeling toward us, and since our capture we have never felt toward them any other feeling but that of friendship. The above is a true statement in so far as I can speak from personal knowledge. What occurred in the bank I can speak of only as it was told to me."[77]

Besides the Youngers, the court considered the freedom of W.J. Jamison of Hennepin County. Jamison had been in the State Reformatory since November 1896 for the crime of grand larceny in the second degree. The ruling following the session read, "Taken under advisement."[78]

Also up for a pardon was Charles Fred of St. Paul. He had been sentenced to the City Workhouse from Municipal Court on July 6, 1897, for thirty days or pay a fine of twenty-five dollars for the crime of disorderly conduct. Fred's application was denied.

Another St. Paulite, Joseph Craig, sentenced to the City Workhouse from St. Paul Municpal Court for twenty days or payment of a twenty-five-dollar fine for the crime of disorderly conduct was denied a pardon.

The case of Lewis Kellihan was also considered by the board. The court felt that because Kellihan was a young man of only twenty years of age, and of weak intellect, that the sentence of death heretofore passed upon him be commuted to imprisonment in the State Prison at Stillwater for the term of his natural life.

Considering the fact that all these prisoners had been denied a pardon by the board, the Youngers may have seen the writing on the wall. Their session began with a meeting from two o'clock until five with the board listening to arguments on the petition for pardon of the Younger brothers. Younger supporters took up the first two hours with arguments for clemency, and at 4:00 P.M., the Northfield delegation, which strongly opposed any pardon, opened their arguments. The Northfield representatives were still presenting their case at time of adjournment, so the board met again the following morning at 9:00 A.M. to continue the hearing.[79]

Among those arguing for a pardon were Warren Carter Bronaugh, Warden Henry Wolfer, all the members of the Board of Prison Managers, Minnesota State Auditor R.C. Dunn, ex-Sheriff Ara Barton of Rice County, Thomas Loyhed (a pursuing posse member from Faribault), and St. Paul Judge James McCafferty. Speaking for Northfield and Rice County against a pardon were F.W. Anderson of St. Paul, Mayor F.H. Noble, C.P. Carpenter, Professor Goodhue, Representative D.F. Kelly of Northfield, Mayor A.D. Keyes of Faribault, Attorney A.L. Keyes of Rice County, and W.R. Estes of Madelia.

James D. O'Brien of Stillwater, president of the board of prison managers, was the first speaker and delivered an effective plea for the Youngers before the fifty people who had crowded into the governor's office: "The board is unanimous in the opinion that these men have been exemplary prisoners. If freed, we believe they would make honest, respectable citizens. Their conduct has been beyond reproach, and I, for one, am ready to go on record as saying that if pardoned they will prove themselves good citizens. Our board considers that they have served time enough for the crime of which they were convicted. We do not believe that people should go beyond that in the consideration of this question. We unanimously recommend their pardon."[80]

Attorney General Childs asked O'Brien how many life convicts had been pardoned, and O'Brien replied that in the eight years he had served on the board, he remembered two such cases.

Warden Wolfer then read from a typewritten document he had prepared. Wolfer maintained that, normally, prisoners guilty of the kind of crimes committed by the Youngers should be locked up for life. But then the warden praised their character and blamed their fate on early bad association. He said he could not excuse any of their crimes, but had they been given a chance as younger men, they would never have become criminals.

Wolfer ended his reading with a plea for justice: "I will not further trespass upon your time, but before closing I desire to say that, in justice to my own conscience and to these men, I could not say less than I have said. To have remained silent would have been cowardice, believing in the justice of their cause as I do."[81]

Judge McCafferty followed with an hour-long history of the Youngers' early life and presented several endorsements for a pardon from Missourians. The judge gave reasons why the boys should be pardoned. First, they were victims of environment, and he placed the blame on the peculiar conditions of Missouri during the Civil War. "They were not naturally bad boys or possessed of criminal tendencies," he claimed.

Secondly, said Judge McCaffery, their punishment had been ample, and the law had been vindicated. "They had been grievously wounded in the affair at Northfield, when the people there took the law into their own hands, and had suffered intensely thereby for years," he said.

"You mean that they were injured by the people of Northfield while the latter were defending their property, don't you?" snapped Chief Justice Charles M. Start. Judge McCaffery admitted that the question presented a fairer statement of the case and went on with his argument.

McCaffery's third argument maintained that the prisoners' reformation was complete, but he was again interrupted by Judge Start, who considered the statement misleading: "If that is the case," he said, "how is it in a case when the governor signs a warrant for execution? Is that done with the object of reformation? Reformation, as I understand it, is intended to apply to those sentenced for limited or definite terms. Is the principle of reformation intended to include life convicts?"

James O'Brien, president of the prison board of managers, suggested that the pardon board shift the responsibility of the boys' fate to the prison board, by commuting the sentence to a definite term of years, and the prison board "would do the rest." The "rest" was granting a quick pardon. The chief justice and the attorney general, however, emphatically rejected the proposal, stating that the board of pardons would maintain responsibility over such cases.

State Auditor R.C. Dunn spoke next, stating that he was speaking for the people of northern Minnesota. Dunn said he had traveled throughout the northern part of the state and interviewed the people there. Nine out of ten, he claimed, favored a Younger pardon.

Thomas Loyhad of Faribault, one of the pursuers of the robbers in 1876, also spoke on behalf of the prisoners. Loyhad said he and his companions came too close for comfort when they stumbled upon the outlaws who were concealed in a thicket. Cole saved their lives by preventing Charlie Pitts from shooting them.

Former Sheriff of Rice County, Ara Barton, was the final speaker on the Youngers' behalf. Barton described the Youngers' "manly qualities" while they were his prisoners. He also stated that he had talked with the physician who had examined the body of Gustavson and was told that the Swede had been killed by a ricocheting bullet. Barton ended his argument saying he had interviewed 1,000 citizens of Faribault and four-fifths advocated a pardon.

Warren Carter Bronaugh, leading the fight for a Younger pardon, was much encouraged by his side's presentation on the first day. Bronaugh was confident his group had a made a strong case for the prisoners and was hopeful they had been successful. Many others felt the Youngers' cause was doomed, and believed that both the chief justice and the attorney general were opposed to the pardon. The general opinion was that the board would be reluctant to grant a pardon because of the Northfield opposition.

Bronaugh read a four-page speech he had prepared in defense of the Youngers on the thirteenth. He declared at one point: "It is the consenses [sic] of opinion and has found expression almost universal that the Younger Bros. have been to a large extent victims of circumstances. This is particularly true as regards their history in the State of Missouri. I have lived in the State of Missouri all my life, and have been in public life for years. I have a very large and extensive acquaintance throughout the whole state, and I desire to say that I am fully acquainted with the sentiment of the state. I have no interest in the Younger Bros. except that which has been prompted by a feeling of justice and humanity. I know the history of the Youngers and their family. They come from good stock in which no criminal taint has ever appeared until this unfortunate affair. It is true that many crimes were currently charged to the Youngers because of their unfortunate connection during their war experiences with Quantrill and others of like character. These influences, together with their unfavorable consequences have been fully set forth in the letters and petitions that have been presented here for your consideration."[82]

George N. Baxter, prosecuting attorney during the Youngers' 1876 trial, sent a telegram to Governor Clough on the thirteenth. He had gone to Northfield to find evidence to indict the brothers for shooting Nicolaus Gustavson but could find no one who knew if he was killed by the robbers' or citizens' fire. It was decided a stray bullet had killed Gustavson, and no indictment was found.[83]

The opposition voiced an opinion that the pardon would be a grave mistake and that such action would tarnish the state's legal reputation. The opposing delegation felt the boys had forfeited their lives to the state, and it was sufficient mercy to them, that they were allowed to live.

St. Paul's F.W. Anderson opened the case for the opposition. Anderson, a banker for years, spoke for the country bankers who were often the victims of outlaw raids.

Anderson felt that if the Youngers were released, any protection for the banking institutions would be weakened. He then read a letter from Charles Parsons of St. Louis, president of the American Association of Bankers, who was also protesting any would-be pardon. "Their punishment should have been death," wrote Parsons. "I believe in the enforcement of the law and making the way of the transgressor hard. I hope the Youngers will be made to serve out their lives in prison."

Mayor F.A. Noble of Northfield then took the floor and attacked Cole Younger's statement that he had not killed anyone. "Those men were there in Northfield to kill," explained Noble. "Their record in prison has nothing to do with the case. Any fellow would be an exemplary chap there. You all know they were a gang of cut-throats and devils."

Noble then introduced R.C. Carpenter, an eloquent speaker who went right to work in his opening remarks. "These men turned hell loose in our streets," bellowed Carpenter. "The high tide of brigandage in this country passed away when they were put behind the bars at Stillwater. Their record since then has been so good that we believe it to their advantage to stay there. Indeed, they should be very grateful to the State of Minnesota for the chance it has given them to become such good men and make such exemplary records. Cole Younger is now seeking pardon through false statements and seeking public sympathy for misrepresentations."[84]

A number of affidavits were then presented by R.C. Carpenter from eye witnesses of the Northfield raid, all of which declared Cole Younger was the man who had shot and killed Nicholaus Gustavson. All the eye witnesses maintained they had actually seen Cole raise his revolver, fire at Gustavson, and the man then fell to the ground.

The first came from Dr. D.J. Whiting, the dentist who witnessed the raid from his office above the bank. Dr. Whiting said he saw Cole throughout the robbery attempt, and at no time did the outlaw order any of his men to stop shooting, as claimed by Cole. He said he did see Bob Younger take several shots at Anselm Manning, and he heard Cole shout to Bob that he should "charge upon him" and "shoot through the door." The dentist also said he heard Cole order another of his men to "shoot that man in the window."

Another man, P.S. Doherty said he saw Cole Younger shoot Gustavson. John Norton said he also witnessed the shooting of Gustavson, and insisted the man who took the pistols from the dead robber in the street was the one who did it. He added he had seen Cole in jail and recognized him as the killer. Other affidavits were presented from Mrs. Ellen A. Ames, W.H. Riddell, and the bank clerk, Frank Wilcox. Professor Goodhue and Representative D.F. Kelly also voiced strong opinions against a pardon.

In addition to the affidavits, several protests to the pardon were filed by people who had known the Youngers before their incarceration. Three of the protests came from residents of Lawrence, Kansas, who had been victims of the Quantrill raid. Two others were from the wife and sister of Pinkerton Captain Louis J. Lull of Chicago, who in 1874 with Pinkerton's James Wright and others attempted to arrest the Youngers near Roscoe, Missouri. Lull and Sheriff Daniels of Osceola, Missouri, and John Younger were all killed.

The closing speaker of the afternoon, Mayor A.D. Keyes of Faribault, said, "No doubt, it is the best thing for the Younger boys themselves to pardon them, but they are a very small part of the people of the state of Minnesota numerically. What particular good, I would like to ask, will come to the people of the state by the pardon of these men, either now or in the future? It will either tend to prevent crime or it will promote it."

Keyes and other Rice County representatives felt that if Cole was really sincere, he should admit to the court that the killer of Joseph Heywood was Frank James. Warren Bronaugh was angered by this and wrote a letter to the *St. Paul Pioneer Press* the following day: "I do not understand why the people of Northfield should make this claim, inasmuch as it has been frequently asserted they are fully aware who these parties were, and that, acting upon reliable information, a requisition has been made by the governor of this state upon the Governor of Missouri, over twelve years ago, for the body of the prisoner who it was claimed was the only living person, aside from the Youngers, who participated in the bank robbery."[85]

Bronaugh went on to say that the Youngers were not the type of men who would turn informants to gain clemency for themselves. The Youngers, he said, felt they were responsible for their part in the raid and would suffer the penalty without implicating others. "I honor the Youngers for this position," said Bronaugh, " and I believe that every fair-minded man will do the same."

Alonzo Bunker, the bank teller wounded at Northfield, on the other hand, was angry over the possibility of a Younger pardon. In an interview with a Minneapolis newspaper, he especially took umbrage to Cole's remark that he had saved lives by not shooting during the robbery attempt and that a certain man on a buckskin horse had done the killing. Bunker said Cole had made these statements with the purpose of securing a pardon, and he was shocked that some Minnesota newspapers favored a pardon.[86]

Bunker felt the statements made by respectable citizens of Northfield should take credence over those of a convicted murderer. He then added that if Cole really tried to prevent the killings, he should prove it by naming the man on the buckskin horse and the last man to leave the bank. "Then I think he [Cole] overdoes the matter considerably in showing how many people's lives he saved by simply not shooting them," he explained. "He would have us believe he was at Northfield on that eventful day, very opportunely, for the purpose of preventing 'the boys' from killing law-abiding citizens."[87]

Bunker went on to debunk Cole Younger's story that he spared the life of Dr. Henry Wheeler by deliberately shooting above his head. If this were true, reasoned Bunker, why did he shoot a defenseless Swede (Gustavson)?[88] He said the community of Northfield was safe as long as the Youngers remained behind bars. "When I think of the murdering of poor Heywood in cold blood, and of the unprovoked assault in the law-abiding citizens of Northfield, to say nothing of other crimes committed by these men, I do not think they will live long enough to pay the penalty. I cannot interfere."[89]

But Bunker did not need to interfere, for on July 13, the board of pardons unanimously voted to deny their pardon. It was 3:30 in the afternoon when the board adjourned and began its discussion behind closed doors. When all members appeared to be in agreement, Chief Justice Start moved that the pardon be refused, and Attorney General Childs seconded the motion. Governor David M. Clough would have voted for the pardon had two board members been favorable, but since he stood alone, Clough did not vote.[90] An hour later, the decision was announced, but no explanations were offered as to how the decision had been reached and upon what grounds it was based. Later, however, a board member consented to speak about it.[91]

"While under the law the board of pardons is not required to make a statement of its reasons in a case where a pardon is denied," said the board member. "It is perhaps just as well that the public should know the grounds on which the board based its refusal of a pardon to the Younger brothers. The petitioners in law and in fact were murderers. This proposition was established by a plea of guilty and the final judgment of a court of competent jurisdiction. It is the exclusive province of the legislature to prescribe punishment for murder—either death or imprisonment."[92]

The board member said his group did not buy the statement that the Youngers were forced into crime by the horrid Civil War environment of Missouri. Eleven years had passed since the surrender at Appomattox, and still the boys had refused to accept the "magnanimous" terms offered by General Ulysses S. Grant. If they had indeed reformed, the law would then have to require a pardon for anyone serving twenty-one years in prison.

Another board member said the appeal was denied since the "character of the crime renders it one absolutely without extenuating circumstances. . . . No one claimed that there was any injustice done here, and the only reason urged for a pardon meriting serious consideration was the fact of the early environment of the petitioners and that they are now reformed."[93]

Bronaugh and Harry Jones, a nephew of the Youngers, were waiting in the office of Minnesota Governor David M. Clough when the decision was reached. Warden Wolfer had already boarded a train for Stillwater, confident the pardon attempt had failed. No one was surprised by the verdict, although the Youngers had thought they had a friend on the board.[94]

"It was eleven years ago when we took up the work of seeking a pardon for my uncles," said nephew Jones. "I had some hope that we would meet with success this time. But after the hearing of yesterday afternoon I realized that we could not expect a pardon this time. It was perfectly plain to me that Judge Start was against us, and I had fears that the attorney general was also not favorably inclined. But I did think the governor [David Clough] would give us his vote."[95]

Warden Wolfer had prepared the Youngers for the situation, explaining to them that although he had left before a decision had been reached, he was confident there was no hope for them. Bronaugh and Jones delivered the bad news two hours later. Both Cole and Jim laughed pleasantly, neither at all surprised by the outcome.

Bronaugh and Jones visited with Warden Wolfer and departed for Minneapolis. In the city, they were the guests of prison physician Dr. Bebee, who considered himself an intimate acquaintance of the Youngers. A brother-in-law of Dr. Bebee, in anticipating the parole of Cole and Jim, had prepared a supper in his home, intending that the Youngers be present as guests of honor. Although everyone was disappointed, the supper went on with Bronaugh serving as guest of honor.[96]

During a visit to Governor Clough the following day, Bronaugh and Jones were astonished when the executive related to them that he had erred when asked to sign the pardon for the Youngers. Clough, according to Bronaugh, concluded, "I have but one time to regret my action, and that will be all my life."

But the Youngers proved to be in better spirits:

"There is one mighty good thing about it all," remarked Cole in a newspaper interview, "and that is we know we have got some good friends left on earth. I feel more sorry for them than I do for myself. We are deeply grateful to all who have tried to assist us in getting a pardon, and in this hour of our disappointment we have not one unkind word or feeling for anyone. We have got to stay here, evidently, to the end of the chapter, and we will stand it as well as we can."[97]

Another life prisoner, a man named Rose, was called in and informed he had been pardoned. Rose laughed hysterically and almost went into convulsions. Rose, the official rat catcher of the institution, had been a federal soldier, and he and Cole had planned to walk out of Stillwater together—a mingling of the blue and the gray as Cole called it. "Well, the blue has beat us out again," Cole told Rose in congratulating his more fortunate friend.

According to the *Prison Mirror*, most prisoners were given little hope of securing a pardon. Rose, of course, was one of the exceptions.

"Exercising clemency toward convicted persons is a subject that arouses many editorial writers," wrote a convict in the prison newspaper. "These newspapermen are creators of public opinion, and it would seem possible for them to calmly, impartially consider the subject instead of disseminating personal ideas immature in reasoning and founded on the erroneous conception that every person in prison has received a fair impartial trial and that the sentences must be warranted upon the trial court's proceedings. In fact, the majority of editorial writers should refrain from casting reflections upon the pardon power because it seems too lenient or applaud it for refusing leniency toward prisoners. Their attitude shows plainly a lack of discernible ability. Few prisoners appeal to the pardon power of a state for clemency. Clemency is a term used for pity. Prisoners, as a rule, detest being considered seekers after pity. This is the concealed ideas of many editorials, and thereby erroneous. The prisoner appeals to the pardon power because it is a lawfully created power to entertain his opinion, which is based upon his opinions concerning the justice of a sentence as opposed to the injustice of the trial court's imposed sentence. The appellant is not after pity, but expects justice. He has a right to the benefits of the law, and has a right, not only to ask for, but to demand justice. And no class of persons should exploit these facts more than editorial writers. Today they are greatly responsible for the necessity of wives, children, and mothers practically begging for pity for some loved one in prison. We need Websters to interpret the law and demand justice for clients not wives, mothers and friends to beg for pity."[98]

One of the petitioners for a Younger pardon told the *Northfield News* that if the signers from Missouri had spent more time creating sentiment in Minnesota, the decision might have been different. Next time they would canvass the state thoroughly. However, no further efforts at a pardon could be made until after the expiration of the term of Chief Justice Start, which was December 31, 1900. Governor Clough and his attorney general would leave office at the end of 1898, but the Chief Justice would bar a pardon, even if the other two voted for it, since the vote had to be unanimous.[99]

An angry Bronaugh published a letter in the *St. Paul Pioneer Press* on July 15. He stated that had the Board of Pardons known the Youngers and the "penitent spirit" possessing them, they would have pardoned them. He attacked an affidavit read by C.P. Carpenter of Northfield, charging Cole Younger as the deliberate killer of the "inoffensive" Swede,

Nicholaus Gustafson. According to Bronaugh, this affidavit and others like it, were read only to discredit Cole. He added that right after the robbery, no one in Northfield came forward that could identify Cole or Jim Younger as the murderer. In his lengthy piece, Bronaugh called the decision a "sad case," concluding with:

"We shall return to our homes and meet our friends in sorrow. If it is the will of the good people of Minnesota to keep these men in prison until they are ripe for the grave, their will is law. We have done our best.

"We leave the field with regret, but we hope that the good people of this state, unasked and unsolicited by us at any future time, will determine that the limit of punishment should be fixed, and that there may be a ray of hope spanning their horizon—a hope that sometime before the grim reaper shall claim them for his own, they may be liberated and allowed to return to their homes to die among their friends and relatives."[100]

Notes

[1]Northfield Historical Society.

[2]W.C. Bronaugh, *The Youngers' Fight for Freedom*, p. 160.

[3]*Prison Mirror*, January 16, 1890.

[4]James Taylor Dunn, "The Minnesota State Prison during the Stillwater Era, 1853-1914," *Minnesota History*, December 1960.

[5]*Liberty Tribune*, July 31, 1891.

[6]Cole Younger, *The Story of Cole Younger by Himself,*" p. 92.

[7]Robert K. DeArment, *Bat Masterson: The Man and the Legend*, Norman, The University of Oklahoma Press, 1980, pp. 330-331.

[8]*Creede Candle*, April 22, 1892.

[9]Judith Ries, *Ed O'Kelley, The Man Who Murdered Jesse James' Murderer*, Marble Hill, Missouri, Stewart Printing & Publishing Company, p. 42.

[10]James D. Horan and Paul Sann, *Pictorial History of the Wild West*, New York, Crown Publishers, Inc., 1971, p. 45.

[11]*Denver Republican*, June 9, 1892.

[12]Frank G. Robertson and Beth Kay Harris, *Soapy Smith King of the Frontier Con Men*, New York, Hastings House Publishers, 1961, pp. 111-112.

[13]Fred Huston, "Death of the Coward Killer," *Real Frontier,* August 1971, pp. 52, 54; Carl W. Breihan, *The Complete and Authentic Life of Jesse James,* New York, Frederick Fell, Inc., Publishers, 1953, pp. 204-205.

[14]Dallas Cantrell, *Northfield, Minnesota: Youngers' Fatal Blunder,* pp. 127-128.

[15]Ibid.

[16]W.C. Bronaugh, *The Youngers' Fight for Freedom,* pp. 310-312

[17]Ibid, pp. 316-317.

[18]W.C. Heilbron, *Convict Life at the Minnesota State Prison,* p. 147.

[19]W.C. Bronaugh, *The Youngers' Fight for Freedom,* pp. 276-277.

[20]*Stillwater Messenger,* June 9, 1884, p. 5.

[21]Ibid.

[22]W.C. Bronaugh, *The Youngers' Fight for Freedom,* pp. 319-320.

[23]E.F. Rogers letter to Governor of Minnesota dated October 30, 1894. Northfield, Minnesota, Bank Robbery of 1876. Selected Manuscripts Collections and Government Records, Microfilm Edition, Roll 3, Minnesota Historical Society.

[24]E.F. Rogers letter to Governor Knut Nelson dated November 21, 1894. Northfield, Minnesota, Bank Robbery of 1876. Selected Manuscripts Collections and Government Records, Microfilm Edition, Roll 3, Minnesota Historical Society.

[25]Theodore C. Blegen, *Minnesota: A History of the State,* Minneapolis, University of Minnesota Press, 1963, pp. 388-389.

[26]B.G. Yates letter to Governor Knute Nelson dated December 14, 1894. Northfield, Minnesota, Bank Robbery of 1876. Selected Manuscripts Collections and Government Records, Microfilm Edition, Roll 3, Minnesota Historical Society.

[27]George T. Barr, "Account of Northfield Bank Robbery in 1876," Unpublished manuscript in archives of Blue Earth County Historical Society, Mankato, Minnesota.

[28]W.C. Bronaugh, *The Youngers' Fight for Freedom,* p. 176.

[29]Ibid; Marley Brant, *The Outlaw Youngers,* pp. 256-257.

[30]W.C. Bronaugh, *The Youngers' Fight for Freedom,* p. 325.

[31]Dallas Cantrell, *Northfield, Minnesota: Youngers' Fatal Blunder,* pp. 128-129.

[32]Nicholas A. Nelson letter to Governor David M. Clough dated December 8, 1896. Northfield, Minnesota, Bank Rob-

bery of 1876. Selected Manuscripts Collections and Government Records, Microfilm Edition, Roll 3, Minnesota Historical Society.

[33]A.E. Hedback, M.D., June 7, 1921, "Cole Younger's Story of the Northfield Raid in his own Handwriting," William Watts Folwell and Family Papers, Northfield (Minnesota) Bank Robbery of 1876: Selected Manuscripts Collections and Government Records. Microfilm Edition. Minnesota Historical Society.

[34]Ibid.

[35]Peter Brennan letter to Retta Younger dated September 23, 1891, Bronaugh-Younger Papers, Northfield (Minnesota) Bank Robbery of 1876: Selected Manuscripts Collections and Government Records. Microfilm Edition. Minnesota Historical Society.

[36]W.C. Bronaugh, *The Youngers' Fight for Freedom*, p. 326-327.

[37]L.L. Pitts, Missouri State Treasurer letter to Minnesota Governor David M. Clough, Chief Justice Charles M. Start, and Attorney General H.W. Childs dated February 10, 1897, in Washington County Historical Society Collection, Stillwater.

[38]W.C. Heilbron, *Convict Life at the Minnesota State Prison*, p. 150.

[39]W.C. Bronaugh, *The Youngers' Fight for Freedom*, pp. 277-278.

[40]Ibid., pp. 275-282.

[41]Arthur Pomeroy letter to Governor David M. Clough dated June 24, 1897. Northfield, Minnesota, Bank Robbery of 1876. Selected Manuscripts Collections and Government Records, Microfilm Edition, Roll 3, Minnesota Historical Society.

[42]Dr. G.A. Newman letter to Governor Clough dated June 26, 1897. Northfield, Minnesota, Bank Robbery of 1876. Selected manuscript Collections and Government Records, Microfilm Edition, Roll 3, Minnesota Historical Society.

[43]W.H. Harrington letter to Board of Pardons dated July 1897. Northfield, Minnesota, Bank Robbery of 1876. Selected Manuscripts and Government Records, Microfilm Edition, Roll 3, Minnesota Historical Society.

[44]A.T. Cole letter to Warden Henry Wolfer dated July 6, 1897. Northfield, Minnesota, Bank Robbery of 1876. Selected Manuscripts Collections and Government Records, Microfilm

Edition, Roll 3, Minnesota Historical Society.

[45]W.C. Bronaugh, *The Youngers' Fight for Freedom*, pp. 178-179.

[46]William H. Wallace letter to Board of Pardons dated July 6, 1897. Northfield, Minnesota, Bank Robbery of 1876. Selected Manuscripts Collections and Government Records, Microfilm Edition, Roll 3, Minnesota Historical Society.

[47]E.D. Wheelock letter to Warden Henry Wolfer dated July 7, 1897, Northfield, Minnesota, Bank Robbery of 1876. Selected Manuscripts Collections and Government Records, Microfilm Edition, Roll 3, Minnesota Historical Society.

[48]Citizens of Preston petition to Board of Pardons July 8, 1897. Northfield, Minnesota, Bank Robbery of 1876. Selected Manuscripts Collections and Government Records, Microfilm Edition, Roll 3, Minnesota Historical Society.

[49]E.B. Ellison letter to Governor David M. Clough dated July 9, 1897. Northfield, Minnesota, Bank Robbery of 1876. Selected Manuscripts Collections and Government Records, Microfilm Edition, Roll 3, Minnesota Historical Society.

[50]Robert Forbes letter to Governor Clough dated July 9, 1897; W.W. Snow letter to Board of Pardons dated July 9, 1897; Burr Duell letter to Board of Pardons dated July 10, 1897; Thomas H. Loyhed letter to Board of Pardons dated July 10, 1897; Robert Mee letter to Board of Pardons dated July 10, 1897; H.M. Barton letter to Board of Pardons dated July 10, 1897; R.A. Mott letters to Board of Pardons and Governor Clough dated July 10, 1897. Northfield, Minnesota, Bank Robbery of 1876. Selected Manuscripts Collections and Government Records, Microfilm Edition, Roll 3, Minnesota Historical Society.

[51]George P. Wilson letter to Warden Henry Wolfer dated July 10, 1897. Northfield, Minnesota, Bank Robbery of 1876. Selected Manuscripts Collections and Government Records, Microfilm Edition, Roll 3, Minnesota Historical Society.

[52]George W. Newell letter to Board of Pardons dated July 10, 1897; George W. Batchelder letter to Charles W. Start dated July 10, 1897; D. Cavanaugh letter to Board of Pardons dated July 10, 1897; C.O. Cooley letter to Governor David M. Clough dated July 10, 1897; Northfield, Minnesota Bank Robbery of 1876. Selected Manuscripts Collections and Government Records, Microfilm Edition, Roll 3, Minnesota Historical Society.

[53]George W. Tressler leter to Governor Clough dated July 10,

1876. Northfield, Minnesota, Bank Robbery of 1876. Selected Manuscripts Collections and Government Records, Microfilm Edition, Roll 3, Minnesota Historical Society.

[54]Hector McLean letter to Judge Start dated July 11, 1897; W.N. Cosgrove letter to Board of Pardons dated July 12, 1897; Signatures of business and professional men on letterhead of William R. Estes sent Board of Pardons, July 12, 1897; D.M. Sabin letter to Board of Pardons dated July 12, 1897; C. Kendrick Letter to Governor Clough dated July 12, 1897; T.T. Crittenden, et al, telegrams to Governor Clough and Chairman, State Board of Pardons dated July 12, 1897; John Q. Crisp letter to Board of Pardons dated July 12, 1897. Northfield, Minnesota, Bank Robbery of 1876. Selected Manuscripts Collections and Government Records, Microfilm Edition, Roll 3, Minnesota Historical Society.

[55]Affidavit of George M. Bennett to Board of Pardons dated July 12, 1897. Northfield, Minnesota, Bank Robbery of 1876. Selected Manuscripts and Government Records, Microfilm Edition, Roll 3, Minnesota Historical Society.

[56]Ibid.

[57]Carl W. Breihan, *Ride the Razor's Edge: The Younger Brothers Story,* pp. 245-246.

[58]A Friend, telegram to Governor Clough sent July 13, 1897. Northfield, Minnesota, Bank Robbery of 1876. Selected Manuscripts Collections and Government Records, Microfilm Edition, Roll 3, Minnesota Historical Society.

[59]J.N. Rogers letter to Governor Clough dated July 12, 1897; Henry Wolfer letter to Roland H. Hartley filed July 22, 1897 with enclosures: Nicholas A. Nelson letter dated July 3, 1897; W.H. Pratt letter to the Board of Pardons dated July 1, 1897; and a letter from H.A. Jones to Wolfer dated July 1, 1897. Northfield, Minnesota, Bank Robbery of 1876. Selected Manuscripts and Government Records, Microfilm Edition, Roll 3, Minnesota Historical Society.

[60]Affidavit of F.J. Wilcox dated June 10, 1897. Northfield, Minnesota, Bank Robbery of 1876. Selected Manuscripts Collections and Government Records, Microfilm Edition, Roll 3, Minnesota Historical Society.

[61]Affidavit of D.J. Whiting dated July 7, 1897. Northfield, Minnesota, Bank Robbery of 1876. Selected Manuscripts Collections and Government Records, Microfilm Edition, Roll 3, Minnesota Historical Society.

[62] Affidavit of John Morton dated July 8, 1897. Northfield, Minnesota, Bank Robbery of 1876. Selected Manuscripts Collections and Government Records, Microfilm Edition, Roll 3, Minnesota Historical Society.

[63] Affidavit of P.S. Dougherty dated July 8, 1897. Northfield, Minnesota, Bank Robbery of 1876. Selected Manuscripts Collections and Government Record, Microfilm Edition, Roll 3, Minnesota Historical Society.

[64] Affidavit of W.H. Riddell dated July 8, 1897. Northfield, Minnesota, Bank Robbery of 1876. Selected Manuscripts Collections and Government Records, Microfilm Edition, Roll 3, Minnesota Historical Society.

[65] D.B. Thurston letter to Governor dated July 7, 1897; H.A. Brill letter to Charles M. Start dated July 8, 1897; Anson L. Keyes letter to Board of Pardons dated July 9, 1897; F.A. Smith letter to Board of Pardons dated July 9, 1897; John McKinley letter to Attorney General Childs dated July 9, 1897; Charles C. Otis letter to Charles M. Start dated July 9, 1897; William B. Dean and J. Ross Nichols letter to C.M. Start dated July 9, 1897. Northfield, Minnesota, Bank Robbery of 1876. Selected Manuscripts Collections and Government Records, Microfilm Edition, Roll 3, Minnesota Historical Society.

[66] Ed A. Paradis letter to Henry W. Childs dated July 10, 1897. Northfield, Minnesota, Bank Robbery of 1876. Selected Manuscripts Collections and Government Records, Microfilm Edition, Roll 3, Minnesota Historical Society.

[67] *The Midway News,* July 10, 1897.

[68] "Not Safe to Give My Name" letter to Henry W. Childs dated July 10, 1897; Citizens of Howard Lake petition to Board of Pardons dated July 10, 1897; J.W. Mason letter to H.W. Childs dated July 10, 1897; William Louis Kelley letter to Charles M. Start dated July 10, 1897; C.R. Barns letter to H.W. Childs dated July 10, 1897. Northfield, Minnesota Bank Robbery of 1876. Selected Manuscripts Collections and Government Records, Microfilm Editions, Roll 3, Minnesota Historical Society.

[69] Ellen M. Ames affidavit dated July 10, 1897. Northfield, Minnesota, Bank Robbery of 1876. Selected Manuscripts Collections and Government Records, Microfilm Edition, Roll 3, Minnesota Historical Society.

[70]Chuck Parsons letter to F.W. Anderson, asking to please pass his sentiment to the Board of Pardons and Governor Clough dated July 10, 1897. Northfield, Minnesota, Bank Robbery of 1876. Selected Manuscripts Collections and Government Records, Microfilm Edition, Roll 3, Minnesota Historical Society.

[71]Fred Bloom letter to Governor D.M. Clough dated July 10, 1897. Northfield, Minnesota, Bank Robbery of 1876. Selected Manuscripts Collections and Government Records, Microfilm Edition, Roll 3, Minnesota Historical Society.

[72]Marian B. Lull letter to Governor David M. Clough dated July 8, 1897. Northfield, Minnesota, Bank Robbery of 1876. Selected Manuscripts Collections and Government Records, Microfilm Edition, Roll 3, Minnesota Historical Society.

[73]Fanny Lull Henderson, Minerva Lull, and Julia Lull Royce letters to Governor Clough dated July 9, 1897. Northfield Bank Robbery of 1876. Selected Manuscripts Collections and Government Records, Microfilm Edition, Roll 3, Minnesota Historical Society.

[74]July 12, 1897, Petitions to Board of Pardons: Citizens of Madelia (2), Dassel, Faribault, Northfield, and Rice County Board of County Commissioners. Northfield, Minnesota, Bank Robbery of 1876. Selected Manuscripts Collections and Government Records, Microfilm Edition, Roll 3, Minnesota Historical Society.

[75]Samuel M. Davis letter to Charles M. Start dated July 12, 1897; C.A. Patterson letter to Governor Clough dated July 12, 1897; G.W. Plank letter to governor Clough and Board of Pardons dated July 12, 1897; F.E. Dudley letter to Board of Pardons dated July 13, 1897; Martha G. Ripley letter to Board of Pardons dated July 12, 1897. Northfield, Minnesota, Bank Robbery of 1876. Selected Manuscripts Collections and Government Records, Microfilm Edition, Roll 3, Minnesota Historical Society.

[76]Kathleen White Miles, *Annals of Henry County, Volume 1, 1885-1900*, p. 220.

[77]*The Northfield Bank Raid September 7, 1876*, Northfield, Northfield News Publishing Company, Inc., 1995, p. 23.

[78]Regular Meeting of the Board of Pardons, July 12, 1897. Summary in Northfield, Minnesota, Bank Robbery of 1876. Selected Manuscripts Collections and Government Records, Microfilm Edition, Roll 3, Minnesota Historical Society.

[79]*St. Paul Pioneer Press*, Tuesday, July 13, 1897, "Arguments on the Younger Pardon."

[80]Ibid.

[81]Ibid.

[82]Remarks of Col. Bronaugh to the Board of Pardons July 13, 1897. Northfield, Minnesota, Bank Robbery of 1876. Selected Manuscripts Collections and Government Records, Microfilm Edition, Roll 3, Minnesota Historical Society.

[83]G.N. Baxter telegram to Governor David M. Clough dated July 13, 1897. Northfield, Minnesota, Bank Robbery of 1876. Selected Manuscripts Collections and Government Records, Microfilm Edition, Roll 3, Minnesota Historical Society.

[84]*St. Paul Pioneer Press*, Tuesday, July 13, 1897.

[85]*St. Paul Pioneer Press*, Wednesday, July 14, 1897, "Held Fast in Prison."

[86]*Minneapolis Journal*, Friday, July 9, 1897, "Victim of Youngers Speaks Out."

[87]Ibid.

[88]The "defenseless Swede" is referred to in the article as Anderson, a misnomer. It should have read Nicolaus Gustavson.

[89]*Minneapolis Journal*, Friday, July 9, 1897.

[90]*Northfield News*, Saturday, July 17, 1897, "Pardon Denied."

[91]*St. Paul Pioneer Press*, Wednesday, July 14, 1897, "Pardon is Denied."

[92]Ibid.

[93]Walter N. Trenerry, *Murder in Minnesota*, p. 103.

[94]*St. Paul Pioneer Press*, Wednesday, July 14, 1897.

[95]Ibid.

[96]W.C. Bronaugh, *The Youngers' Fight for Freedom*, pp. 227-228.

[97]*St. Paul Pioneer Press*, Wednesday, July 14, 1897.

[98]W.C. Heilbron, *Convict Life at the Minnesota State Prison*, pp. 150-151.

[99]*Northfield News*, Saturday, July 17, 1897.

[100]*St. Paul Pioneer Press*, July 15, 1897.

VII

1898 to 1900

*"It would help to maintain the proper equilibrium if on
the day the Youngers are let out on parole the train
robbers in Montana could be shut up in jail."*

—*Minneapolis Journal*[1]

uring the first half of 1898, several persons penned
letters praising Cole Younger for his war service and
kindness to the enemy. Among these was Gideon
W. Thompson of Barry, Missouri, who issued a
statement on March 5, 1898. Thompson, issued a colonel's
commission in the Confederate army, was ordered to Missouri
from Arkansas in July 1862. According to Thompson, Cole
Younger served under him there and was an excellent soldier
and humane individual.[2]

William N. Gregg of Kansas City wrote George M.
Bennett on April 9, stating that he knew Cole and Jim
Younger, "two as brave chivalrous soldiers as the Confederate
(or any other army) had," during the war. Gregg related that
he and Cole were sworn into service together at Widow
Ingraham farm, Jackson County, Missouri, about the fourteenth day of August 1862, by Colonel Gid Thompson for
three years or the duration of the war. Gregg wrote of Cole

The dining hall at the Stillwater Prison, ca. 1900. (Courtesy of the Minnesota Historical Society)

saving Major Emory Foster's life during the Battle of Lone Jack before reporting to General E. Kirby Smith for assignment on the Mississippi River in Louisiana. Cole, he alleged, went then to California and did not return until the fall of 1865; thus, he could not have participated in the Missouri battles where he had been accused of playing a role.[3]

E.G. Bower of Dallas, Texas, wrote George M. Bennett on April 25. Bower had served as Cole's messmate during Confederate service. According to Bower, Cole could not have committed atrocities in 1864 Missouri because he was not in the state the entire year. The writer insisted that Cole with Shelby's Brigade of Missouri Cavalry spent the latter part of 1863 in winter quarters on the Ouachita River near Camden, Arkansas. Cole went to Bonham, Texas, with his men, and during the spring of 1864, proceeded southwest to the Rio Grande River, through Old Mexico to Guaymas on the Pacific Coast and north to California.

Following the war, 1868, Cole came to Dallas County, Texas, with his brothers Jim, John, and Bob, and their sister, Henrietta and the friendship between Bower and Cole was renewed. No one stood higher in the estimation of the local citizens than Cole Younger, alleged Bower. When Cole, however, left the county, his brother Jim, who was under the influence of liquor, killed Colonel Charles Nichols, a deputy sheriff and old soldier comrade and friend of Cole's. It was a sad blow to Cole Younger.

Bower was quite impressed by Cole, especially when they served together in the Civil War. "[We] were under Gen'l Joe Shelby and knew him [Cole] as well as any man could," wrote Bower, "knew his kindly nature, his warm friendships, his entire truthfulness and heroic gallantry; on the battlefield, he is as calm, thoughtful, sober, cool and intrepid as any man that ever lived. There was never a charge of wrong-doing in Texas against him; he was on the side of law and order."[4]

Emory S. Foster wrote George M. Bennett on May 7, 1898. Foster had been a Union officer during the war, and he praised Cole Younger for keeping him from being shot. Foster, major of the Seventh Cavalry Missouri State Militia, related that on August 15, 1862, he was in command of 740 Union troops searching for a Confederate force moving from Lexington to Sedalia, Missouri. He found the enemy at Lone Jack. His orders were to attack and hold the Southerners until General Warren, moving from Clinton, could join him. Foster's forces attacked the scattered Confederates, but learned from prisoners that a larger force of Confederates was camped only three miles away.[5]

Expecting General Warren to arrive during the night, the Union troops slept in line at Lone Jack. In the morning, they were attacked by, according to Foster, 3,000 Confederate troops. Foster was mesmerized by a brave young Confederate riding in front of his line, distributing ammunition to his men. Foster and his brother, both wounded, were soon captured and locked in a nearby house. A Confederate officer entered their room and said he was going to shoot them with his pistol. Cole Younger rushed in and "seizing the fellow, thrust him out of the room." Cole then placed a guard at the house so no one would disturb the captives.

"Cole Younger was then certainly a high type of manhood, and every inch a soldier, who risked his own life to protect that of wounded and disabled enemies," wrote Foster. "I believe he still retains those qualities and would prove himself as good a citizen as we have among us if set free."[6]

On June 6, 1898, S.B. Elkins, U.S. Senator, wrote Governor Clough advocating a pardon, despite the refusal of the Board of Pardons only one-year earlier. Elkins summarized Cole's good conduct in prison, and added:

"I knew Cole Younger when a boy, and his family before him. He came of good stock, and it was a matter of surprise that he should have done what he did. I feel especially indebted to him, because during the war I fell into the hands of the enemy, and Cole Younger, I think, saved my life, and for this and his good character when I knew him, and the standing of his family, I feel I can take the liberty of asking such executive clemency as could be extended under the circumstances."[7]

Elkins, inspired by Foster's letter relating Cole's war experiences, was moved to author another letter, this time to Charles M. Start, on July 4. Elkins stated he had witnessed the closing moments of the Battle of Lone Jack, in which Foster was commanding the Union side. He also conveyed being taken as a prisoner during the summer of 1862 by Quantrill's men and brought into camp by his pickets.[8] The first person he saw in camp that he knew was Cole Younger, who did not seem to be a member of Quantrill's band.[9]

Elkins knew he was to be shot, and the men composing the picket divided his possessions—his horse, boots, and coat. Recalled Elkins:

"As soon as I saw Cole Younger, I felt a sense of relief because I had known him and his parents long and favorably, and as soon as I got a chance I told him frankly what I feared and that I hoped he would manage to take care of me and save me from being killed. He assured me he would do all he could to protect me."

Quantrill came into camp and asked Elkins his name. Cole interjected that Elkins' father and brother were in the Confederate army and were good fighters, and that he had remained at home to care for his mother; that he was a good fellow and noncombatant. When Quantrill left, Cole told Elkins he would stay with him and helped him to escape. Elkins had always felt that but for Cole Younger's intercession in his behalf, he would have been killed.

On August 6, 1898, Marshall P. Wright of Jackson County, Missouri, signed an affidavit stating that the Youngers were in Missouri the day they allegedly robbed a train, 250 miles away, in Adair, Iowa. According to Wright, the Youngers were blamed continually for crimes they did not commit. On the day of the train robbery, Wright, who knew the brothers well, stated that he met the boys at Monegaw Springs, St. Clair County, Missouri.

"I had with me a copy of the early morning paper giving an account of the robbery," recalled Wright. "Cole and Jim Younger were both there and read the newspaper containing the account of the aforesaid train robbery attributing the act to the Younger brothers. I read the article to the boys and remarked [at] their ability to be in so many places at the same time. The place where the robbery was committed, Adair, Iowa, was more than two hundred and fifty (250) miles from where I found them in St. Clair, County, Missouri, which distance (if guilty) they must traverse in much less than twenty-four hours on horseback. It was then stated by people living there whom I knew that the Youngers had not been away. There were then no cross lines of railroad making it possible for them to cover the distance by rail."[10]

Cora McNeill's novel, *Mizzoura: The Youngers*, was published in 1898, the only book on their lives approved by the Youngers. Through the book, Cora McNeill found an opportunity to appeal for a Younger pardon: "To keep men like the Youngers shut behind prison doors more than twenty years voices a vicious desire of torturing persons for personal gratification. So far as physical punishment is concerned, these men have suffered more than a dozen deaths could bring to them; especially is this true of James Younger, the roof of his mouth and a portion of his upper jaw having been torn away by a gun-shot and the wound never having healed, he is never for a moment without pain; even now there are pieces of bone occasionally taken from his jaw. Pardon cannot relieve him from this condition; he must suffer on to the end of his life whether in or out of prison. If out of prison have we a sane man or boy in Minnesota who could or would feel an ambition to follow his example and repeat his bitter experiences or those of his brother . . ."[11]

Jesse Edwards James, son of the noted outlaw, was arrested for his alleged participation in the holdup of a Missouri-Pacific train at Belt Junction, near Leeds, Missouri, on September 23, 1898. T.T. Crittenden, the former governor of Missouri, testified to the young man's innocence. His son,

The warden and his dog at the old state prison at Stillwater, ca. 1900. (Courtesy of the Minnesota Historical Society)

T.T. Crittenden, Jr., who had given the young man his first job, also worked hard in Jesse, Jr's., behalf. Although the boy's chances looked pretty bleak, he was acquitted of all charges. The Youngers must have followed the trial closely in the newspapers.[12]

Henry W. Ashton, a prominent Chicago attorney, wrote W.C. Bronaugh on October 20, stating he was in a position to do the Youngers some good in regard to securing their freedom. He assured Bronaugh he wished no remuneration for his services and asked for names of friends that might be supportive of a pardon for the brothers.[13]

Minneapolis attorney George W. Bennett also wrote Bronaugh, stating he had a fantastic scheme for securing the freedom of Cole Younger. With the United States at war with Spain (the Spanish-American War), he suggested he visit Generals Fitzhugh Lee and Joseph Wheeler. He hoped he could influence the military leaders to request that Cole be released to fight under them in the war, since he was an experienced soldier. The plan, however, fizzled before it had begun.

In another letter, Bennett related to Bronaugh that Denman Thompson, a renowned actor of "Old Homestead" fame and others, had volunteered to assist Cole financially. Bennett had visited Thompson at the Southern Hotel in St. Louis and discussed the matter with him. The actor gave Bennett one-hundred dollars for the Younger cause and invited him to his play at Havlin's Theatre that same evening.

Former Minnesota Governor Andrew R. McGill (1887 to 1889) published the following statement on December 28, 1898:

"While the crime for which the Younger brothers are being punished cannot be atoned, it seems to me that the many years of their imprisonment, and their advanced age, it would be both proper and wise in the board of pardons to fix upon a time not far in the future when their confinement shall be deemed sufficient to answer the demands of justice, and commute their sentences to expire at that time."[14]

"Honest John" Lind, after being defeated by David M. Clough for governor in 1896, became the new Minnesota chief executive in 1899 while running as a fusion candidate. Lind, who one year earlier had served in the Spanish-American War, became the first non-Republican to capture the Minnesota governorship since pre-Civil War days.[15]

Jesse Edwards James at his father's grave, Kearney, Missouri. (Courtesy of Armand DeGregoris Collection)

Honest John did not carry out large reforms while in office. He did, however, urge state reforms in taxation, introduced increased care of the mentally ill and retarded, advocated support for education, forestry, and agriculture, and supported direct democratic controls of the state government by the people. Since he took no interest in the issue of prison reform, Bronaugh and Younger supporters relaxed their campaign during his single term in office.

On July 30, B.G. Yates, one of the Younger captors and superintendent of the American District Telegraph Company in St. Paul, wrote W.C. Bronaugh, assuring him that when the legislature reconvened, he and his constituents would canvass every man for his influence in the Younger affair. With John Lind in office, however, he feared nothing could be achieved until a new governor was elected.[16]

In 1899, shortly after Governor Clough's term of office had expired, George M. Bennett introduced a bill to the Minnesota General Assembly calling for the parole of life prisoners who would have been eligible for release had they been sentenced to thirty-five years. Known as the Wilson Parole Bill, because of support from Senator George P. Wilson, the bill passed in the senate chambers by a vote of forty-eight to five but was defeated in the house thirty-one to sixty-eight. Wilson had been attorney general at the time of the Northfield raid and had assisted with the prosecution of the Youngers in 1876.[17]

St. Paul Postmaster Henry A. Castle wrote George P. Wilson immediately upon learning of his bill. "I write briefly to express my gratification that you have initiated measures that may result in the release of the Younger Brothers, now confined in the State Prison at Stillwater," wrote Castle. "I have felt for several years past that the ends of justice and the demands of example have been fully complied with by their imprisonment."[18]

Minneapolis attorney A.T. Ankeny also wrote Wilson favoring his bill. Ankeny agreed that the conceded object of punishment was not revenge but reformation. He was afraid that the state was in danger of placing a stigma upon its "fair" name.[19]

The *Stillwater Gazette* conveyed its support of the Wilson Bill: "George P. Wilson of Minneapolis, who as attorney general of the state of Minnesota, prosecuted the Younger

boys in 1876, yesterday introduced a bill in the Senate providing for the parole of these men, who are life prisoners. He
fought the case to convict them twenty-two years ago; today
he stands for them and seeks to have a bill passed that will
release them from the penitentiary, which is not covered by
the law now, as it does not provide for the parole of life prisoners. There has always been a determined and bitter fight
against granting the boys their liberty, usually coming from
Northfield. That the bill will be opposed by some there is no
doubt, but in the able hands of Senator Wilson we hope to see
the bill passed and Cole and Jim Younger once more restored
to liberty. . . ."[20]

An article in the *Mankato Free Press* reported that
England had similar features in her laws regarding life prisoners being released because of good conduct over several years.
The system, according to the newspaper, had no blemishes on
its record, and the process was working fine.[21]

Letters for and against the Wilson Bill flooded the *St.
Paul Pioneer Press*. The most controversial was a letter signed
simply B.G.Y., which was thought to be the work of former
Madelia resident B.G. Yates. But presumed-dead outlaw Bill
Stiles had also been hailed by the name of Yates. Whoever the
writer, B.G.Y. argued vehemently for a Younger pardon:

"There is now in prison at Stillwater only one life convict who was there when the Youngers were committed; all
have been pardoned, only one having died, among them some
of the most cold-blooded murderers known. It seems difficult
to understand why there is such opposition to the pardon of
the best prisoners we ever committed, while we raise no voice
in protest when the most vicious are pardoned by the dozen."[22]

Outraged by the "Yates" letter, other citizens challenged the effort. One writer explained the circumstances of
the lifer who had been there longer than the Youngers. The
lifer was a poor man without friends or money, and the writer
stated that if Yates was sincere about pardoning good men, he
should also be asking for the poor man's parole as well. Most
of the writers, however, were concerned that once the
Youngers were paroled and sent home to Missouri, they would
be forever free since Missouri always refused to recognize requisition papers from Minnesota.

The (Minneapolis) *Representative* published an article
favoring the passage of the Wilson Bill and a Younger pardon

that same year. The *Journal* rationalized: "Since they [Youngers] were convicted nearly one hundred 'lifers' have been pardoned—some after serving only three or four years. But there was no mercy for the Youngers. Their offense was that they robbed a BANK! That was 'the sin against the Holy Ghost!'"[23]

The *Fairmont Daily* concurred by crying, "Let them go back to their own state" as did many other Minnesota newspapers.[24] The *Crookston Journal* followed suit by exclaiming, "We say let them leave the prison walls and get a glimpse again of heaven's sunshine."[25] The *Lake Crystal Union* used humor to get their point across: "We were compelled to have two packages, each weighing scant 4½ pounds, sent from Minneapolis last week, upon which we paid [thirty-five] cents expressage for each package. If this is not highway robbery then count the Younger gang saints."[26]

Early in 1899, Cole commenced a correspondence with Senator M.J. Daly, an avid supporter of a pardon for the brothers. Daly had just delivered a powerful speech in the Youngers' behalf in the state senate, and the brothers were grateful. M.J. Daly was born on March 13, 1861, in St. Paul, and twenty-five years later, graduated from Iowa State University. He immediately began practicing law in Perham, served as vice-president of the First National Bank, and was engaged as county attorney from 1891 to 1899. In 1899, he served a four-year term as state senator.[27] Cole wrote Daly the following letter in March 1899:

Mr. McNeil, Mr. Greave, and Hon[orable] E.H. Schurmeier was [sic] here today. Wish I could repeat all they said in regard to the speech you made in the Senate in favor of the Wilson Bill. I had read what little the papers give and felt very grateful. But if possible I now feel still more after hearing them speak so highly. They were wishing I could have herd [sic] you. I told them I would feel very happy as it was if you could only here [sic] them praising you. They said everyone said it was one of the best speeches made in the Senate during the session. Let me assure you there will never be any act of ours in or out of prison that will caus [sic] you to regretted [sic] having [sic] extended a helping hand to us in this our hour of distress. And our heart felt gratitude is yours in full and our wish will ever be that God's best blessings will fall upon you and your family. And believe us truly your true and greatful [sic] but unfortunet [sic] friends. Cole Younger (over)

One thing gave me pleasure in your speech and in that of Senator Stochuralls. You both referring to Senator Wilson and his effort in such high terms. God bless him for he has acted from the highest standpoint that of humanity and without many and without praise.

Your friend always,
Cole Younger[28]

The enigma of convicted killer Bill Ryan made news in 1899. Cole, of course, would have known the truth regarding the mystery, but he never made mention of Ryan. Bill Ryan had entered the Missouri State Penitentiary on October 16, 1881, for his role in the 1879 Glendale robbery. In 1888, he convinced the prison board he was dying of tuberculosis, and on January 4, 1889, his sentence was commuted by Missouri Governor Albert P. Morehouse in accord with the Missouri Three-Fourths Law. Following the dynamiting of a Missouri Pacific express car on September 23, 1898, the Pinkertons were called in, and they began investigating the movements of Ryan. The Pinkertons, while searching through photographs at the Minnesota State Penitentiary at Stillwater, uncovered a likeness of Ryan taken in the prison in 1895. According to a *Kansas City Star* article, Ryan had served a short term for burglary at Stillwater under the alias of Harry A. Glenn. The Bertillion measurements taken at the prison reportedly matched the Pinkerton's description of Ryan to some degree.[29]

According to the story, Ryan used his Glenn alias at Stillwater. After his release in 1897, he went to Kansas City, using the name John Murphy. If Ryan were in fact Harry Glenn, he would have been in direct contact with Cole and Jim Younger during his confinement. The Ryan-Glenn account, however, has never been proven, or, on the other hand, disproved. The newspaper article reads:

Bill Ryan at Stillwater

A PHOTO OF THE BANDIT TAKEN WHEN HE WAS IMPRISONED THERE.

Bud Pitcher, who knew him well, gladly testifies it. The wily old bandit had many aliases—In jail here, yet none knew him.

Bill Ryan, alias Harry Glen, alias John Murphy, alias Bill Evans, alias Bill Jennings

---

As the record of the career of Bill Ryan, former member of the James gang, slowly unwinds itself to the detectives who are fastening the Macomb and the Leeds train robberies on the wily old bandit, it develops that he is indeed a remarkable criminal.

Ryan is known to have found his way to return under four aliases. Each time he has succeeded in keeping his identity from the officers, and his cunning now causes some to doubt that he is really the Glendale robber of years ago.

It is remarkable that crime and fate should have thrown Ryan into Stillwater prison, where the Younger brothers for their members of the same Missouri band of outlaws, are locked up for life, and that he should have served out a sentence beside those more famous criminals without their identity becoming known. However, this is true, Ryan was arrested for burglary in Minneapolis in 1895 and served a short sentence in Stillwater prison. He was known to the Minnesota officiates as Harry A. Glen alias Murphy, and the police records of Minneapolis contain the information that he was in the Oregon prison previously under the name of John Murphy.

No Doubts There

Stillwater is the most carefully conducted prison in the United States. The Bertillon system of measurements is used there. When Ryan was taken there he was photographed and a most minute description of him placed in the records. But the prison keeper never had any idea that they had another Missouri train robber in the walls.

Ryan, of course, knew the Youngers. He was secure under his aliases. He came almost directly to Kansas City and was not recognized about his old haunts. When he was shot and fell into the hands of the police as Murphy last spring, nobody knew him. He was in jail right under the nose of Marshall Chiles and his deputies, most any of whom would have said offhand that they knew Bill Ryan. He managed to conceal his identity from them, or if anyone around the jail knew him nothing was ever said about it. He even went before the grand jury and was released, although he had been shot and captured in the act of burglary.

His Work as Evans

Ryan had only been out of the Kansas City jail a few days when he was in the Leeds holdup as Evans. That robbery was probably planned in the county jail. Ryan was in no hurry about leaving Kansas City and while Evans was looked for high and low he was in and out of town several times. When he turned up as Bill Jennings in the Macomb robbery, he was recognized as Ryan for the first time by George Bryant, the veteran detective.

The Pinkertons were certain that Ryan had been in prison elsewhere, and they began to search their records and Ryan's photograph taken at Stillwater came to light. It is as good a likeness of Ryan as could be made. By this picture Jennings, Evans, and Murphy were easily brought together as one and the same man.

A reporter for the *Star* took this photograph today to Bud Pitcher, salesman for the W.W Morgan Clothing Company. Mr. Pitcher knew Ryan as a boy; saw him in the Missouri penitentiary, saw him in Kansas City in 1890 after he was pardoned by Governor Morehouse, and saw him again last November. Mr. Pitcher knows Ryan. He was waiting on two customers when the photograph was handed to him.

"Do you know the man?" He was asked, without any explanation whatever. "That's Bill Ryan!"

The instant that his eyes fell on the photograph, Mr. Pitcher said "That's Bill Ryan".

Adjusting his eyeglasses, Mr. Pitcher scrutinized the picture closely.

"Yes, that's a good likeness I ever saw," he said. "Where did you get it?"

"It came from Stillwater prison," the reporter replied.

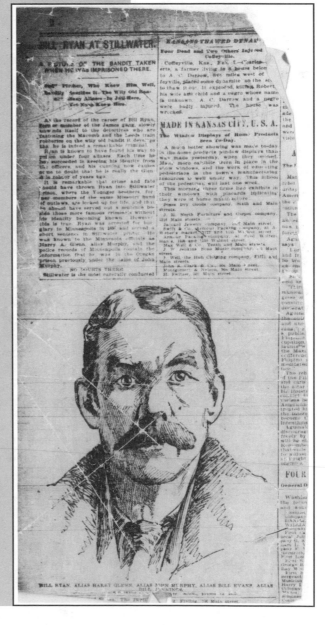

"Well, wherever it came from, it is Bill Ryan's picture alright," he said.

"It is an excellent likeness of the man in jail at Springfield now."

"Then they have Ryan in jail, for if that isn't Bill Ryan's face on that card I don't know him."

"How well do you know him?"

"I recognized him in the store here last fall. I know him that well."

Mr. Pitcher called the attention of his customers who happened to be from Lee's Summit to the picture, and told them they need not have any doubt that Ryan was in jail.

Where the Doubt Came In

The whole trouble about Ryan's identification comes from the fact that an error was made in describing him when he was released from the Missouri penitentiary. The police have been looking for a Bill Ryan with "black hair and whiskers and brown eyes." Ryan is a red faced, blue-eyed Irishman, with a red moustache and reddish, sandy hair. The Minnesota officials had his description correct. They had took a good photograph of him. Those little precautions are neglected in the Missouri penitentiary, just as an identification was neglected at the county jail when Ryan was released from that place. If he were to escape from jail now the Stillwater photograph would be the only likeness of him. He has not been photographed since his last arrest.[30]

Whether Ryan was in fact in Stillwater for a brief term may never be known. The prison had its share of celebrity convicts even without the likes of the Youngers and Bill Ryan. On June 9, 1899, convict Rafael Ortiz, whose case had attracted some national attention, entered the gates of Stillwater Prison escorted by First Sergeant John Harris and Private Grady of the Eleventh United States Regulars. During the U.S. occupation of Puerto Rico following the Spanish-American War, Ortiz was struck twice across the face by an American soldier. Responding, he pulled a razor and killed the man as he sat in a café. He was ordered to be shot. At the execution, Secretary of State Alger stopped his carriage in seeing a large crowd of people before him.[31]

According to *Harper's Weekly*, "The assembled people fell upon their knees."[32] A bystander approached Alger and explained why Ortiz was being executed and begged him to commute the sentence to life imprisonment. Alger telegraphed San Juan to cancel execution orders and President William McKinley commuted his sentence to life. Sent to Stillwater, Ortiz became prisoner 5168.[33]

While numerous friends of the Youngers wrote letters requesting a Younger parole or pardon in 1900, others took up the cause of Ortiz. Among those was Warden Henry Wolfer, who advocated paroles for the Youngers as well as Ortiz. A large group of citizens in Stillwater also campaigned for Ortiz's release. Mrs. Celia Kenny and former District Court Judge John W. Willis of St. Paul, representing a group of citizens in Puerto Rico, crusaded for a pardon for Ortiz. (He was released in 1904.)[34]

Samuel R. Van Sant, "a genial, experienced, and popular riverman," narrowly defeated Governor Lind in his bid for reelection in 1900. Van Sant had run as a progressive Republican on a platform that differed little from Lind's. Eliminating partisan considerations, the Republican legislature quickly enacted a number of progressive measures, including increased railroad taxation and primaries for all except statewide offices.[35]

Van Sant, last of the Civil War veterans, was an advocate of fiscal reform, and he quickly recommended the abolishment of the Board of Corrections and Charities. He proposed in its place a new salaried State Board of Control with "the responsibility of the charitable reformatory and penal institutions of the state." The legislature adopted the program.[36]

Samuel Rinnah Van Sant. (Courtesy of the Minnesota Historical Society)

With a new century came a new passion. Alix J. Muller, a reporter for the *St. Paul Pioneer Press*, arrived at Stillwater Prison to interview Jim Younger for a story she was a doing on crime and procedure. Miss Muller, an expert on police procedure, including the Bertillon System for the Identification of Criminals, was quite taken with Younger, and the two began corresponding regularly. Before long, they had fallen in love, and they planned to marry should Jim obtain a parole or pardon at any time. Neither was aware, however, of a Minnesota ruling denying ex-prisoners on parole a marriage certificate.[37]

Alix J. Muller was but a year old when the James-Younger Gang attempted to rob the First National Bank of Northfield, Minnesota, in September 1876. A daughter and

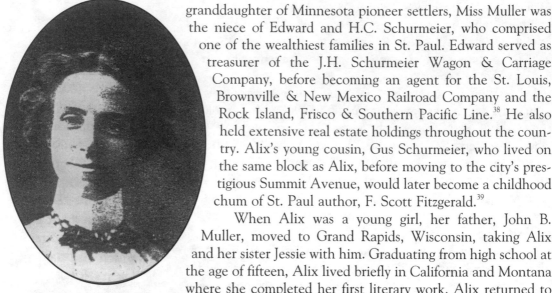

Alix J. Muller. (Courtesy of the *St. Paul Pioneer Press*)

Below, Alix Muller painted as a hobby. Pictured here is a self-portrait. (Photo by the author)

granddaughter of Minnesota pioneer settlers, Miss Muller was the niece of Edward and H.C. Schurmeier, who comprised one of the wealthiest families in St. Paul. Edward served as treasurer of the J.H. Schurmeier Wagon & Carriage Company, before becoming an agent for the St. Louis, Brownville & New Mexico Railroad Company and the Rock Island, Frisco & Southern Pacific Line.[38] He also held extensive real estate holdings throughout the country. Alix's young cousin, Gus Schurmeier, who lived on the same block as Alix, before moving to the city's prestigious Summit Avenue, would later become a childhood chum of St. Paul author, F. Scott Fitzgerald.[39]

When Alix was a young girl, her father, John B. Muller, moved to Grand Rapids, Wisconsin, taking Alix and her sister Jessie with him. Graduating from high school at the age of fifteen, Alix lived briefly in California and Montana where she completed her first literary work. Alix returned to St. Paul in 1895 and went to work as a reporter for the *St. Paul Pioneer Press*. The following year she became a special writer for the *Salt Lake Herald* during the Bryan campaign, and while in Utah, she became heavily engrossed in the Equal Suffrage cause. She soon became coeditor and publisher of the *Pacific Empire* of Portland, Oregon, the only workman's weekly then issued between Portland and San Francisco.[40]

Returning to Minnesota, Alix became associate editor of the *Spring Valley Vidette*. When the paper changed hands, she returned to the *Pioneer Press*, contributing articles and book reviews, and it was said of her that "she is a young woman of whom one may very safely say that her whole heart is bound up in her chosen life work."[41] Throughout the first half of 1901, she visited Jim regularly and wrote him several letters, hoping and praying that a parole or pardon was not long in coming.

Alix worked tirelessly to secure a parole, then, later, a pardon, for the Youngers. In one of her letters to the Board of Pardons, Alix wrote:

"Gentleman—Enclosed please find letters from Senators L.H. Schellbach and J.N. Smith, two friends of the Younger brothers, to whom I wrote in their behalf. Also a petition sent me by Senator Daly, which was circulated on the last day of the session in the Senate, and is therefore very incomplete.

"Trusting you will see your way clear toward granting the prayer of the Youngers and their many friends. . . ."[42]

While those for and against a Younger pardon battled via letters, a Minneapolis newspaper commented on the stalemate in an article entitled, "Perennial Bill for their Release will soon Appear:"

"Senator Wilson may spring the Younger boys' pardon bill again, and he may not. While satisfied that a large number of those who opposed the measure last term could now be induced to withdraw, he has not yet had time to give the matter due attention. But the veteran bill is expected at the proper time."[43]

The year ended on a sad note when Zerelda Amanda "Zee" Mimms James, wife of Jesse, fell into a coma and passed away on November 13, 1900. Jesse's widow had been bedridden for nearly a year with rheumatism and nervous prostration. Her daughter-in-law law, Stella, said of her:

"She had been a devoted and courageous mother who had guided her children tenderly and watched over them prayerfully, determined that they should grow up respected citizens."[44]

Notes

[1]*Minneapolis Journal*, July 13, 1901.

[2]Statement of Gideon W. Thompson, March 5, 1898. Northfield, Minnesota, Bank Robbery of 1876. Selected Manuscripts Collections and Government Records, Microfilm Edition, Roll 4, Minnesota Historical Society.

[3]William N. Gregg letter to George M. Bennett dated April 9, 1898. Northfield, Minnesota, Bank Robbery of 1876. Selected Manuscripts Collections and Government Records,

Microfilm Edition, Roll 4, Minnesota Historical Society.

[4]E.G. Bower letter to George M. Bennett dated April 25, 1898. Northfield, Minnesota, Bank Robbery of 1876. Selected Manuscripts Collections and Government Records, Microfilm Edition, Roll 4, Minnesota Historical Society.

[5]Emory S. Foster letter to George M. Bennett dated May 7, 1898. Northfield, Minnesota, Bank Robbery of 1876. Selected Manuscripts Collections and Government Records, Microfilm Edition, Roll 4, Minnesota Historical Society.

[6]Ibid.

[7]S.B. Elkins letter to David M. Clough dated June 6, 1898. Northfield, Minnesota, Bank Robbery of 1876. Selected Manuscripts Collections and Government Record, Microfilm Edition, Roll 3, Minnesota Historical Society.

[8]Ibid.

[9]S.B. Elkins letter to Charles M. Start dated July 4, 1898. Northfield, Minnesota, Bank Robbery of 1876. Selected Manuscripts Collections and Government Records, Microfilm Edition, Roll 4, Minnesota Historical Society.

[10]Affidavit of Marshall P. Wright dated August 6, 1898. Northfield, Minnesota, Bank Robbery of 1876. Selected Manuscripts Collections and Government Records, Microfilm Edition, Roll 4, Minnesota Historical Society.

[11]Cora McNeill, *Mizzoura: The Youngers*, Minneapolis, Mizzoura Publishing Company, 1898, p. 382.

[12]Carl W. Breihan, *Saga of Jesse James*, Caldwell, Idaho, The Caxton Printers, Inc., 1991, p. 148.

[13]W.C. Bronaugh, *The Youngers' Fight for Freedom*, p. 278.

[14]Statement of A.R. McGill, December 28, 1898. Northfield, Minnesota, Bank Robbery of 1876. Selected Manuscripts Collections and Government Records, Microfilm Edition, Roll 4, Minnesota Historical Society.

[15]Theodore C. Blegen, *Minnesota: A History of the State*, pp. 433-434.

[16]W.C. Bronaugh, *The Youngers' Fight for Freedom*, pp. 278-279.

[17]Marley Brant, *The Outlaw Youngers*, p. 260.

[18]Henry A. Castle letter to George P. Wilson dated February 20, 1899. Northfield, Minnesota, Bank Robbery of 1876. Selected Manuscripts Collections and Government Records, Microfilm Edition, Roll 4, Minnesota Historical Society.

[19]A.T. Ankeny letter to George P. Wilson dated March 23,

1899. Northfield, Minnesota, Bank Robbery of 1876. Selected Manuscripts Collections and Government Records, Microfilm Edition, Roll 4, Minnesota Historical Society.

[20]*Stillwater Gazette*, February 11, 1899.

[21]*Mankato Free Press*, February 17, 1899.

[22]*St. Paul Pioneer Press*, date unknown.

[23]*The Representative* (Minneapolis), undated 1899.

[24]*Fairmont Daily*, undated 1899.

[25]*Crookston Journal*, March 2, 1899.

[26]*Lake Crystal Union*, February 22, 1899.

[27]John W. Mason, Editor, *History of Otter Tail County Minnesota: Its People, Industries and Institutions*, pp. 284-285.

[28]Cole Younger letter to M.J. Daly dated March 26, 1899. Original letter property of Mary Shasky; copies The History Museum of East Otter Tail County, Perham.

[29]Ted P. Yeatman, *Jesse James and Bill Ryan at Nashville*, Nashville, Depot Press, 1981, pp. 8-12.

[30]*Kansas City Star*, February 7, 1899.

[31]White Bear Lake, *St. Croix Valley Press*, July 2001, Brent Peterson, "Rafael Ortiz: Stillwater's Federal Convict."

[32]*Harper's Weekly*, May 6, 1899.

[33]White Bear Lake, *St. Croix Valley Press*, July 2001, Brent Peterson.

[34]Brent Peterson telephone interview with author August 24, 2001.

[35]Theodore C. Blegen, *Minnesota: A History of the State*, pp. 434-437; Clifford E. Clark, Jr., *Minnesota in a Century of Change*, p. 364.

[36]Theodore C. Blegen, *Minnesota: A History of the State*, pp. 434-437.

[37]Undated letter from Jim Younger to Warden Henry Wolfer, Stillwater State Prison Case File: Younger brothers, Selected Manuscripts Collection and Government Records, Microfilm Division, Minnesota Historical Society.

[38]*The St. Paul Pioneer Press*, Saturday, April 9, 1904, obituary of Alix J. Muller; St. Paul City Directories 1903-1920.

[39]John J. Koblas, *F. Scott Fitzgerald in Minnesota: His Homes and Haunts*, St. Paul, Minnesota Historical Society Press, 1978, Appendix.

[40]Alix J. Muller, *A History of the Police and Fire Departments in the Twin Cities*, 1899, St. Paul; *St. Paul Pioneer Press*, Saturday, April 9, 1904.

[41]Ibid.

[42]Alix J. Muller letter to Board of Pardons dated January 8, 1902. Northfield, Minnesota, Bank Robbery of 1876. Selected Manuscripts Collections and Government Records, Microfilm Editor, Roll 4, Minnesota Historical Society.

[43]*Minneapolis Journal*, January 19, 1901.

[44]Marley Brant, *Jesse James: The Man and the Myth*, pp. 248-249.

VIII

1901

*"I am feeling so happy that I hardly know what to say.
One thing I can say and that is I feel like a new man."*

—Cole Younger[1]

F. Rogers, in Cole's behalf, wrote George M. Bennett regarding the outlaw's war service on January 24, 1901. Rogers related he had in fact been with Major Emory S. Foster at the Battle of Lone Jack when the commander was wounded and taken prisoner. Rogers recalled:

"During that time there were several attempts made by a gang of ruffians to enter the house and kill some of the wounded; Major Foster being a special object of their hatred (some of them having been his personal enemies before the war), and their efforts were persistent and determined."[2]

Rogers said he remembered one incident Foster may have forgotten, since he had been seriously wounded at the time. Some of the "ruffians" did enter the house and began abusing the wounded. Cole Younger, on guard, drew his sabre and rushed the men, ordering them to get out quick, and he called them cowardly fiends. Cole told the men he would slaughter every one of them if they did not leave; and added he would protect them over his own dead body if need be. The room was cleared quickly. Had it not been for Cole,

The warden's house, 2000 (above). (Photo by Kristin Scheffert) The warden's residence at the old state prison (right), ca. 1900. (Courtesy of the Minnesota Historical Society)

rationalized Rogers, the prisoners would have all been slaughtered.

On February 11, the *Minneapolis Journal* carried an editorial criticizing any pardon for the brothers under the heading, "The Life Sentence":

"We are unable to appreciate as an argument in favor of the release of the Younger brothers the fact that they have survived in the penitentiary longer than was expected. These men were sentenced for atrocious murder. They were principals in an attempt to rob a bank in broad daylight, and in order to carry out their design the robbers were prepared to kill anyone who interfered, and did commit murder. It is to the credit of Minnesota that these men have been held in confinement as long as they have, and that misplaced sympathy has not set them free. It will be worth much to the reputation of Minnesota as a place where crime is punished, justice is done, and where criminals are not made the beneficiaries of sickly sentimentality, if these notorious bandits are compelled to end their days just where they are. If they had died eight to ten years ago there would have been no question as to the justice of the penalty. The fact that they have survived till this time and are still in the enjoyment of life and making themselves useful to the state against the state which they committed so great a crime fails to present sufficient reason why they should now be released from the penalty which it was decreed they should pay. A life sentence should mean a life sentence if it was a just sentence when imposed."[3]

In March 1901, Cole again wrote a letter to M.J. Daly whom he now referred to as "My Noble Friend." Daly, although living in Perham, was at the senate chambers in St. Paul:

"Your kind favor was received yesterday eve. Many thanks for the kind words and let me assure you and all the Noble Members of the Senate and House and all friends that we appreciate your good work in behalf of humanity with all our heart. And time will prove whether we were worthy or not. We hope Mrs. Daly and the senator's children are well and happy. And believe one all ways [sic] your true and greatful [sic] but unfortunet [sic] friend.   Cole Younger"[4]

Another fire broke out in the prison on March 24, in Shop H of W.B. and W.G. Jordan, who operated the prison shoe shops. The cell housekeeper sounded the alarm, and the extreme heat set off the automatic sprinklers, which prevented the flames from spreading. The damage was about one thousand dollars, most of which was caused by water from the sprinkling system. The blaze, unlike the January 1884 fires believed set by inmates, was caused by spontaneous combustion.

On March 25, friends of the Younger effort began circulating a petition to be sent directly to the president of the United States requesting a pardon. The group planned to present papers to the chief executive urging clemency and showing "the injustice and hardship of the sentence imposed." The group's spokesman said there was no way that the case could again be brought before the Supreme Court. The Circuit Court of Appeals could reverse or modify its sentence but the group was certain it would take no action. This lack of action by the courts induced the group to go directly to the president.[5]

On April 10, 1901, Attorney H.T. Williams of Sedalia, Missouri, wrote Governor Van Sant protesting a parole or pardon for the Youngers. In concluding his three-page epistle, Williams added:

"You can't train a rattlesnake to be good by petting and warming him. Such action increases strength and venom. The remedy for the rattlesnake is execution. I believe that until something better is discovered, the remedy for crime is proper punishment—*certain, swift and sure.*"[6]

On the same day, Archibald Carnagher of Kansas City, in favor of a Younger parole, wrote the governor. Carnagher based his argument on the unfortunate experience suffered by the boys during the Kansas-Missouri Border War and the Civil War. He stated that he was a "free-state-man" living in Olathe, Kansas, before the war and was and knew the father of the Youngers by reputation. Like himself, "Old Man" Younger was a Union man. When Carnagher was serving with the Kansas cavalry during the war, he frequently passed the Younger farm while on raids and protected his property as best he could.

Shot by Quantrill men in 1861, Carnagher was taken to the U.S. Hospital in Kansas City. During the summer, the Youngers' father came to the city and sold the quartermaster $3,000 worth of mules and started home. En route, he was murdered for his money. According to Carnagher, the men who killed him found no money upon his body, but when his body was being prepared for funeral, the morticians discovered $3,000 tied in a red handkerchief around his body. The killers had opened his shirt at the neck and inspected his trousers, thus missing the money tied around his waist.

According to Carnagher, this cruel deed turned the Youngers to outlawry. Before the murder of their father, the Youngers comprised one of the most highly respected families in the county. Carnagher believed there would have been no tragedy at Northfield had the murder of their father not taken place.[7]

Also in April, the bill introduced to the Minnesota legislature by C.P. Deming of Minneapolis, calling for parole eligibility of life prisoners who had served at least twenty-four years, was reviewed by Governor Samuel Rinnah Vant Sant and passed on to the Speaker of the House of Representatives. In his letter to House Speaker, M.J. Dowling, Van Sant penned:

"Pursuant to your request, I have the honor to herewith return to your Honorable Body, House File No. 234, being 'a bill for an act to amend Section 7510 of the 1894 General Statutes of Minnesota, the same being Section 4, of Chapter 9, of the General Laws of Minnesota for the year 1893, relating to the parol [sic] of prisoners."[8]

With the Youngers in mind, the House amended the bill to prohibit a paroled prisoner from exhibiting himself "in any dime museum, circus, theater, opera house, or any other place of public amusement or assembly, where a charge is made for admission."[9]

The bill passed with unanimous approval that same month—eighty to thirty-seven in the House and forty to seventeen in the Senate. Assisting with the bill's passage was Representative J.W. Phillips, who, in 1876, was driven from the streets of Northfield as the James-Younger Gang robbed the bank.

Minnesota Attorney General Wallace B. Douglas returned the file to Governor Van Sant with a letter stating the bill had passed both houses. The bill, which stated men such as the Youngers were eligible for parole, also read "that no such life convict shall be paroled under the provisions of this act without the unanimous consent, in writing, of the members of the Board of Pardons."[10]

The bill also raised a very important issue. Did the power to pardon, in part conferred upon the Chief Justice of the Supreme Court, include the power to parole or assent to the parole of prisoners with life sentences? If the pardoning power did include the power to parole, the legislative enactment in question was a delegation by the legislature of executive powers to the Board of Prison Managers, which by the Constitution, was vested in the Governor, the Chief Justice, and the Attorney General. Douglas asked the governor to approve the act, or inform the friends of the bill of the objections.

The bill had passed although there were questions to be argued in both houses regarding some of the finer points. But, Cole and Jim Younger took advantage of the bill's passing. This time, they applied for parole, rather than pardon, to the Board of Managers of the State Prison on May 6, 1901. The Board of Managers forwarded a resolution of support to the Board of Pardons. Cole and Jim, in separate applications, each asked that a parole be granted upon the grounds:

"That he has been confined in the Minnesota State Prison for nearly twenty-five years. And for the further reason that he has always obeyed all of the rules of the State Prison, and has shown every evidence of reform. That he has reformed, and is desirous of proving his ability and purpose to live a law-abiding life. He believes that the punishment already inflicted ought to satisfy the requirements of justice, and he feel that society cannot be benefited by longer incarceration.

"And for the further reason that he is growing old and desires to prove his fitness to be trusted with his liberty and give proof that he is fully reformed before it is too late to do so."[11]

The resolution authored by the Board of Managers of the State Prison, which was forwarded to the Board of Pardons, offered a strong endorsement for a Younger parole. The resolution stated that the brothers had impeccable records during their confinement and had served "more than thirty-five years less than the diminution which they would have been allowed by law for good conduct had they been sentenced to a term of thirty-five years."[12]

The *St. Louis Post-Dispatch* carried an article on the Youngers in May. The article was sympathetic to the Younger cause and quoted them at some length. Jim was quoted as stating:

"There has not been one day here in which I have not put my mind to the problem of preserving myself to enjoy those years of freedom which I feel we shall have. I have put my old life as far from my thoughts as the prison has put it from my hands. I have not read one single story of crime. I have made patience, cheerfulness, kindness habits of my life. I have put bitterness down, and I have no bitterness. I have learned the whole lesson of self-control."[13]

Cole's statement was somewhat similar in context:

"It was a long way up here, but it has been a longer way home. We have been here [twenty-five] years. I was [thirty-one] when we came and Jim was [twenty-eight]. We have taken our medicine. We have never whimpered. We have been strict with ourselves and kept the rules. And our hope of pardon, parole, forgiveness is in the record of these [twenty-five] years. There is not one mark against us. No other prisoner has ever been here so long and preserved his mind. We have done it because we feel that we were in measure the product of extraordinary conditions and that, if given the opportunity, we can in our last few years prove the things expected of men in this day are not beyond us—that we were by acquirement and not inherently bad."[14]

The board of prison managers, however, did not parole the Youngers. Their action was merely a resolution requesting the written consent of the board of pardons. Two resolutions were passed, one for each of the brothers. They reached the governor's office the following morning and were put on file pending the actions of the three members of the board of pardons.[15]

The governor, attorney general, and chief justice refused to discuss the matter with the press. A meeting of the board was not required, as the law only required the written consent of the individual members. Most persons familiar with the case speculated that the board would meet to discuss the question.

The board of prison managers declared it would not meet again until June 6. Pro-pardon persons were concerned that, should the board of pardons delay action until August 1, when the board of prison managers was to give way to the board of control, the fate of the Youngers would rest in the hands of three men—Morey, Lee, and Leavitt. It was quite doubtful, however, that the board of pardons would indorse the application at any stage during the proceedings.

Winona Attorney O.B. Gould wrote Governor Van Sant protesting a parole on May 10. Gould felt "the quality of mercy had already been strained" since these men should have been hanged at the gallows and sent to Hell. He believed it was folly to talk of reformation and good conduct, insisting:

"When the devil was sick—the devil a monk would be,
When the devil was well—the devil a monk was he."[16]

A New Salem, North Dakota, man, who signed his letter simply "A Christian," wrote Governor Van Sant the same day, and unlike Gould, this man (discovered to be B. Lueder) favored a Younger release. "A Christian" based his argument upon the Bible and believed the teachings of Jesus Christ advocated a parole for the boys.[17]

A *Minneapolis Journal* article, published on May 11, touched upon the citizens of Northfield's opposition to a Younger parole:

"The steps taken to parole the Younger brothers have not caused the outspoken opposition of the citizens of this locality, which the attempts of former years created. It is true that some, perhaps many, have grown indifferent to the matter. This may be accounted for in various ways. Former movements to parole the Youngers have systematically failed, and many feel that this attempt will meet a like fate. Again, many have confidence in the board of pardons and in the governor sufficient to put their minds at ease. The locality as a whole may be said to be opposed to pardoning the men who are responsible for the crime here some twenty-five years ago. The community is not at all vindictive and fewer are opposed to the pardon of three men than ever before, but the locality at large still contains a good, strong majority who are against the parole."[18]

An article, "Bitter at Northfield," published in the same newspaper three days later, however, contradicted the earlier story. Reverend G.L. Morrill of the Baptist Association of Northfield was playing the organ when a reporter entered. Frank Wilcox, one of three First National Bank employees on duty the day of the September 7, 1876, holdup attempt, was leading the singing of the congregation and choir. Following the service, Dr. Morrill was asked about the feelings of Northfield citizens regarding a Younger parole. One man, who had lived in Northfield during the raid, bellowed, "Just let them be paroled and walk down this way. Judge Lynch is right here and will be ready for them."[19]

The *Northfield Independent* concurred in an article published May 17. The editors regretted that the indictment against the Youngers for the "brutal murder of the inoffensive Swede in the streets . . ." was not maintained on the calendar of the court. It was believed that the same loophole that saved their necks before would do so again, "but it would insure them a continued residence at Stillwater, where they have developed into such distinguished and exemplary citizens."[20]

On June 8, W.C. Bronaugh journeyed again to Minneapolis, this time calling upon Senator Wilson at his office in the Lumber Exchange Building. Although they had never met face to face before, the two men engaged in relaxed conversation. Wilson suggested that Bronaugh should meet some of the members of the legislature and arranged a meeting in his office for the following afternoon.[21]

At the meeting, Wilson told those present that he had recently had a meeting with Governor Van Sant, who had received a letter from a Sedalia, Missouri, attorney blasting any would-be pardon of the Youngers. To counteract this letter, Wilson advised Bronaugh to return to Missouri and gather all the letters he could in favor of a pardon. As Bronaugh departed, Wilson reminded him that letters from important politicians in Missouri could be beneficial to their cause.

Bronaugh returned to St. Paul in time for the Youngers' case before the Board of Pardons, registering at the Merchants Hotel under the name, "W.C. Carter, Dallas, Texas." A large number of documents were presented to Governor S.R. Van Sant, including a petition to release the Youngers signed by many prominent men: Bishop Whipple, the late Bishop Gilbert, former Governor Alexander Ramsey, Archbishop John Ireland, Henry A. Castle and General Flower. Among the signers were three survivors of the Madelia shootout—W.C. Murphy, George A. Bradford and C.A. Pomeroy—as well as Dr. Henry M. Wheeler who had shot and killed Clell Miller during the Northfield raid. Letters from other prominent men such as the late Henry H. Sibley, the late C.K. Davis,

Reverend H.B. Whipple. (Courtesy of the Rice County Historical Society)

Alexander Ramsey. (Courtesy of the *Chicago Record-Herald*, April 23, 1903)

and General Elkins were presented as well as affidavits showing the conduct of the Youngers during the prison fire.[22] Bronaugh even presented a joint letter addressed to the pardoning board signed by nearly every attorney in Sedalia.

A reporter from the *Lexington* (Kentucky) *Morning Herald* also visited the Youngers in June. This journalist, unlike most of the others who came to Stillwater, was anything but objective; and was, in fact, caught up in hero worship of the former outlaws.

"I visited the Younger boys at Stillwater a month before they were pardoned [sic]," related the reporter two years later. "I found Cole carrying water on one of the streets in the prison yard. He was then [fifty-seven] years old, a fellow fat with good cheer. He laughed about the twenty-five years he had spent there. He laughed about the prospect of getting out. He laughed about the old life and his ha, ha was loud and hearty when I asked him what he would do if he were freed.

"Everybody about the prison was fond of Cole. He was the cheeriest soul in those grim walls. He always said 'certainly' when someone asked him to tell the story of the wild life in Missouri. But he never told anything, and I feel safe in saying he never will. He has been sounded on the subject so many times, and he has chased the devil around the stump with his answers so much that his skill at telling you all about it and still never telling a thing is so keen that you laugh in his face, and he laughs with you understanding that you see the point. What can you do with a man who talks like this."[23]

The *Lexington* reporter asked Cole about the great deal of money he had made before he was caught and what he had done with it.

"Money!" blurted Cole. "Why, my dear fellow, I hid great fortunes in hollow trees, but pshaw! Those hollows have all grown to be lumps by this time. You see I have been here twenty-five years."

According to the reporter, every time a movement to free the Youngers received great impetus, the "fighting doctor" [Henry Wheeler] who killed outlaw Clell Miller during the raid, was the first person to arrive in St. Paul and Stillwater. "His admiration for Cole, born in the heat of the battle at Northfield, has not abated from that day to this," wrote the reporter. "He attributes the success of the whole movement to the reputation which that day made for Cole in Minnesota. The whole state incensed with the raiders, but there was still a little corner in the popular heart for the man who would go back for his brother."

But, of course, "that tiny little corner in the popular heart" did not include everyone. Another anonymous wordsmith, this one signing his name as "A friend of right and justice," wrote Governor Van Sant and the Board of Pardons on July 7. This writer said he did not include his name because he was afraid of retribution from gang members. He stated he and his fellow Missourians did not want the Youngers to return to their state where they could wreak havoc. Instead he proposed, "But Them two Men Deserve to be Hung."[24]

L.B. Valliant, Supreme Court Justice of the State of Missouri, wrote Supreme Court Justice Charles M. Start requesting a Younger parole on June 12. On June 15, E.F. Rogers of Kansas City wrote again to Charles Start, also asking for a parole. Rogers related his experiences as an officer in the federal army fighting Cole Younger, when "not a blot stained his character." Early in the war, Rogers was stationed at Harrisonville, Missouri, where he and Captain Walley attended a dance. Walley, after dancing with a lady, asked for another, but she informed him she was "engaged" to Cole Younger for that particular dance. Captain Walley was enraged, told Cole he would make no disturbance that evening but would kill him the first opportunity. The captain, according to Rogers, was a vicious man. Cole remained a gentleman through the affair.[25]

Rogers added he had seen and heard Cole stand up and raise his voice to insults by his men at the Battle of Lone Jack, Missouri. He protected the Union prisoners at the risk of his own life.

On June 25, Attorney George M. Bennett presented what the newspapers called a "monster petition" to Governor Van Sant in support of a Younger parole. Written on the backside of the petition was the heading, "The Youngers Petition for Relief—from Rt. Rev. H.B. Whipple, Hon. C.K. Davis, Ex. Gov. Alex Ramsey, et al. Filed by Geo. M. Bennett." The last signature on the petition was that of Archbishop Ireland.[26]

The petition called for a Younger parole but was designed for use in the campaign for a pardon under the provisions of the Deming Bill. Bennett informed the governor that he intended to appear before the board of pardons at their next meeting, July 8, in support of the parole application, which had already been endorsed by the board of prison managers.[27]

Bennett's opponents, however, insisted that the bill had never legally passed. The House of Representatives had in fact called the bill back, and it had never been signed by the governor. The bill was printed in the laws but its legality was being challenged. Chief Justice Start also raised a question. Did the bill impose on governor's hands? Was the imposition of the bill warranted by the Constitution? But if the chief justice were to raise the point, he would not perhaps have to act under the bill, as according to all precedent, paroling was not an exercise of the pardoning power, which was the only judicial duty the constitution imposed on the chief justice.

The Youngers' quest for parole received a tremendous boost from Bishop Henry B. Whipple, who wrote Charles Start about the same time as the Bennett petition. The bishop asked not for parole but for a pardon for the brothers and believed they were victims of geography and time. According to Bishop Whipple:

"I know the conditions of Missouri during the Civil War. My cousin General [Henry Wager] Halleck was in command. The previous conflict in Kansas had ripened into the bitterest hatreds and vendetta. The family of the Younger Brothers were sufferers. They joined the free lancers of the Confederacy. I believe their subsequent history was the outcome of those days of guerilla warfare, and so far as I know and believe the Younger brothers were not guilty of personal acts of cruelty or murder. I believe that in the Northfield bank robbery, the murder of the cashier was the act of a drunken member of the gang. Since the day they entered prison they have lived exemplary lives, and men like General Sibley, Gov[ernor] Marshall and others have expressed to me their belief that they had received their punishment in such manner as to guarantee their good behavior and were proper subjects of clemency."[28]

The *Minneapolis Journal* interviewed Cole on Sunday, July 7. Cole informed the reporter that he was glad he called and that he hadn't been feeling very well for a week or so and had been down with a bad back. About all he was capable of doing, he said, was move around enough to carry food from the prison kitchen to the hospital.

He said when the state board of pardons considered their case the next day, he hoped they would recognize the merit of their appeal and issue a pardon. He was surprised at the great number of influential people of the northwest who were fighting for him and his brother's freedom.

"Just think of it, we have been in this prison for near- ly twenty-five years, and this is one of the first times we have seen a ray of light shining forth from the darkness that has sur- rounded us," related Cole. "I don't mean by that that we have had any cause for complaint, for we have not. During our stay in prison we have been well treated by every warden and every prison official under the warden, and neither Jim nor I could possibly have a word of fault to offer. We have tried to meet every requirement, and I believe that the prison records will show that there is not a black mark against us. Jim and I have always tried to make it easy for the officers over us, and I think we have won the friendship and good will of every one of them. The late Ben Cayou was our keeper for many years, and not long before his death he called at the prison and said to me, 'Cole, my only hope now is that I will live long enough to see you and Jim from prison, for you are certain entitled to consideration because of your remarkable record.'"[29]

Cole related that when he and his brothers came to Stillwater Prison on November 21, 1876, the population in the institution was about 175. The brothers were put in the tub and pail shop where they worked for two years. Over the next eight years they were employed in the belt shop where they made all the belts, sieves, and straw stackers used by the thresher company. Warden Reed then put them to work in the storeroom and tailor shop for the next ten months, but when Stordock became warden, he gave them jobs in the library. He said he was put in charge of the library, Jim in charge of the mail, and Bob was given a position as clerk in the office of Steward Benner. Cole remained with the library for six years and was then given a position as head nurse in the prison hos- pital. While he had been "dishing out pills" for many months, he felt he had not acquired any great knowledge of medicine.

"I weighed 175 pounds when I came to this prison and I now weigh 234 pounds," he continued. "I begin to feel my advancing age, but on the whole I feel pretty good, and I think

I would be able to live a few years more if I were released. I have had only one severe illness while here, and that was an attack of lumbago. Jim has been sick several times, but he is now feeling fine and weighs more than he ever did."[30]

Cole conveyed that he was born in Jackson County, Missouri, January 15, 1844. Jim was born at the same place, January 15, 1848, and Bob October 29, 1855. He talked about Bob's death in prison of consumption. Cole told how all fourteen children in the family were still living in 1860, and he had relatives in Missouri, Texas, and California. He added that since coming to the prison, he had been outside the walls on three occasions only—twice at the warden's house and once in the county jail.

"I would like to visit my home in Missouri," said Cole, "but if the parole says that we must stay in this state, why we shan't feel bad and will accept it with gratification."[31]

Dr. Frank Powell of St. Paul penned a letter to Governor Van Sant on July 8 requesting a Younger pardon. Powell was concerned that further imprisonment of the Youngers would lead to "vengeance, not justice."[32]

Governor Vant Sant received other letters favoring a Younger release and so did the Board of Pardons in the first two weeks of July. The bankers of Sedalia, Missouri, sent a petition on July 2, and the lawyers of the same city followed suit that day as well. Attorney William J. Stone of St. Louis and C.E. Faulkner of Minneapolis wrote, asking that their names be added to those favoring a parole. George M. Bennett again wrote the Board of Pardons offering to find employment for the Youngers.

F.E. Kenaston, President of the Minneapolis Threshing Machine Company wrote an interesting letter to Governor Van Sant on July 10, rebuking a statement he had read regarding employment for the Youngers at his company.

"My attention has been called to an article published in this evening's *Minneapolis Times* stating that one of our employees had telephoned you offering work to the Younger Bros if pardoned, in our shops at Hopkins," penned Kenaston. "I beg to inform you that such offer, if made, was wholly unauthorized. My company would under no circumstances have these murderous thieves in its employ in any capacity. They are in the only place proper for them to be, and the writer sincerely hopes that the Hon. Board of Pardons will use its best backbone at all sittings when this subject is under discussion."[33]

Alix Muller, Jim Younger's lady friend, induced her uncle, Edward J. Schurmeier to write on the boys' behalf listing propositions in regard to the employment of the brothers should they be granted a parole. Schurmeier said he would furnish Cole and Jim with a fine store in a suitable location for a cigar and tobacco business. He would allow them to run the business in his name and would furnish them a "first-class man" to help them run the store. He added, he would give the boys all the money needed to run the store, let them keep all the profits or shares, and make his home their home.[34]

Schurmeier stated that if they were instead employed at the Andrew Schoch Grocery Company in St. Paul, they could still live at his home. Schoch had offered the Youngers sixty dollars a month apiece to start work. According to Schurmeier, Schoch was "a Christian gentleman, kind and humane and one for whom it would be a pleasure to work.

No matter where employed in St. Paul, Schurmeier insisted the brothers live in his home. He called his residence "very retired," bounded by Central Avenue, Robert Street, and Aurora Avenue, across from the Convent of Visitation, "and very little exposed to the public." As an added inducement, he related that he had a library of 1,000 volumes, which the boys in their leisure could enjoy.

But Cole Younger, perhaps, helped his own cause by writing his life story while still in prison and by writing as a man who had realized his mistakes: "There is little to inspire mirth in prison. For a man who has lived close to the heart of nature, in the forest, in the saddle, to imprison him is like caging a wild bird. And yet imprisonment has brought out the excellencies of many men. I have learned many things in the lonely hours there. I have learned that hope is a divinity; I have learned that a surplus of determination conquers every weakness; I have learned that you cannot make a white dove to a blackbird; I have learned that vengeance is for God and not for man. . . ."[35]

As the three-member board of pardons took up the boys' case on July 8, newspaper headlines gave them little chance of attaining their freedom: "Dark for Youngers"; "Hope for the Parole not Bright"; "Start Chief Obstacle"; "The Chief Justice Does Not Believe in Letting Them Out"; and "May Hold Parole Law Invalid."[36]

According to at least one newspaper, the feeling at the State Capitol was that the Youngers would have to wait awhile longer. Members of the board were still very much disgusted with the action of the legislature earlier that year. The majority of the House members were opposed to freeing the Youngers but dodged their responsibility by tacking on the amendment to the Deming Bill, which required the unanimous consent of the board of pardons. These men counted on the well-known opposition of Chief Justice Start, and one of them informed him that he expected him to block the way. The chief justice was highly indignant and denounced the member as a coward for shifting his responsibility in such a way. According to Attorney General Douglas, the act was invalid. Chief Justice Start had only to rest on that decision and it was believed he would.

The Younger brothers looked to the validity situation with a mingling of hope and fear. They had been disappointed many times, and they felt the board of pardons would not release them, but the parole proposition was entirely different from an absolute pardon. Cole Younger divulged his hopes to the press:

"After twenty-five years it looks as though there may be a rift in the cloud that has overshadowed our unfortunate and luckless lives, and oh, what a glorious awakening this break of a new day would be.

"I have been sick for the past week or two, and with regard to our possible parole, I am in such a confused frame of mind that I don't know what to say.

"One thing I would like to have you print is that we desire to thank our friends in Minnesota, who have taken such an active interest in our welfare.

"Among the many hundreds to whom we are indebted are Dr. Wheeler of Northfield, who shot Jim, and who shot at me, and who signed our petition for a pardon: Captain B.G. Yates, Captain Murphy, now of Owatonna, and others who assisted in our capture.

"In event of parole we have no plans. In case we are let out our fate will be in the hands of the state agent and the warden, and we are informed by both gentlemen that we will find plenty of work without delay."[37]

The Board of Pardons met on the eighth with the hearing lasting only half an hour. Chief Justice Start questioned Warden Henry Wolfer over most of that period. No formal plea was made for the Youngers. Those persons representing them—George M. Bennett, Warden Henry Wolfer, John H. Schurmeier of a St. Paul wagon company, and Captain B.G. Yates—were convinced that the board members' minds were already made up and felt their only course was to shed further enlightenment on the case.[38]

Chief Justice Start asked Warden Wolfer if there was anything in the records of the men at Stillwater that might detract from their good time allowance and prevent a parole.

"There is no record against them whatever," replied the warden.

"From the beginning what has been their record with regard to observing the rules of the prison?"

"It has been prefect."

"Is there any employment in view for them, that they can step into in case they are paroled?"

"Not that I know of. I think they would have no difficulty, though, in getting work. I have never discussed it with them."

"What work have they been trained to in the prison?"

"Cole has been a nurse for the past six years. Jim is working in the library and as mailing clerk."

"Would their training open up to them a chance for employment outside?"

"I think not."

"What do they expect to do if they get out?"

"Well, they never mentioned it to me but once. I told them that it was not necessary to discuss it yet."

"There has been an offer of employment for one of them, I believe," said the chief justice. "It was from Dr. Frank Powell."

Mr. Schurmeier said that if the people who were here in 1876 would take a vote, he believed that ninety-nine percent would vote for the release of the boys. He said he would see to it that the brothers had suitable employment if released.

Chief Justice inquired of Warden Wolfer: "Do they have any friends who could help them?"

"Not in this state, I believe."

"Have they in Missouri?"

"Yes, they have friends there who could care for them. I think the matter of employment should be carefully guarded.

They are anxious themselves to avoid notoriety and make a good living."

"Are they in good health?"

"Yes. Cole has had some trouble with his heart the past year. Jim has dyspepsia, due to his difficulty in masticating food; otherwise they are quite well."

"Is it your judgment they are actually changed men?"

"Yes, sir, it is."

"You think they would not be tempted by an offer of money to pose as an advertising scheme, as bartenders in a big saloon, for instance?"

"No! That feature can be entirely eliminated. The board of prison managers controls their employment while on parole."

Attorney General Douglas asked: "Do you know whether the boys have relatives in Missouri with money who are able to take care of them?"

George Bennett answered: "They have a nephew who is doing pretty well and a sister with a little means. They could each take care of them for six months in the year."

The Chief Justice asked Mr. Bennett what interest personally he had in the case. He replied that he was not their attorney, and there was nothing in it for him, but since 1897, he had made a personal investigation and felt deeply interested in them.

"I was here in 1876 myself," answered the Chief Justice, "and I know what the feeling was then. There is no mitigation for their crime."

"I am satisfied of one thing. The father of these boys was a Union man, and was murdered by a captain in the Union army for his money. That does not excuse the crimes they committed, however. All that has been said for them does not mitigate their offense."

Governor Van Sant then announced the board would take the case under advisement and adjourned the session.

The following morning the board of pardons met for a second session without a decision. The question as to the constitutionality of the law was raised, and several hours were devoted to that problem. Their treatment of other cases did not look promising for the Youngers as the board commuted only three cases and did not grant a single pardon. By ten o'clock in the morning, the other cases were finished. There was a moment of silence while the three judges looked at each other and waited for someone to speak. Rocking back and forth in their chairs, they stared at the wall. Spectators took the hint and left the room.

An executive conference followed, which lasted about half an hour. Chief Justice Start and Attorney General Douglas came out and told the press they would take up the Younger case at eight o'clock the next morning. Governor Van Sant added that the board did not feel ready to act on the matter and needed more time for consideration.

On July 10, 1901, Governor S.R. Van Sant, Chief Justice Charles Start, and Attorney General Wallace Douglas approved a Younger parole. The document they authored, "In the Matter of the Parole of Coleman and James Younger," they stated Chapter 234 of the 1901 laws became law, although not approved by the governor. They recognized the "exclusive province of the legislature to extend the parole system to life convicts." The three men reiterated they were satisfied with the conduct of the brothers over a quarter century, and Cole

Governor Samuel R. Van Sant and his staff, ca. 1901. (Courtesy of the Minnesota Historical Society)

and Jim had earned their parole if any life prisoner could ever do so. Although there were still some legal issues of the bill that had not been resolved, the signers decided not to raise those questions at the time.[39]

Warren Carter Bronaugh was not present at the hearing but remained incognito at an ice cream parlor across the street from the Capitol. From the store, he could see through the windows of the Capitol and observe the motions of those at the hearing. His good friend, State Auditor Dunn, helping to preserve his secrecy, popped in to let him know what was going on across the street.[40]

Dunn told Bronaugh there would not be a decision before noon and advised him to go secure lunch. Upon placing his order at a nearby restaurant, Dunn walked in and slapped him on the back with great news.

On July 10, 1901, the *St. Paul Pioneer Press* announced, "Cole and Jim Younger will be paroled this morning, unless the persons who have carefully watched the proceedings of the pardon board are badly mistaken. The questions asked by the members of the board Monday indicated they desired only to be satisfied that the Youngers when released from the restraints of prison walls would be given suitable occupation."[41]

Because of some of the remarks issued by Chief Justice Start, the *Pioneer Press* painted an indefinite picture, but Justice Start was in complete harmony with his associates on the board. The parole was a conditional parole and subject to careful restrictions as to place of residence, employment, and lifestyle. Details of the parole were not announced until later that morning, long after the early edition of the newspaper had gone into circulation.

Ironically, that same morning, the *Pioneer Press* announced that Colonel John S. Mosby, the Confederacy's "Gray Ghost," came to St. Paul under orders from President William McKinley as special agent of the general land office for Minnesota and Nebraska. Whether he met with the Youngers following their parole is not known.

"This was a glad day for two old men who have passed a quarter of a century in prison," declared the *Minneapolis Journal*, "in expiation of desperate crimes done in their youth, when the war of the rebellion had left bitterness and hatred behind as the heritage of the borderland."[42]

220

The *Kansas City Star* reported: "Immediately after church services, while Cole Younger, head nurse, was at his accustomed post in the prison hospital, and Jim, librarian and postman, was in the library, each was informed that he was wanted 'down front.' They supposed that they were to see a visitor in the reception room. But the brothers met a deputy warden, who handed each of them a suit of civilian clothes and a telescope grip.

"'Put these clothes on,' said the warden, and he added, 'you won't have to go back.'

"The brothers put the clothes on without delay."[43]

Because Warden Wolfer was in St. Paul attending the hearing, he directed his son, Harry Wolfer, to give the good news to the Youngers. Wolfer lost no time in seeking out the brothers. Another account records that he addressed the boys together in a single room.

"Boys," he exclaimed with tears in his eyes and a lump in his throat, "you are paroled. The state board has just approved the parole. The warden will be home soon to tell you all the particulars and arrange for your leaving. Probably you will get away tomorrow. Shake."[44]

A slightly different version states that young Wolfer walked into the library and informed Jim Younger he was being freed. Jim appeared unmoved but held out his hand and thanked the bearer of good news. "Of course, I'm pleased," Jim said slowly. "It's the difference between life and death."[45]

As Wolfer approached Cole in the library, the former outlaw looked up from his work as if he knew why the warden's son was coming to him. "Cole, you've been paroled," announced Wolfer. Cole stared a moment in silence, then answered softly, "That's the best news I've had for many a long day. And I can tell you Jim and I will work hard to merit the good will of the people outside. Nobody's going to regret this."[46]

At first, the brothers seemed dazed at hearing the news. They had waited so long with little hope, and now that the moment had come, it was hard for them to realize their good fortune. They had learned during incarceration to conceal their feelings, but a slight quaver in their voices showed their elation as they shook the hand of young Wolfer.

Once the stunned Youngers were informed of their parole, they were interviewed by a Stillwater newspaper reporter. The brothers were anxious to talk with an outsider. "When I get outside the prison door, if I ever do get out, I believe there is agility enough in my old bones to let me turn just one somersault," exclaimed Cole. "I feel like a ten-year-old boy at the mere possibility. Beyond any doubt the actuality will overcome me to the extent of just one old-fashioned handspring."[47]

"Me too," interrupted Jim. "Remember the time they let us go over on the wall to the warden's house that time—must be eight years ago?"

"I can remember the way everything looked right now," chimed in Cole. "It's very strange that long confinement produces on one's idea of space. I don't quite know whether the muscles of the eyes contract, or whether it is refusal of the brain to immediately comprehend what the eyes see, but when a man has been in close confinement between walls for a long time they [don't] seem able to grasp the ideas of distance. I remember staring over at the Wisconsin hills that were all green and beautiful. I wanted to stay there until I could get used to the sensation, but of course [I] couldn't."[48]

Jim was asked how Cole's reflections made him feel. "Feel as if I were about to fall off something high," Jim answered.

"But that will soon wear off," Cole added. "I want to get out of this prison because I have reached the limit of my capacity for taking punishment. We have been kindly and well treated, according to our merits as prisoners, but you people who live on the outside and talk so glibly of life imprisonment—why, not one of you has any conception of its meaning.

"It is burial without death. Only by exercising his will power in a systematic and never-ceasing struggle with the melancholy born of solitude can a man evade insanity. I don't mean violent, straight-jacket insanity, perhaps, though some might come to that, but the dreadful haunting dread of mental failure suggested by introspection.

"I know nothing of mental science except such things as I have read while in jail, without the power to properly digest them, but it seems to me that this fear of becoming insane and the constant strain of trying not to is really the most torturing form of insanity.

"It may be functional, as the doctors say, and not organic, but unless the will of the sufferer is tremendously strong he endures the tortures of the damned."[49]

The reporter asked Cole if he had ever been outside the walls but on that one occasion. He answered that he also had the night of the fire and related that everything modern to him dated from the night of the fire.

"If we are paroled," stated Jim, "we shall get in a quiet corner somewhere, so that all the sights and sounds of the world will be visible and audible, but we have no desire to do aught else than labor quietly to the end of our days. This will afford us the opportunity we have been seeking for a long time—that of showing the world that we know how to live decently and honestly and hold trustworthy positions as men among men.

"I don't think I shall be much disturbed by the mechanical and engineering advances that have occurred in the last [twenty-five] years. You see, engineering is my hobby. I take the *Scientific American* and have had it for many years. Every issue of that paper I have studied carefully. When the first electrical cars were put in use I saw the cuts and plans and diagrams in the *American* and wrestled with them and the descriptions given until I understand the principle. Now, of course, it will look odd to see a carriage running around without horses, or a big car traveling without mules or steam, but for years I have known that these things were, and pictures have familiarized me with their appearance. It will all be novel—very new and novel, but not incomprehensible."[50]

When his brother finished, Cole remarked: "The telephone and Edison's talking machines have always been my limit. Once when I was down in the office, I had orders to telephone over to the warden's house. That tickled me to death, because I had heard them talking at one end of the line, and it was all I could do to keep my face straight at the spectacle of a fellow jabbering into a dumb-bell—'Wha-a-t!—yes—did he?—who said so!—all right—tell him to come down this afternoon.'

"I heard that and never forgot it. When they showed me how to ring for the warden I put my ear to the thing and waited. When the warden said, 'Hello,' at the other end of that line, it sounded so close at hand and the whole thing seemed so absurdly impossible that I was rattled. I couldn't reply for a minute more."[51]

Jim cut in: "Now they have lines from Minneapolis to New York, and you can talk just as easily as to the warden's house."

"I have heard about it," replied Cole. "When I have a chance I am going to try that if it costs a dollar."

"To the man who has been in prison as long as I have," said Jim, "access to all the modern books and magazines is a blessing not unmixed with pain. You see, every magazine story, every novel, every scientific treatise, everything printed, in fact, contains reference to events and things in common everyday use of which the prison reader comprehends nothing. He reads half-comprehendingly, and longs and longs for freedom, if only for a little time, that he may once more get in tune with the world and be at least able to read of it intelligently. Still, the man in prison who reads, must, I think, be held a good critic on some matters. Take the modern march of slang, for instance.

"I have noticed that a slang word appears first, perhaps, in a publication of the lower class. It has probably been accepted by certain classes before it reaches the papers at all. Now, here in the solitude of the prison library, I watch the evolution of that slang word. It crawls insidiously from the newspaper to the cheaper magazines of the day, where it appears most likely in a story of the day. In a subsequent issue of the magazine the editor of the magazine uses it editorially to express some idea. Next month I discover it in one of the heavier publications, quoted most likely, but still there. From that time the position of the word is assured, because writers of ponderous leaders on electrical engineering in the *Electrical Magazine* are not without their weaknesses, and they, too, pick the word up.

"For people outside, the setting of such words as I refer to in conversation may remove the impression of their absurdity, but to a man in jail, with nothing but books to talk to, some of these phrases sound like infant babbling. And to tell the truth, great as my opportunities have been of late years, I still tie to Dickens. He doesn't clip his English, he doesn't slang it, and his writings are full of heartbeats. I have laughed with him and wept with him. Great is Dickens."[52]

The reporter, somewhat surprised, asked the two men if their confinement had really made them fear insanity.

"God knows what it is that men fear who are shut up for life," replied Jim. "I think it is that a man becomes afraid of himself—doubtful of his ability to sustain the awful routine of life under restraint. It is not the prison that hurts—it is a splendid institution. A well-behaved man can live here in entire physical comfort, but the human mind requires a wider range of activity than that possible behind stone walls. The prisoner who desires to live out his sentence without mental deterioration must develop mental activities thought of outside a place like this.

"For many years I have never permitted myself to harbor a bad thought about anyone. Mind, I do not say I have not had such thoughts. They flash into one's mind and would take root and grow there if not cast out. My method has been, when so assailed by my evil genius, to deliberately force a train of thought on another and more pleasant subject. It is hard to do, but it can be done.

"A long time ago, down in Missouri, I knew an old lady about [seventy] years old, whose husband was about [eighty], I should think. People used to say that in all their married life those two had never been angry at each other, nor uttered a cross word. One day I asked the old lady how that was.

"'James,' she said, 'when I married, my mother said to me that I was marrying a man and not an angel. She warned me that if I desired to live a happy life I must look always for the good in my husband and shut my eyes to the bad. Now, I have seen great good in him—I have never seen any bad, and we have never quarreled.'

"I believe in that old lady's philosophy," offered Jim, "and I have looked for the brighter side of things ever since coming in here, otherwise I should have died long ago, a maniac most likely. Both Cole and I have cultivated control until I think either of us could command our feelings in the most awful situation conceivable. Perhaps you can conceive that situation."[53]

The *Minneapolis Journal* announced on July 10:

"After a protracted consideration of the latest petition for their freedom, the state board of pardons at noon today decided to give the Youngers their liberty on the parole plan.

"This means they will be free to come and go within the borders of the state of Minnesota the moment suitable employment is provided for them. Governor Van Sant said this afternoon that he would immediately contact Warden Wolfer of the state prison [to come] to the capitol and make arrangements for the prisoners to leave the penitentiary the moment the preliminaries had been complied with."[54]

Governor Van Sant told the press that, "in taking this action the board was governed by the fact that the state legislature had taken the initiative in this matter along what we believe to be constitutional lines. We reached this conclusion only after mature deliberation, and we believe that the ends of justice have been fully served."[55]

Van Sant said that Warden Wolfer was working toward finding the boys employment. There had been two offers of employment for Cole and Jim, but the governor was noncommittal about whether either would be accepted. He indicated that the employment issue would be settled by Warden Wolfer.

S.H. Sleener, manager of the Minneapolis Threshing Machine Company, which operated a large factory in Hopkins, just west of Minneapolis, telephoned the governor immediately to report that his company stood ready to furnish the Youngers permanent employment at once. The Schurmeier Wagon Company of St. Paul called that same day with a similar offer.

A *Journal* reporter interviewed the Youngers in Deputy Warden Jack Glennon's office, and, in response to a question of how he felt, Cole stated:

"I can't tell you how I feel, but I can tell you this: I am pleased more than words can express. I have not yet been informed when I am to leave the prison, Warden Wolfer being absent in St. Paul, but we will be released in due time, and then by our actions we will demonstrate to the people of the northwest that the action of the pardoning board has not been in vain and that we are deserving of consideration.

"I suppose the outside world will look queer to me when I leave these gates, but I'll make the best of it and try to accustom myself to conditions as I find them. Please state through the column of the *Journal* that both Jim and I are very grateful for everything that has been said and done in our behalf, and there is not a soul on earth against whom we harbor any ill will."[56]

Jim was asked to step into the office, and he, too, expressed elation over getting out. "I feel as though I am going to get a change of venue," said Jim. "I never get excited; I have full control of myself, and wouldn't flinch if I saw a hurricane coming over the hill. I am in the hands of the warden and state agent, and they will determine when I am to be released.

"I am not going to do very much talking, but am going to prove myself by my conduct and actions. I thank all friends from the least to the greatest from the bottom of my heart. I am deeply grateful to everybody."

Cole told the *Journal* that his father, who controlled the mail lines out of Kansas City, was killed at the outbreak of the war, and his mother died shortly after it ended. A bitter feeling lingered in the hearts of the Missouri people. Cole said, however, his father was a Union man and a close friend of General Frank Blair. The Redlegs were committing a number of depredations in their part of the country, related Cole, and his father secured a petition that the commands in that part of the country settling old grudges be removed. When he carried his petition to Washington, the Redlegs robbed the mail line he controlled, and he went to Kansas City to see Colonel Peabody. As he was returning in his buggy, the Redlegs ambushed and murdered him. Colonel Peabody took charge of the body and broke the news to Mrs. Younger. According to Cole, the hostilities commenced at this time.

As to his prison years, Cole said that many persons, who were their bitterest enemies when they were admitted, were now their best friends.

"I expect we will find many changes when we get out, if we do," added Cole. "I imagine I will act like a ten-year-old boy. Just think, we have been unable to keep pace with the progress of the country, except through reading and from reading a person can hardly form a just idea of what the subject matter really is. We have never seen an electric streetcar, excepting from the prison wall. We saw one down the street one day, and it was a surprise to us then, I remember, as we saw it move off without anything pulling, or anything pushing it. Wonderful projects have been undertaken and carried out since we entered the prison, and I guess it will be advisable for us to secure a guide when first we leave the institution. I am anxious to get out to note what has been going on, and I think it will be some time before we can accustom ourselves to things as they really are."[57]

Union Captain Reuben Smith of Asawatomie, Kansas, was interviewed in the same issue of the *Journal,* and he focused upon the early life of the Youngers. He spoke out upon a recent newspaper article blaming their outlaw career upon the burning of the Younger home and murder of their father.

Captain Smith admitted that these events may have rendered the boys more desperate, but, he maintained, the Youngers had already entered their outlaw career before either of the events had taken place.

He alleged that during the first week of January 1862, he was at Harrisonville, Missouri, serving under A.G. Nugent's regiment. He was in charge of the quartermaster and commissary stores, and he kept supplies in a long brick storeroom on the north side of the square. He also kept a barrel of whiskey, which had been found in a straw pile a few miles from town. One morning, his superior officer introduced him to a man, who at once struck him as an old Southern planter. He was tall, well built, gentlemanly in manner, language, and deportment. This man, claimed Captain Smith, was Colonel Harry Younger, father of the "notorious" Younger brothers. As long as the whiskey lasted, the two colonels came every morning for the daily drink.

On one of these mornings, insisted Smith, a young, tall man came in a carriage and entered the back of the storeroom, asking if his father was present. When Smith informed him he was with another colonel upstairs, Cole yelled, "Pap, breakfast is ready, and Mother wants you to come at once." The young man was Cole Younger.

Smith again insisted that the boys' father was not killed for months afterward and the burning of the house, which he himself ordered, did not take place until a year later. Prior to both events, Cole Younger and his gang had bushwhacked an escort of Smith's company near Blue Cut, killing one soldier and wounding six others. Mrs. Younger lived nearby, and when Smith talked with her about the bushwhacking, she said Cole had been there, and she would continue to feed and harbor him. A few days later, said Smith, she cared for another member of the gang and swore she would help any Southern soldier in the bush or in her home. Smith said Mrs. Younger seemed to think she was running the "whole Confederacy." The home was ordered to be burned by Smith's superior officer.

As to the murder of Cole's father, Smith maintained plunder was not the reason for the act. Three of the men were Missourians and two from Kansas, and they killed for separate reasons. Nothing was taken from the body of Colonel Younger but a gold pin. Smith concluded by saying the Youngers were bandits by choice, since after the war, they could have turned in their weapons and become good citizens.

The citizens of Northfield were also angry over the Younger parole. A few citizens were indifferent, but practically none, even those who had grown up after the Northfield raid in 1876, indorsed the release of the prisoners.

One prominent Northfield citizen interviewed by the newspaper expressed the general feeling when he stated: "This is a question of public policy and public right, and I doubt if it is a wise policy to liberate these men. If such criminals are turned loose, the tendency is to promote lawlessness, lynch law, and all that sort of thing."

One young man, however, related: "I was not here at the time of the raid, never saw the Youngers, and don't know anything of them except in a historical way. I have no feeling concerning the outcome. If people who know them best consider it safe to let them out, probably it may be; I have nothing to say on that score. I have said all along that if men were sentenced justly, the sentence is as just now as it ever was and yet present methods of prison discipline recognize the wisdom of giving men the benefit of their good behavior. If they are entitled to be at large, those who know them ought to be able to determine whether it is wise to parole them or not. I don't pretend to know whether it is all right to do so or not, as to the particular cases where parole is to be applied, that is for the state board of pardons to determine."

Anselm R. Manning, Northfield hardware store dealer during the raid, had killed one of the robbers and turned the tide of battle. When asked for his sentiment regarding the Younger parole, Manning said:

"If I had my way at the time they were tried, they would have been hanged. Of course, they have now been in prison for a good many years and whether they ought to stay there or not, I don't know. I haven't anything against the men; they didn't harm me, but they certainly deserved their sentence. Of course, they may be repentant now after undergoing so many years in prison."

Despite the arguments of public opinion, Cole and Jim were paroled the following day, Thursday the eleventh. Governor Van Sant, Chief Justice Start, and Attorney General Douglas stated in a published memorandum that they did not consider the question of the Youngers' guilt, nor whether they had been sufficiently punished. "The board carried out the wishes of the legislature that passed the parole bill," they said. "According to that bill the Youngers were entitled to parole. They had been imprisoned more than twenty years, their conduct in prison had been 'almost perfect,' and the board of state prison managers had recommended the parole."[58]

The principal conditions of the parole were as follows:

"He shall not exhibit himself in any dime museum, circus, theater, opera house, or any place of public amusement or assembly where a charge is made for admission.

"He shall on the twentieth day of each month write the warden of the state prison a report of himself, stating whether he had been constantly at work during the last month, and if not, why not; how much he has earned, and how much he has expended, together with a general statement as to his surroundings and prospects, which must be endorsed by his employer.

"He shall in all respects conduct himself honorably, avoid evil associations, obey the law, and abstain from the use of intoxicating liquors.

"He shall not go outside the state of Minnesota."[59]

The boys had been outside the walls only three times during their quarter century of imprisonment. Twice they had been allowed to go to the warden's house; the third time was their 1884 transfer to the Washington County Jail following the prison fire.

George M. Bennett was one of the first persons to greet the governor as he left the board meeting.

"Thank you, governor; thank you," he exclaimed, gripping the executive's hand.

"Don't thank me," answered Van Sant. "Thank the legislature."

Colonel Bronaugh was the first Missourian to congratulate the brothers. When the Youngers joined Bronaugh and others in Deputy Warden Jack Glennon's office, Cole shared his feelings with everyone present: "I feel like shaking hands with the whole world. As I stand here today, I ain't got a grudge against any human being alive or dead. Men, I'm happy."[60]

According to the *Kansas City Star,* the following conversation took place between Bronaugh and Cole:

"I said I'd be the first Missourian to shake hands with you, Cole," said a choked up Captain Bronaugh.

"You sure are," replied Cole, shaking hands a second time.

"Well, I reckon you'll keep your promise to walk down the prison steps between us?"

"You bet I will, and I would have waited twenty-five years more to do it."

"Reckon they know it in Jackson?"

"Yes, you bet!"

"Bronaugh, did you send any telegrams to Missouri?"

"Lots of 'em, and not a one to anybody that is not your friend."

"I sent one myself," replied Cole.

"Who to?"

"Lizzie Daniel, down at Harrisonville. You know I knew her when she was a little child —so high. She's a noble girl, too, good Methodist, too."[61]

Lizzie Daniel was the wife of a Harrisonville, Missouri, successful attorney. Her husband, Judge Henry Clay Daniel, had served as a prosecuting attorney as well as judge during the years of the Youngers' incarceration. The Daniels had eight children. Lizzie had been a close friend of Cole's for more than thirty-five years, and upon learning of a possible parole for him in 1901, she recommenced a correspondence with him.[62]

George M. Bennett, eager to spread the news to out of-state Younger relatives and friends, sent a telegram to the boys' sister, Mrs. A.B. Rollins [Retta] in Dallas, Texas, stating, "Pardon granted; papers signed; failure is now impossible." Mrs. Rollins, during her brothers' twenty-five years of incarceration, had visited them several times and worked hard for their release.

Bennett did an interview with the *Minneapolis Journal* that same afternoon. Said Bennett:

"I want to say at the outset to do justice to Justice Start, who has been regarded all along as the stumbling block in the way of the release of the Younger brothers, the charges which have been made against Chief Justice Start in this regard are not true. He is evidently a man who exercises on all occasions those truly judicial virtues—silence and circumspection. He refused to agree to absolute pardon in 1897. Never from that time to this has he changed his position in that connection. He never said he would not vote to parole or release these men."

Bennett added that by Start issuing the parole, he had done nothing inconsistent with the position he had originally taken. He discussed the early attempts of ex-Governor Marshall of Minnesota and several citizens of Missouri to free the Youngers. According to Bennett, he became interested in the Younger cause following the rejection of the 1897 parole bid. He said he began communicating with Union officers who had first hand knowledge of Cole Younger in the Civil War and added he received information from Major Foster of St. Louis; Colonel Rogers of Kansas City; and others. He learned that Cole and his men were regular soldiers of the Confederate army, men of good conduct and not the cutthroats they were made out to be.

Assured that he and his followers could not procure a parole in 1899, he drafted the Wilson Parole Bill, presented by George P. Wilson of Minneapolis, which was defeated in the House. At the last session of the legislature, he joined with Representative Deming of Minneapolis, and together they produced the new bill.

"I have been interested in this case solely from motives of humanity, and I believe the intelligent public will be glad to know that the Youngers are about to get a look at this great, round world, from which they have been so long shut out."[63]

Jesse James, Jr., son of the noted outlaw, was behind the counter of his cigar store in Kansas City when he received the news of the parole. "I'm glad of it," he said, looking happy but not surprised. "I think that twenty-five years in prison is ample amends to justice for almost any crime." T. Crittenden, Jr., son of the former governor, was in James' store at the time and told a reporter ninety percent of Missourians had been in favor of a pardon. Crittenden also expressed a certainty that the Youngers would make good solid Minnesota citizens.[64]

Warden Wolfer decided to keep the hour of the boys' release from the press. In an address to several reporters, who had congregated in his office, Wolfer announced, "I will take the Younger boys over the walls of this prison at twelve o'clock at night if necessary to prevent you fellows getting onto it. You fellows can camp around here six weeks if you want to but I will guarantee you that I will get them out without your knowledge even if [I] have to wait that long. These boys are to go out of this institution with as little notoriety and publicity as possible, and I mean to protect them in every way."[65]

232

Several of the correspondents, especially those representing Southern newspapers, attempted to urge the warden that he was pursuing the wrong policy, but he remained obdurate and said he would not flinch from his duty. He said his chief fear was that, when the boys were released, a "morbid and curious crowd" would gather at the prison and along the streets. A rumor circulated among the journalists that not even the Youngers would learn of their release time until less than an hour before, and their prospective place of employment would initially be kept a secret. Although no one had an inkling of what city the warden would take the boys, many persons believed the site would be outside the Twin Cities.

Warden Wolfer said he had instructed Cole and Jim not to talk for publication upon their release and to drop out of sight from newsmen and curious citizens. He said this policy would be rigidly enforced. Wolfer stated that this was not only the wish of the board of pardons and board of prison managers but of the Youngers themselves, who wanted the matter dropped.

Cole did tell the press a night earlier that, "After I get out of this place, my mouth will be closed like that of an oyster, and no newspaper reporter will be able to get an interview out of me with a pair of tongs. What I have already said can be used, but from the moment I leave the prison doors silence will be my motto."[66]

Reporters felt that the Youngers would be taken from the prison secretly some time between Saturday evening and Monday morning and taken to their place of employment. Speculation focused upon alternate methods the boys could reach the street from without passing through the front gates. A gate at the upper end of the prison yard was a likely spot and was watched by some newsmen. Another theory was that Wolfer would take them over the wall on the north, south, or west side with ropes and ladders under cover of darkness. The reporters, despite representing competing newspapers, agreed to work together and camp at several areas around the prison in relays. They also watched the home of hack driver William Herron, the man who had driven them to the prison in 1876.

Wolfer was angry with certain prominent St. Paul citizens whom he said seemed to have the impression they were to have their way as to where and how the Youngers would be employed. The *Journal* correspondent asked Wolfer if he had read the article that morning in the *Pioneer Press*, which stated that the Youngers would be going to work in Hopkins at the threshing machine company. Wolfer spoke out:

"The whole article is false, and without the slightest foundation in fact, and the person giving the information must have known he was lying. I am surprised that the *Pioneer Press* used information of that kind without first taking the precaution to inform itself of the truth. I do not wish to do anyone an injustice, but in view of the persistent efforts of E.J. Schurmeier of St. Paul to gain control of the Youngers, I believe he is the author of the matter contained in the *Pioneer Press*.

"Ever since the parole board acted favorably in giving a parole to the Youngers, Mr. Schurmeier persistently maneuvered to gain control of the Youngers and their services. He has conceived an idea that if he can get control of them and fit out a tobacco and cigar store for them at the location of his property in St. Paul, it would be a great stroke of business policy. Whenever he breached the matter to me, I have quietly but firmly refrained from discussing it, telling him that all applications made for the services of the Youngers would be given careful consideration.

"I do not own any interests at Hopkins, and I have no motive in locating the Youngers except for their own good and the best interests of society. I have not discussed the place with them, but my understanding with them is that when all the applications are in, we will talk the matter over and decide which will be the best for them. The Youngers have expressed no preference to work in the Twin Cities over other points, and at this time it is impossible for me to say where they will be employed. The board of pardons and the board of prison managers will be consulted with reference to this matter before the men are released."[67]

While the warden moved secretly with his plans to release them, the Youngers continued doing their work within the prison walls. They did not seem to be disturbed in the least as to when they would be released.

On July 13, the *Minneapolis Journal* ran a lengthy editorial questioning the release of the Youngers as good policy. The article examined the decision from three viewpoints. The first was whether further detention would protect the public from future crimes. The second question considered was whether the twenty-five years in prison had reformed them. Third, whether their release would generate a good or bad effect on prison discipline and public morale.

The consensus of the editor was that on points one and two, there was no danger in paroling the boys since they were no longer the hardened criminals they were when entering prison in 1876. On the third, the paroling of men whose outlook was once so hopeless might have a salutary effect on other longtime prisoners and lead to good conduct. On the other hand, the editor felt that the two Youngers, who were once the most notorious criminals in the country, did not ever deserve to be given freedom.[68]

But the decision had already been made, and Cole and Jim Younger were to at last have a future, despite their ages and lack of knowledge regarding a very different world outside prison walls. Shortly before Warden Wolfer put a ban on their speaking to journalists, the brothers were asked about that short, but very real, future.

Said Cole Younger: "I am not exactly a dead man, but I have been shot twenty-eight times and am now carrying in my body fourteen bullets that physicians have been unable to extract. Twelve of these wounds I received while wearing the gray, and I have ever been proud of them, and it has been one of my keenest regrets that I did not receive the rest of them during the war with Spain."[69]

Notes

[1]*Stillwater Messenger*, February 7, 1903.
[2]E.F. Rogers letter to George M. Bennett dated January 24, 1901. Northfield, Minnesota, Bank Robbery of 1876. Selected Manuscripts Collections and Government Records, Microfilm Edition, Roll 4, Minnesota Historical Society.
[3]*Minneapolis Journal*, February 11, 1901.
[4]Cole Younger letter to M.J. Daly dated March 1901. Mary Shasky and the History Museum of East Ottertail County, Perham.
[5]*Minneapolis Journal*, March 25, 1901.
[6]H.T. Williams letter to Governor Van Sant dated April 10, 1901. Northfield, Minnesota, Bank Robbery of 1876. Selected Manuscripts Collection and Government Records, Microfilm

Edition, Roll 4, Minnesota Historical Society.

[7]Archibald Carnagher letter to Governor Van Sant dated April 10, 1901. Northfield, Minnesota, Bank Robbery of 1876. Selected Manuscripts Collections and Government Records, Microfilm Edition, Roll 4, Minnesota Historical Society.

[8]S.R. Van Sant letter to Hon. M.J. Dowling dated April 5, 1901. Northfield, Minnesota, Bank Robbery of 1876. Selected Manuscripts and Government Records, Microfilm Edition, Roll 4, Minnesota Historical Society.

[9]Walter N. Trenerry, *Murder in Minnesota,* p. 103.

[10]W.B. Douglas letter to Governor S.R. Van Sant dated April 5, 1901. Northfield, Minnesota, Bank Robbery of 1876. Selected Manuscripts Collections and Government Records, Microfilm Edition, Roll 4, Minnesota Historical Society.

[11]Parole Applications of Thomas Coleman Younger and James Hardin Younger to the State Prison Board of Managers dated May 6, 1901. Northfield, Minnesota, Bank Robbery of 1876. Selected Manuscripts Collections and Government Records, Microfilm Edition, Roll 4, Minnesota Historical Society.

[12]Board of State Prison Managers Resolution forwarded to Board of Pardons (no date). Northfield, Minnesota, Bank Robbery of 1876. Selected Manuscripts Collections and Government Records, Microfilm Edition, Roll 4, Minnesota Historical Society.

[13]*St. Louis Post-Dispatch,* Sunday, May 19, 1901.

[14]Ibid.

[15]*Minneapolis Journal,* May 8, 1901.

[16]O.B. Gould letter to Governor Van Sant dated May 10, 1901. Northfield, Minnesota, Bank Robbery of 1876. Selected Manuscripts Collections and Government Records, Microfilm Edition, Roll 4, Minnesota Historical Society.

[17]"A Christian" letter to Governor Vant Sant dated May 10, 1901. Northfield, Minnesota, Bank Robbery of 1876. Selected Manuscripts Collections and Government Records, Microfilm Edition, Roll 4, Minnesota Historical Society.

[18]*Minneapolis Journal,* May 11, 1901.

[19]Ibid., May 14, 1901.

[20]*Northfield News* article reprinted in the *Minneapolis Journal,* May 17, 1901.

[21]W.C. Bronaugh, *The Youngers' Fight For Freedom,* pp. 235-237.

[22]Madelia newspaper, title and date unknown.

[23]*Lexington Morning Herald*, August 9, 1903.

[24]"A friend of right and justice" letter to Governor Van Sant and Board of Pardons dated July 7, 1901. Northfield, Minnesota, Bank Robbery of 1876. Selected Manuscripts Collections and Government Records, Microfilm Edition, Roll 4, Minnesota Historical Society.

[25]E.F. Rogers letter to Charles M. Start dated June 15, 1901. Northfield, Minnesota, Bank Robbery of 1876. Selected Manuscripts Collections and Government Records, Microfilm Edition, Roll 4, Minnesota Historical Society.

[26]George M. Bennett petition to Governor S.R. Van Sant dated June 25, 1901. Northfield, Minnesota, Bank Robbery of 1876. Selected Manuscripts Collections and Government Records, Microfilm Edition, Roll 4, Minnesota Historical Society.

[27]*Minneapolis Journal*, June 28, 1901.

[28]Bishop Henry B. Whipple undated letter to C.M. Start. Northfield, Minnesota, Bank Robbery of 1876. Selected Manuscripts Collections and Government Records, Microfilm Edition, Roll 4, Minnesota Historical Society.

[29]*Minneapolis Journal*, July 10, 1901.

[30]Ibid.

[31]Ibid.

[32]Dr. Frank Powell letter to Governor Van Sant dated July 8, 1901. Northfield, Minnesota, Bank Robbery of 1876. Selected Manuscripts Collections and Government Records, Microfilm Edition, Roll 4, Minnesota Historical Society.

[33]F.E. Kenaston letter to Governor S.R. Van Sant dated July 10, 1901. Northfield, Minnesota, Bank Robbery of 1876. Selected Manuscripts Collections and Government Records, Microfilm Edition, Roll 4, Minnesota Historical Society.

[34]Edward J. Schurmeier letter to Warden Henry Wolfer dated July 12, 1901. Northfield, Minnesota, Bank Robbery of 1876. Selected Manuscripts Collections and Government Records, Microfilm Edition, Roll 4, Minnesota Historical Society.

[35]*Lee's Summit Journal*, Friday, July 3, 1981, "Cole Younger Tells His Life Story."

[36]*Minneapolis Journal*, July 8, 1901.

[37]Ibid.

[38]Ibid, July 9, 1901.

[39]"In the Matter of the Parole of Coleman and James

Younger." Northfield, Minnesota, Bank Robbery of 1876. Selected Manuscripts Collections and Government Records, Microfilm Edition, Roll 4, Minnesota Historical Society.

[40]W.C. Bronaugh, *The Youngers' Fight for Freedom*, pp. 239-240.

[41]*St. Paul Pioneer Press*, Wednesday, July 10, 1901, "Youngers to be Paroled."

[42]*Minneapolis Journal*, July 10, 1901.

[43]*Kansas City Star*, July 11, 1901.

[44]*Minneapolis Journal*, July 10, 1901.

[45]*St. Paul Pioneer Press*, Thursday, July 11, 1901.

[46]Ibid.

[47]*Stillwater Messenger*, July 13, 1901, p. 4.

[48]Ibid.

[49]Ibid.

[50]Ibid.

[51]Ibid.

[52]Ibid.

[53]Ibid.

[54]*Minneapolis Journal*, July 10, 1901.

[55]Ibid.

[56]Ibid.

[57]Ibid.

[58]*St. Paul Pioneer Press*, Thursday, July 11, 1901, "Prison Doors are Opened."

[59]Cole Younger, *The Story of Cole Younger by Himself*, p. 96.

[60]*Stillwater Gazette*, July 12, 1901.

[61]*Kansas City Star*, July 11, 1901.

[62]Dr. William A. Settle, *Cole Younger Writes to Lizzie Daniel*, Liberty, Missouri, James-Younger Gang, 1994, p. 2.

[63]*Minneapolis Journal*, July 10, 1901.

[64]*St. Paul Pioneer Press*, Thursday, July 11, 1901, "Will Make Good Citizens."

[65]*Minneapolis Journal*, July 11, 1901.

[66]Ibid.

[67]Ibid.

[68]*Minneapolis Journal*, July 13, 1901.

[69]W.C. Heilbron, *Convict Life at the Minnesota State Prison*, pp. 147-148.

Epilogue

*"I've led an adventurous and turbulent life. The war
brought on hate and strife and killing around here. I
have been blamed for a lot of it with which I had nothing to do. They murdered my father and I was
launched into a life of shooting and reprisals and
rough riding, winding up with twenty-five years in the
Penitentiary. I was brought up in a Christian home.
Now I am an old man and I've come by God's mercy,
back to the place of my childhood to end my days."*

—Cole Younger[1]

fter failing at a number of jobs and being denied the
opportunity of marrying his sweetheart, Alix
Muller, Jim's depression grew unbearable. On
October 14, 1902, Jim gave fifty cents for the social-
ist cause to street violinist Adolph Grether and said, "Well,
goodbye, Adolph. I won't see you again." Grether assumed Jim
had received his pardon and was leaving Minnesota.[2] The following morning, Jim fired a bullet into his head. He was dead
at the age of fifty-four.

"Jim Younger's body, unrestrained by the laws of parole, passed beyond the boundary of Minnesota today to its last resting place," reported an article in a St. Louis newspaper. "Without any religious ceremony, the corpse was taken from the undertaking rooms to the railway station and placed aboard a baggage car of a Northwestern train for Kansas City."[3]

Following Cole's 1901 release from Stillwater Prison, he, too, worked a variety of jobs including one as tombstone salesman for the Peter N. Peterson Granite Company, an assistant manager at the Interstate Institute for Liquor and Morphine Habits, and supervisor of workmen at the home of St. Paul Police Chief John J. O'Connor. On February 4, 1903, Cole was awarded a conditional pardon and went home to Missouri on February 16.

A free man, Cole remained active with several endeavors. He authored his own autobiography, *Cole Younger by Himself,* and established the Cole Younger and Frank James Wild West Show. He was instrumental in engineering an electric railroad—The Kansas City, Lee's Summit and Eastern Railroad—in August 1905. Following a brief affiliation with the Lew Nichols Carnival Company, Cole, in 1909, took to the lecture circuit. He passed away at 8:45 in the evening on March 21, 1916, at the age of seventy-two.[4]

A St. Louis newspaper eulogized: "Cole Younger was one of the last of the members of the robber bands that infested western Missouri during and after the Civil War. . . . Younger, after a long term in the Penitentiary, became a law-abiding Missouri citizen."[5]

Notes

[1]*St. Louis Daily Globe-Democrat,* March 22, 1916.
[2]Washington County Historical Society Files, Stillwater.
[3]*St. Louis Republican,* Wednesday, October 22, 1902.
[4]Marley Brant, *The Outlaw Youngers,* pp. 287-314.
[5]*St. Louis Daily Globe-Democrat,* March 22, 1916.

Bibliography

Books

Blegen, Theodore C., *Minnesota: A History of the State*, Minneapolis, University of Minnesota Press, 1963.

Brant, Marley, *Jesse James: The Man and the Myth*, New York, Berkley Books, 1998.

Brant, Marley, *Outlaws: The Illustrated History of the James-Younger Gang*, Montgomery, Alabama, Elliott & Clark Publishing, 1997.

Brant, Marley, *The Outlaw Youngers: A Confederate Brotherhood*, Lanham, New York & London, Madison Books, 1992.

Breihan, Carl W., *The Complete and Authentic Life of Jesse James*, New York, Frederick Fell, Inc., Publishers, 1953.

Breihan, Carl W., *Outlaws of the Old West*, New York, Bonanza Books, 1957.

Breihan, Carl W., *Ride the Razor's Edge: The Younger Brothers Story*, Gretna, Pelican Publishing Company, 1882.

Breihan, Carl W., *Saga of Jesse James*, Caldwell, Idaho, The Caxton Printers, Inc., 1991.

241

Breihan, Carl W., *Younger Brothers: Cole, James, Bob, John*, San Antonio, The Naylor Company, 1961.

Bronaugh, W.C., *The Youngers' Fight For Freedom*, Columbia, Missouri, E. W. Stephens Publishing Company, 1906.

Bruns, Roger A., *The Bandit Kings From Jesse James to Pretty Boy Floyd*, New York, Crown Publishers, Inc., 1995.

Cantrell, Dallas, *Northfield, Minnesota: Youngers' Fatal Blunder*, San Antonio, The Naylor Company, 1973.

Clark, Jr., Clifford E., *Minnesota: In a Century of Change*, St. Paul, Minnesota Historical Society Press, 1989.

Croy, Homer, *Jesse James Was My Neighbor*, New York, Duell, Sloan and Pearce, 1949.

Croy, Homer, *Last of the Great Outlaws*, New York, The New American Library, 1958

Croy, Homer, *Cole Younger: Last of the Great Outlaws*, Lincoln, University of Nebraska Press, 1999.

DeArment, Robert K., *Alias Frank Canton*, Norman and London, University of Oklahoma Press, 1996.

DeArment, Robert K., *Bat Masterson: The Man and the Legend*, Norman, The University of Oklahoma Press, 1980.

Drago, Harry Sinclair, *Outlaws on Horseback*, Lincoln & London, University of Nebraska Press, 1998.

Dunn, James Taylor, *Marine on the St. Croix: 150 years of Village Life*, Marine on the St. Croix, Marine restoration Society, 1989.

Dunn, James Taylor, *The St. Croix Midwest Border River*, New York, Holt, Rinehart & Winston, 1965.

Folwell, William Watts, *A History of Minnesota*, Volume I, St. Paul, Minnesota Historical Society Press, 1956.

Folwell, William Watts, A *History of Minnesota,* Volume II, St. Paul, Minnesota Historical Society Press, 1961.

Fradin, Brindell, and Fradin, Judith Bloom, *From Sea to Shining Sea: Minnesota,* Chicago, Childrens Press, 1994.

Heilbron, Bertha L., *The Thirty-Second State: History of Minnesota,* St. Paul, Minnesota Historical Society, 1958.

Heilbron, W.C., *Life at the Minnesota State Prison,* W.C. Heilbron, St. Paul, 1909.

Henry, Will, *Jesse James: Death of a Legend,* New York, Leisure Books, 1996.

The History of Henry and St. Clair Counties, Missouri, St. Joseph, MO., National Historical Company, 1883.

Holmquist, June D. and Holbert, Sue E., *A History Tour of 50 Twin City Landmarks,* St. Paul, Minnesota Historical Society Press, 1966.

Horan, James D. and Sann, Paul, *Pictorial History of the Wild West,* New York, Crown Publishers, Inc., 1971.

Horan, James D., ed., *The Trial of Frank James for Murder with Confessions of Dick Liddil and Clarence Hite and History of the "James Gang,"* New York, Jingle Bob/Crown Publishers, Inc., 1977.

Huntington, George, *Robber and Hero,* Minneapolis, Ross & Haines, Inc., 1962.

James, Stella Frances James, *In the Shadow of Jesse James,* Thousand Oaks, California, The Revolver Press, Dragon Books, 1989.

Johnston, Patricia Condon, *Stillwater: Minnesota's Birthplace,* Afton, Afton Historical Society Press, 1995.

Jones, Evan, *The Minnesota,* Minneapolis, University of Minnesota Press, 1990.

Kiester, J.A., *History of Faribault County, Minnesota*, Minneapolis, Haiman & Smith, 1896.

Koblas, John J., *F. Scott Fitzgerald in Minnesota: His Homes and Haunts*, St. Paul, Minnesota Historical Society Press, 1978, Appendix.

H.F. Koeper, *Historic St. Paul Buildings*, St. Paul, St. Paul City Planning Board, 1964.

Kunz, Virginia Brainard, *The First 150 Years*, St. Paul, The St. Paul Foundation, Inc., 1991.

Lass, William E. *Minnesota: A History*, New York & London, W.W. Norton & Company, 1983.

Love, Robertus, *The Rise and Fall of Jesse James*, Lincoln & London, University of Nebraska Press, 1925.

Mason, John W., Editor, *History of Otter Tail County Minnesota, Its People, Industries and Institutions*.

McNeill, Cora, *Mizzoura: The Youngers*, Minneapolis, Mizzoura Publishing Company, 1898

Miles, Kathleen White, *Annals of Henry County, Volume 1, 1885-1900*, 1973.

Montana, Sybil, *Bob Ford was his Name, Jesse James was his Game*, Springfield, Missouri, Sybil Montana, 2001.

Muller, Alix J., *A History of the Police and Fire Departments in the Twin Cities*, St. Paul, 1889.

Nolan, Dick, *Benjamin Franklin Butler: The Damnedest Yankee*, Novato, California, Presidio Press, 1991.

The Northfield Bank Raid September 7, 1876, Northfield, Northfield News Publishing Company, Inc., 1995.

Peterson, Brent T. & Thilgen, Dean R., *1843-1993 Stillwater: A Photographic History*, Stillwater, Valley History Press, 1992.

Ries, Judith, *Ed O'Kelley, The Man Who Murdered Jesse James' Murderer*, Marble Hill, Missouri, Stewart Printing & Publishing Company.

Robertson, Frank G. and Harris, Beth Kay, *Soapy Smith King of the Frontier Con Men*, New York, Hastings House Publishers, 1961.

Rosenfelt, Willard E., *Washington: A History of the Minnesota County, Stillwater*, The Croixside Press, 1977.

Ross, James R., *I, Jesse James*, Dragon Publishing Company, 198.

Smith, Robert Barr, *The Last Hurrah of the James-Younger Gang*, Norman, University of Oklahoma Press, 2001.

Sterett, Betty, *Scenes from the Past*, 1985.

St. Paul City Directories 1903-1920.

Time-Life Books, "Long Cruel Roads."

Trenerry, Walter D., *Murder in Minnesota*, St. Paul, Minnesota Historical Society, 1962.

Wellman, Paul I., *A Dynasty of Western Outlaws*, New York, Bonanza Books, 1961.

Williams, J. Fletcher, *A History of the City of St. Paul to 1875*, St. Paul, Minnesota Historical Society Press, 1983.

Williams, J. Fletcher, *History of Washington County & the St. Croix Valley*, Minneapolis, North Star Publishing Company, 1881.

Yates, Buster, *Seventy-Five Years on the Watonwan*, No publisher given, 1986.

Yeatman, Ted P., *Frank and Jesse James: The Story Behind the Legend*, Nashville, Cumberland House, 2000.

Yeatman, Ted P., *Jesse James and Bill Ryan at Nashville*, Nashville, Depot Press, 1981.

Younger, Cole, *The Story of Cole Younger By Himself*, St. Paul, Minnesota Historical Society Press, 2000.

Magazines and Pamphlets

James Taylor Dunn, "The Minnesota State Prison during the Stillwater Era, 1853-1914," *Minnesota History*, December 1960, Volume 37, Number 4.

Fred Huston, "Death of the Coward Killer," *Real Frontier*, August 1971.

Thurston James, "Frank James—The Post-Outlaw Years," *James-Younger Gang Journal*, Spring 2001.

Brent Peterson, "Rafael Ortiz: Stillwater's Federal Convict," White Bear Lake *St. Croix Valley Press*, July 2001.

A. Hermina Poatgieter and James Taylor Dunn, editors, *Gopher Reader*, St. Paul, Minnesota Historical Society and Minnesota Statehood Centennial Commission, 1966.

Nancy B. Samuelson, "How the James Boys Fled the Disaster at Northfield and the Capture of 'Frank James,'" *The Journal*, Official Publication of the Western Outlaw-Lawman History Association, Spring-Summer 1993.

Dr. William A. Settle, *Cole Younger Writes to Lizzie Daniel*, Liberty, Missouri, James-Younger Gang, 1994.

Ruth Rentz Yates, editor, *Before Their Identity*, No publisher given, 1996.

Dr. William A. Settle (ed. Marley Brant), *Cole Younger Writes to Lizzie Daniel*, James-Younger Gang, Liberty, Missouri, 1994. Bob Warn, "Historical Bank Raid Centered on Ames Family," in "Nuggets from Rice County, Southern Minnesota History," *Golden Nugget*, May 17, 1972.

Correspondence

J.H. Albert to Governor Merriam dated June 24, 1889. Northfield, Minnesota, Bank Robbery of 1876. Selected manuscripts Collections and Government Records, Microfilm Edition, Roll 3, Minnesota Historical Society.

Ellen M. Ames affidavit dated July 10, 1897. Northfield, Minnesota, Bank Robbery of 1876. Selected Manuscripts Collections and Government Records, Microfilm Edition, Roll 3, Minnesota Historical Society.

A.T. Ankeny to George P. Wilson dated March 23, 1899. Northfield, Minnesota, Bank Robbery of 1876. Selected Manuscripts Collections and Government Records, Microfilm Edition, Roll 4, Minnesota Historical Society.

C.R. Barns to H.W. Childs dated July 10, 1897. Northfield, Minnesota, Bank Robbery of 1876. Selected Manuscripts Collections and Government Records, Microfilm Editions, Roll 3, Minnesota Historical Society.

Capt. Ara Barton to Governor W.R. Merriam dated June 21, 1889. Northfield, Minnesota, Bank Robbery of 1876. Selected Manuscripts Collections and Government Records, Microfilm Edition, Roll 3, Minnesota Historical Society.

H.M. Barton to Board of Pardons dated July 10, 1897. Northfield Bank Robbery of 1876. Selected Manuscripts Collections and Government Records, Microfilm Edition, Minnesota Historical Society.

G.W. Batchelder, Attorney, Faribault, to Governor William R. Merriam dated June 22, 1889. Northfield, Minnesota, Bank Robbery of 1876. Selected Manuscripts Collections and Government Records, Microfilm Edition, Roll 3, Minnesota Historical Society.

George W. Batchelder letter to Charles W. Start dated July 10, 1897. Northfield, Minnesota, Bank Robbery of 1876. Selected

Manuscripts Collections and Government Records, Microfilm Edition, Minnesota Historical Society.

G.N. Baxter telegram to Governor David M. Clough dated July 13, 1897. Northfield, Minnesota Bank Robbery of 1876. Selected Manuscripts Collections and Government Records, Microfilm Edition, Roll 3, Minnesota Historical Society.

George M. Bennett affidavit to Board of Pardons dated July 12, 1897. Northfield, Minnesota, Bank Robbery of 1876. Selected Manuscripts and Government Records, Microfilm Edition, Roll 3, Minnesota Historical Society.

George M. Bennett petition to Governor S.R. Van Sant dated June 25, 1901. Northfield, Minnesota, Bank Robbery of 1876. Selected Manuscripts Collections and Government Records, Microfilm Edition, Roll 4, Minnesota Historical Society.

H.M. Blaisdell letter to Board of Pardons dated July 15, 1889. Northfield, Minnesota, Bank Robbery of 1876. Selected Manuscripts Collections and Government Records, Microfilm Edition, Minnesota Historical Society.

Fred Bloom to Governor D.M. Clough dated July 10, 1897. Northfield, Minnesota, Bank Robbery of 1876. Selected Manuscripts Collections and Government Records, Microfilm Edition, Roll 3, Minnesota Historical Society.

E.G. Bower to George M. Bennett dated April 25, 1898. Northfield, Minnesota, Bank Robbery of 1876. Selected Manuscripts Collections and Government Records, Microfilm Edition, Roll 4, Minnesota Historical Society.

Peter Brennan to Retta Younger dated September 23, 1891, Bronaugh-Younger Papers, Northfield (Minnesota) Bank Robbery of 1876: Selected Manuscripts Collections and Government Records. Microfilm Edition. Minnesota Historical Society.

John R. Bresett to Governor Merriam dated July 18, 1889. Northfield, Minnesota, Bank Robbery of 1876. Selected Manuscripts Collections and Government Records, Microfilm Edition, Roll 3, Minnesota Historical Society.

H.A. Brill to Charles M. Start dated July 8, 1897. Northfield, Minnesota, Bank Robbery of 1876. Selected Manuscripts Collections and Government Records, Microfilm Edition, Minnesota Historical Society.

H.W. Brower to Governor Merriam dated July 5, 1889. Northfield, Minnesota, Bank Robbery of 1876. Selected Manuscripts Collections and Government Records, Microfilm Edition, Roll 3, Minnesota Historical Society.

E.G. Butts to Governor Merriam dated June 24, 1889. Northfield, Minnesota, Bank Robbery of 1876. Selected Manuscripts Collections and Government Records, Microfilm Edition, Roll 3, Minnesota Historical Society.

U.S. Marshal W.M. Campbell to Governor Merriam dated July 3, 1889. Northfield, Minnesota, Bank Robbery of 1876. Selected Manuscripts Collections and Government Records, Microfilm Edition, Roll 3, Minnesota Historical Society.

Archibald Carnagher to Governor Van Sant dated April 10, 1901. Northfield, Minnesota, Bank Robbery of 1876. Selected Manuscripts Collections and Government Records, Microfilm Edition, Roll 4, Minnesota Historical Society.

Henry A. Castle to George P. Wilson dated February 20, 1899. Northfield, Minnesota, Bank Robbery of 1876. Selected Manuscripts Collections and Government Records, Microfilm Edition, Roll 4, Minnesota Historical Society.

Capt. D. Cavanaugh to Governor W.R. Merriam dated June 22, 1889. Northfield, Minnesota, Bank Robbery of 1876. Selected Manuscript Collections and Government Records, Microfilm Edition, Roll 3, Minnesota Historical Society.

D. Cavanaugh to Board of Pardons dated July 10, 1897. Northfield, Minnesota, Bank Robbery of 1876. Selected Manuscript Collections and Government Records, Microfilm Edition, Minnesota Historical Society.

"A Christian" to Governor Vant Sant dated May 10, 1901. Northfield, Minnesota, Bank Robbery of 1876. Selected

Manuscripts Collections and Government Records, Microfilm Edition, Roll 4, Minnesota Historical Society.

"A Citizen" to Governor Merriam dated July 12, 1889. Northfield, Minnesota, Bank Robbery of 1876. Selected Manuscripts Collections and Government Records, Microfilm Edition, Roll 3, Minnesota Historical Society.

John Clark to Governor Merriam dated July 18, 1889. Northfield, Minnesota, Bank Robbery of 1876. Selected Manuscripts Collections and Government Records, Microfilm Edition, Minnesota Historical Society.

Dr. T.C. Clark to Governor Merriam dated June 24, 1889. Northfield, Minnesota, Bank Robbery of 1876. Selected manuscripts Collections and Government Records, Microfilm Edition, Roll 3, Minnesota Historical Society.

Harold I. Cleveland to Governor Merriam dated July 13, 1889. Northfield, Minnesota, Bank Robbery of 1876. Selected Manuscripts Collections and Government Records, Microfilm Edition, Minnesota Historical Society.

A.T. Cole to Warden Henry Wolfer dated July 6, 1897. Northfield, Minnesota, Bank Robbery of 1876. Selected Manuscripts Collections and Government Records, Microfilm Edition, Roll 3, Minnesota Historical Society.

C.O. Cooley to Governor David M. Clough dated July 10, 1897; Northfield, Minnesota, Bank Robbery of 1876. Selected Manuscripts Collections and Government Records, Microfilm Edition, Roll 3, Minnesota Historical Society.

Dr. C.O. Cooley to Governor Merriam dated July 10, 1889. Northfield, Minnesota, Bank Robbery of 1876. Selected Manuscripts Collections and Government Records, Microfilm Edition, Minnesota Historical Society.

W.N. Cosgrove to Board of Pardons dated July 12, 1897. Northfield, Minnesota, Bank Robbery of 1876. Selected Manuscripts Collections and Government Records, Microfilm Edition, Minnesota Historical Society.

John Q. Crisp to Board of Pardons dated July 12, 1897. Northfield, Minnesota, Bank Robbery of 1876. Selected Manuscripts Collections and Government Records, Microfilm Edition, Roll 3, Minnesota Historical Society.

T.T. Crittenden, et al., telegrams to Governor Clough and Chairman, State Board of Pardons dated July 12, 1897. Northfield, Minnesota, Bank Robbery of 1876. Selected Manuscripts Collections and Government Records, Microfilm Edition, Roll 3, Minnesota Historical Society.

W.S. Culbertson to Governor Merriam dated July 8, 1889. Northfield, Minnesota, Bank Robbery of 1876. Selected Manuscript Collections and Government Records, Microfilm Edition, Roll 3, Minnesota Historical Society.

Robert M. Culloch and Michael K. McGrath to W.H. Harrington dated August 31, 1887. Northfield, Minnesota, Bank Robbery of 1876. Selected Manuscripts and Government Records, Microfilm Edition, Roll 3, Minnesota Historical Society.

Samuel M. Davis to Charles M. Start dated July 12, 1897. Northfield, Minnesota, Bank Robbery of 1876. Selected Manuscripts and Government Records, Microfilm Edition, Roll 3, Minnesota Historical Society.

David Day to Governor Merriam dated July 2, 1889. Northfield, Minnesota, Bank Robbery of 1876. Selected Manuscripts Collections and Government Records, Microfilm Edition, Roll 3, Minnesota Historical Society.

William B. Dean and J. Ross Nichols to C.M. Start dated July 9, 1897. Northfield, Minnesota, Bank Robbery of 1876. Selected Manuscripts Collections and Government Records, Microfilm Edition, Roll 3, Minnesota Historical Society.

A.K. Doe to Hon. W.R. Merriam dated May 27, 1889. Northfield, Minnesota, Bank Robbery of 1876. Selected Manuscripts Collections and Government Records, Microfilm Edition, Roll 3, Minnesota Historical Society.

A.K. Doe to Governor Merriam dated June 24, 1889. Northfield, Minnesota, Bank Robbery of 1876. Selected Manuscripts Collections and Government Records, Microfilm Edition, Roll 3, Minnesota Historical Society.

Ignatius Donnelly to Governor Merriam dated July 18, 1889. Northfield, Minnesota, Bank Robbery of 1876. Selected Manuscripts Collections and Government Records, Microfilm Edition, Roll 3, Minnesota Historical Society.

P.S. Dougherty affidavit dated July 8, 1897. Northfield, Minnesota, Bank Robbery of 1876. Selected Manuscripts Collections and Government Record, Microfilm Edition, Roll 3, Minnesota Historical Society.

W.B. Douglas to Governor S.R. Van Sant dated April 5, 1901. Northfield, Minnesota, Bank Robbery of 1876. Selected Manuscripts Collections and Government Records, Microfilm Edition, Roll 4, Minnesota Historical Society.

F.E. Dudley to Board of Pardons dated July 13, 1897. Northfield, Minnesota, Bank Robbery of 1876. Selected Manuscripts Collections and Government Records, Microfilm Edition, Roll 3, Minnesota Historical Society.

Burr Duell letter to Board of Pardons dated July 10, 1897. Northfield, Minnesota, Bank Robbery of 1876. Selected Manuscripts Collections and Government Records, Microfilm Edition, Minnesota Historical Society.

Mayor E.E. Durant of Stillwater to Governor William R. Merriam dated June 24, 1889. Northfield, Minnesota, Bank Robbery of 1876. Selected Manuscripts Collections and Government Records, Microfilm Edition, Roll 3, Minnesota Historical Society.

James H. Easton to Governor Merriam dated July 11, 1889. Northfield, Minnesota, Bank Robbery of 1876. Selected Manuscripts Collections and Government Records, Microfilm Edition, Roll 3, Minnesota Historical Society.

Colonel A.W. Edwards, editor *The Argus,* Fargo, North Dakota, to W.R. Merriam dated June 12, 1889. Northfield, Minnesota, Bank Robbery of 1876. Selected Manuscripts Collections and Government Records, Microfilm Edition, Roll 3, Minnesota Historical Society.

S.B. Elkins to David M. Clough dated June 6, 1898. Northfield, Minnesota, Bank Robbery of 1876. Selected Manuscripts Collections and Government Record, Microfilm Edition, Roll 3, Minnesota Historical Society.

S.B. Elkins to Charles M. Start dated July 4, 1898. Northfield, Minnesota, Bank Robbery of 1876. Selected Manuscripts Collections and Government Records, Microfilm Edition, Roll 4, Minnesota Historical Society.

E.B. Ellison to Governor David M. Clough dated July 9, 1897. Northfield, Minnesota, Bank Robbery of 1876. Selected Manuscripts Collections and Government Records, Microfilm Edition, Roll 3, Minnesota Historical Society.

W.R. Estes to Governor Merriam dated July 11, 1889. Northfield, Minnesota, Bank Robbery of 1876. Selected Manuscripts Collections and Government Records, Microfilm Edition, Minnesota Historical Society.

W.R. Estes letter and unsigned petition to Governor Merriam dated July 14, 1889. Northfield, Minnesota, Bank Robbery of 1876. Selected Manuscripts Collections and Government Records, Microfilm Edition, Roll 3, Minnesota Historical Society.

W.R. Estes letter to Governor Merriam dated July 16, 1889. Northfield, Minnesota, Bank Robbery of 1876. Selected Manuscripts Collections and Government Records, Microfilm Edition, Minnesota Historical Society.

Signatures of business and professional men on letterhead of William R. Estes sent Board of Pardons, July 12, 1897. Northfield, Minnesota, Bank Robbery of 1876. Selected Manuscripts Collections and Government Records, Microfilm Edition, Minnesota Historical Society.

Adam Fetsch to Governor Merriam dated July 2, 1889. Northfield, Minnesota, Bank Robbery of 1876. Selected Manuscripts Collections and Government Records, Microfilm Edition, Roll 3, Minnesota Historical Society.

H.G. Finkle to Governor Merriam dated July 4, 1889. Northfield, Minnesota, Bank Robbery of 1876. Selected Manuscripts Collections and Government Records, Microfilm Edition, Roll 3, Minnesota Historical Society.

M.D. Flower to Governor Merriam dated July 17, 1889. Northfield, Minnesota, Bank Robbery of 1876. Selected Manuscripts Collections and Government Records, Microfilm Edition, Roll 3, Minnesota Historical Society.

Robert Forbes to Governor Clough dated July 9, 1897. Northfield, Minnesota, Bank Robbery of 1876. Selected Manuscripts Collections and Government Records, Microfilm Edition, Minnesota Historical Society.

Emory S. Foster to George M. Bennett dated May 7, 1898. Northfield, Minnesota, Bank Robbery of 1876. Selected Manuscripts Collections and Government Records, Microfilm Edition, Roll 4, Minnesota Historical Society.

A Friend, telegram to Governor Clough sent July 13, 1897. Northfield, Minnesota, Bank Robbery of 1876. Selected Manuscripts Collections and Government Records, Microfilm Edition, Roll 3, Minnesota Historical Society.

"A friend of right and justice" to Governor Van Sant and Board of Pardons dated July 7, 1901. Northfield, Minnesota, Bank Robbery of 1876. Selected Manuscripts Collections and Government Records, Microfilm Edition, Roll 4, Minnesota Historical Society.

O.B. Gould to Governor Van Sant dated May 10, 1901. Northfield, Minnesota, Bank Robbery of 1876. Selected Manuscripts Collections and Government Records, Microfilm Edition, Roll 4, Minnesota Historical Society.

W.H. Grant to Governor Merriam dated July 1, 1889. Northfield, Minnesota, Bank Robbery of 1876. Selected Manuscripts Collections and Government Records, Microfilm Edition, Roll 3, Minnesota Historical Society.

William N. Gregg to George M. Bennett dated April 9, 1898. Northfield, Minnesota, Bank Robbery of 1876. Selected Manuscripts Collections and Government Records, Microfilm Edition, Roll 4, Minnesota Historical Society.

W.W. Griswold to Governor Merriam dated July 4, 1889. Northfield, Minnesota, Bank Robbery of 1876. Selected Manuscripts Collections and Government Records, Microfilm Editions, Roll 3, Minnesota Historical Society.

Liberty Hall to Governor Merriam dated June 24, 1889. Northfield, Minnesota, Bank Robbery of 1876. Selected Manuscripts Collections and Government Records, Microfilm Edition, Roll 3, Minnesota Historical Society.

W.H. Harrington to W.R. Merriam dated June 1889. Northfield, Minnesota, Bank Robbery of 1876. Selected Manuscripts Collections and Government Records, Microfilm Edition, Roll 3. Minnesota Historical Society.

W.H. Harrington to Governor Merriam dated July 1889. Northfield, Minnesota, Bank Robbery of 1876. Selected Manuscripts Collections and Government Records, Microfilm Edition, Roll 3, Minnesota Historical Society.

W.H. Harrington letter to Board of Pardons dated July 1897. Northfield, Minnesota, Bank Robbery of 1876. Selected Manuscripts and Government Records, Microfilm Edition, Roll 3, Minnesota Historical Society.

L.M. Hazen to Governor Merriam dated July 23, 1889. Northfield, Minnesota, Bank Robbery of 1876. Selected Manuscripts Collections and Government Records, Microfilm Edition, Roll 3, Minnesota Historical Society.

Fanny Lull Henderson, Minerva Lull, and Julia Lull Royce letters to Governor Clough dated July 9, 1897. Northfield Bank

Robbery of 1876. Selected Manuscripts Collections and Government Records, Microfilm Edition, Roll 3, Minnesota Historical Society.

Edward J. Hodgson to Governor Merriam dated July 4, 1889. Northfield, Minnesota, Bank Robbery of 1876. Selected Manuscripts Collections and Government Records, Microfilm Edition, Roll 3, Minnesota Historical Society.

H.P. Hynes to Governor Merriam dated June 24, 1889. Northfield, Minnesota Bank Robbery of 1876. Selected Manuscripts Collections and Government Records, Microfilm Edition, Roll 3, Minnesota Historical Society.

Lyndon Irwin to author dated August 5, 2001.

H.A. Jones to Henry Wolfer dated July 1, 1897. Northfield, Minnesota, Bank Robbery of 1876. Selected Manuscripts and Government Records, Microfilm Edition, Roll 3, Minnesota Historical Society.

William Louis Kelley to Charles M. Start dated July 10, 1897. Northfield, Minnesota, Bank Robbery of 1876. Selected Manuscripts and Government Records, Microfilm Edition, Roll 3, Minnesota Historical Society.

F.E. Kenaston to Governor S.R. Van Sant dated July 10, 1901. Northfield, Minnesota, Bank Robbery of 1876. Selected Manuscripts Collections and Government Records, Microfilm Edition, Roll 4, Minnesota Historical Society.

C. Kendrick to Governor Clough dated July 12, 1897. Northfield, Minnesota, Bank Robbery of 1876. Selected Manuscripts Collections and Government Records, Microfilm Edition, Minnesota Historical Society.

Anson L. Keyes to Board of Pardons dated July 9, 1897. Northfield, Minnesota, Bank Robbery of 1876. Selected Manuscripts Collections and Government Records, Microfilm Edition, Minnesota Historical Society.

S.A. Langum to Governor Merriam dated July 9, 1889. Northfield, Minnesota, Bank Robbery of 1876. Selected Manuscripts Collections and Government Records, Microfilm Edition, Minnesota Historical Society.

S.B. Lovejoy to Governor Merriam dated July 1, 1889. Northfield, Minnesota, Bank Robbery of 1876. Selected Manuscripts Collections and Government Records, Microfilm Edition, Roll 3, Minnesota Historical Society.

Thomas H. Loyhed to Board of Pardons dated July 10, 1897. Northfield, Minnesota, Bank Robbery of 1876. Selected Manuscripts Collections and Government Records, Microfilm Edition, Minnesota Historical Society.

Marian B. Lull to Governor David M. Clough dated July 8, 1897. Northfield, Minnesota, Bank Robbery of 1876. Selected Manuscripts Collections and Government Records, Microfilm Edition, Roll 3, Minnesota Historical Society.

J.W. Mason to H.W. Childs dated July 10, 1897. Northfield, Minnesota, Bank Robbery of 1876. Selected Manuscripts Collections and Government Records, Microfilm Edition, Minnesota Historical Society.

Samuel Mathus to Governor Merriam dated June 30, 1899. Northfield, Minnesota, Bank Robbery of 1876. Selected Manuscripts Collections and Government Records, Microfilm Edition, Roll 3, Minnesota Historical Society.

John McKinley to Attorney General Childs dated July 9, 1897. Northfield, Minnesota, Bank Robbery of 1876. Selected Manuscripts Collections and Government Records, Microfilm Edition, Minnesota Historical Society.

Hector McLean to Judge Start dated July 11, 1897. Northfield, Minnesota, Bank Robbery of 1876. Selected Manuscripts Collections and Government Records, Microfilm Edition, Roll 3, Minnesota Historical Society.

William O. Mead to W.H. Harrington dated August 23, 1887, Northfield, Minnesota, Bank Robbery of 1876. Selected

Manuscripts and Government Records, Microfilm Edition, Roll 3, Minnesota Historical Society.

Robert Mee letter to Board of Pardons dated July 10, 1897. Northfield, Minnesota, Bank Robbery of 1876. Selected Manuscripts Collections and Government Records, Microfilm Edition, Minnesota Historical Society.

John Morton affidavit dated July 8, 1897. Northfield, Minnesota, Bank Robbery of 1876. Selected Manuscripts Collections and Government Records, Microfilm Edition, Roll 3, Minnesota Historical Society.

R.A. Mott to Governor Marshall (notation on letter—"Respectfully referred to Gov. Merriam"), dated June 22, 1889. Northfield, Minnesota, Bank Robbery of 1876. Selected Manuscripts Collections and Government Records, Microfilm Edition, Roll 3, Minnesota Historical Society.

R.A. Mott to Board of Pardons and Governor Clough dated July 10, 1897. Northfield, Minnesota, Bank Robbery of 1876. Selected Manuscripts Collections and Government Records, Microfilm Edition, Roll 3, Minnesota Historical Society.

Alix J. Muller to Board of Pardons dated January 8, 1902. Northfield, Minnesota, Bank Robbery of 1876. Selected Manuscripts Collections and Government Records, Microfilm Editor, Roll 4, Minnesota Historical Society.

M.E. Murphy to Governor Merriam dated June 29, 1889. Northfield, Minnesota, Bank Robbery of 1876. Selected Manuscripts Collections and Government Records, Microfilm Edition, Roll 3, Minnesota Historical Society.

W.W. Murphy to Governor Merriam dated July 11, 1889. Northfield, Minnesota, Bank Robbery of 1876. Selected Manuscripts Collections and Government Records, Microfilm Edition, Minnesota Historical Society.

Nicholas A. Nelson to Governor David M. Clough dated December 8, 1896. Northfield, Minnesota, Bank Robbery of 1876. Selected Manuscripts Collections and Government

Records, Microfilm Edition, Roll 3, Minnesota Historical Society.

Nicholas A. Nelson to Board of Pardons dated July 3, 1897. Northfield, Minnesota, Bank Robbery of 1876. Selected Manuscripts Collections and Government Records, Microfilm Edition, Roll 3, Minnesota Historical Society.

George W. Newell to Board of Pardons dated July 10, 1897. Northfield, Minnesota, Bank Robbery of 1876. Selected Manuscripts Collections and Government Records, Microfilm Edition, Minnesota Historical Society.

Dr. G.A. Newman letter to Governor Clough dated June 26, 1897. Northfield, Minnesota, Bank Robbery of 1876. Selected Manuscripts Collections and Government Records, Microfilm Edition, Roll 3, Minnesota Historical Society.

T.M. Newson to Cole Younger dated July 6, 1889. Northfield, Minnesota, Bank Robbery of 1876. Selected Manuscripts Collections and Government Records, Microfilm Edition, Roll 3, Minnesota Historical Society.

"Not Safe to Give My Name" to Henry W. Childs dated July 10, 1897. Northfield, Minnesota, Bank Robbery of 1876. Selected Manuscripts Collections and Government Records, Microfilm Edition, Minnesota Historical Society.

Charles C. Otis to Charles M. Start dated July 9, 1897. Northfield, Minnesota, Bank Robbery of 1876. Selected Manuscripts Collections and Government Records, Microfilm Edition, Minnesota Historical Society.

Pamela Luster Phillips to author dated August 4, 2001.

Ed A. Paradis to Henry W. Childs dated July 10, 1897. Northfield, Minnesota, Bank Robbery of 1876. Selected Manuscripts Collections and Government Records, Microfilm Edition, Roll 3, Minnesota Historical Society.

Chuck Parsons to F.W. Anderson, asking to please pass his sentiment to the Board of Pardons and Governor Clough dated July

10, 1897. Northfield, Minnesota, Bank Robbery of 1876. Selected Manuscripts Collections and Government Records, Microfilm Edition, Roll 3, Minnesota Historical Society.

C.A. Patterson to Governor Clough dated July 12, 1897. Northfield, Minnesota, Bank Robbery of 1876. Selected Manuscripts Collections and Government Records, Microfilm Edition, Roll 3, Minnesota Historical Society.

Petition by citizens of Howard Lake to Board of Pardons dated July 10, 1897. Northfield, Minnesota, Bank Robbery of 1876. Selected Manuscripts Collections and Government Records, Microfilm Edition, Minnesota Historical Society.

Petitions from citizens of Madelia (2), Dassel, Faribault, Northfield, and Rice County Board of County Commissioners to Board of Pardons dated July 12, 1897. Northfield, Minnesota, Bank Robbery of 1876. Selected Manuscripts Collections and Government Records, Microfilm Edition, Roll 3, Minnesota Historical Society.

Petition by citizens of Preston to Board of Pardons dated July 8, 1897. Northfield, Minnesota, Bank Robbery of 1876. Selected Manuscripts Collections and Government Records, Microfilm Edition, Roll 3, Minnesota Historical Society.

Petition by citizens of St. Paul and nine letters written between June 28 and 30 on Merchants Hotel stationery, mailed July 2, 1889 to Governor Merriam. Northfield, Minnesota, Bank Robbery of 1876. Selected Manuscripts and Government Records, Microfilm Edition, Roll 3, Minnesota Historical Society.

Petition by citizens of St. Paul to Governor Merriam dated July 13, 1889. Northfield, Minnesota, Bank Robbery of 1876. Selected Manuscripts Collections and Government Records, Microfilm Edition, Roll 3, Minnesota Historical Society.

Petition for pardon of Robert Younger sent to Governor William R. Merriam 1889. Northfield, Minnesota, Bank Robbery of 1876. Selected Manuscripts Collections and Government Records, Microfilm Edition, Roll 3, Minnesota Historical Society.

Petitions from State of Missouri Officers to Governor William R. Merriam, 1889. Northfield, Minnesota, Bank Robbery of 1876. Selected Manuscripts and Government Records, Microfilm Edition, Roll 3, Minnesota Historical Society.

L.L. Pitts, Missouri State Treasurer to Minnesota Governor David M. Clough, Chief Justice Charles M. Start, and Attorney General H.W. Childs dated February 10, 1897, in Washington County Historical Society Collection, Stillwater.

G.W. Plank to Governor Clough and Board of Pardons dated July 12, 1897. Northfield, Minnesota, Bank Robbery of 1876. Selected Manuscripts Collections and Government Records, Microfilm Edition, Roll 3, Minnesota Historical Society.

Arthur Pomeroy to Governor David M. Clough dated June 24, 1897. Northfield, Minnesota, Bank Robbery of 1876. Selected Manuscripts Collections and Government Records, Microfilm Edition, Roll 3, Minnesota Historical Society.

Dr. Frank Powell to Governor Van Sant dated July 8, 1901. Northfield, Minnesota, Bank Robbery of 1876. Selected Manuscripts Collections and Government Records, Microfilm Edition, Roll 4, Minnesota Historical Society.

Horace W. Pratt to Governor Merriam dated June 26, 1889. Northfield, Minnesota, Bank Robbery of 1876. Selected Manuscripts Collections and Government Records, Microfilm Edition, Roll 3, Minnesota Historical Society.

W.H. Pratt to Governor Merriam dated June 24, 1889. Northfield, Minnesota, Bank Robbery of 1876. Selected Manuscripts Collections and Government Records, Microfilm Edition, Roll 3, Minnesota Historical Society.

W.H. Pratt to the Board of Pardons dated July 1, 1897. Northfield, Minnesota, Bank Robbery of 1876. Selected Manuscripts Collections and Government Records, Microfilm Edition, Roll 3, Minnesota Historical Society.

Dr. W.H. Pratt to Board of Pardons dated July 3, 1897. Northfield, Minnesota, Bank Robbery of 1876. Selected Manuscripts Collections and Government Records, Microfilm Edition, Roll 3, Minnesota Historical Society.

J.A. Reed circa 1889 to Governor William R$. Merriam. Northfield, Minnesota, Bank Robbery of 1876. Selected Manuscripts and Government Records, Microfilm Edition, Roll 3, Minnesota Historical Society.

A.E. Rice to Governor Merriam dated July 21, 1889. Northfield, Minnesota, Bank Robbery of 1876. Selected Manuscripts Collections and Government Records, Microfilm Edition, Roll 3, Minnesota Historical Society.

W.H. Riddell affidavit dated July 8, 1897. Northfield, Minnesota, Bank Robbery of 1876. Selected Manuscripts Collections and Government Records, Microfilm Edition, Roll 3, Minnesota Historical Society.

Martha G. Ripley to Board of Pardons dated July 12, 1897. Northfield, Minnesota, Bank Robbery of 1876. Selected Manuscripts Collections and Government Records, Microfilm Edition, Roll 3, Minnesota Historical Society.

Thomas P. Ritchie to Governor Merriam dated July 4, 1889. Northfield, Minnesota, Bank Robbery of 1876. Selected Manuscripts Collections and Government Records, Microfilm Edition, Roll 3, Minnesota Historical Society.

E.F. Rogers to Governor of Minnesota dated October 30, 1894. Northfield, Minnesota, Bank Robbery of 1876. Selected Manuscripts Collections and Government Records, Microfilm Edition, Roll 3, Minnesota Historical Society.

E.F. Rogers to Governor Knute Nelson dated November 21, 1894. Northfield, Minnesota, Bank Robbery of 1876. Selected Manuscripts Collections and Government Records, Microfilm Edition, Roll 3, Minnesota Historical Society.

E.F. Rogers to George M. Bennett dated January 24, 1901. Northfield, Minnesota, Bank Robbery of 1876. Selected

Manuscripts Collections and Government Records, Microfilm Edition, Roll 4, Minnesota Historical Society.

E.F. Rogers to Charles M. Start dated June 15, 1901. Northfield, Minnesota, Bank Robbery of 1876. Selected Manuscripts Collections and Government Records, Microfilm Edition, Roll 4, Minnesota Historical Society.

J.N. Rogers to Governor Clough dated July 12, 1897. Northfield, Minnesota, Bank Robbery of 1876. Selected Manuscripts Collections and Government Records, Microfilm Edition, Roll 3, Minnesota Historical Society.

D.M. Sabin to Governor Merriam dated June 24, 1889. Northfield, Minnesota, Bank Robbery of 1876. Selected Manuscripts Collections and Government Records, Microfilm Edition, Roll 3, Minnesota Historical Society.

D.M. Sabin to Board of Pardons dated July 12, 1897. Northfield, Minnesota, Bank Robbery of 1876. Selected Manuscripts Collections and Government Records, Microfilm Edition, Roll 3, Minnesota Historical Society.

Julius A. Schmahl to Governor Merriam dated July 9, 1889. Northfield, Minnesota, Bank Robbery of 1876. Selected Manuscripts Collections and Government Records, Microfilm Edition. Minnesota Historical Society.

Edward J. Schurmeier to Warden Henry Wolfer dated July 12, 1901. Northfield, Minnesota, Bank Robbery of 1876. Selected Manuscripts Collections and Government Records, Microfilm Edition, Roll 4, Minnesota Historical Society.

G.M. Seymour to Governor William R. Merriam dated June 24, 1889. Northfield, Minnesota, Bank Robbery of 1876. Selected Manuscripts Collections and Government Records, Microfilm Edition, Roll 3, Minnesota Historical Society.

F.A. Smith to Board of Pardons dated July 9, 1897. Northfield, Minnesota, Bank Robbery of 1876. Selected Manuscripts Collections and Government Records, Microfilm Edition, Minnesota Historical Society.

Robert A. Smith to Governor Merriam dated July 18, 1889. Northfield, Minnesota, Bank Robbery of 1876 Selected Manuscripts Collections and Government Records, Microfilm Edition, Minnesota Historical Society.

W.W. Snow letter to Board of Pardons dated July 9, 1897. Northfield, Minnesota, Bank Robbery of 1876. Selected Manuscripts Collections and Government Records, Microfilm Edition, Minnesota Historical Society.

F.E. Stratton to daughter Alice, February 1904, published in *Historical Whisperings*, Washington County Historical Society, Vol. 9, No. 1, April 1982.

Elisha Taylor to Governor Merriam dated July 9, 1889. Northfield, Minnesota, Bank Robbery of 1876. Selected Manuscripts Collections and Government Records, Microfilm Edition, Minnesota Historical Society.

D.B. Thurston to Governor dated July 7, 1897. Northfield, Minnesota, Bank Robbery of 1876. Selected Manuscripts Collections and Government Records, Microfilm Edition, Minnesota Historical Society.

George W. Tressler to Governor Clough dated July 10, 1876. Northfield, Minnesota, Bank Robbery of 1876. Selected Manuscripts Collections and Government Records, Microfilm Edition, Roll 3, Minnesota Historical Society.

S.R. Van Sant to Hon. M.J. Dowling dated April 5, 1901. Northfield, Minnesota, Bank Robbery of 1876. Selected Manuscripts and Government Records, Microfilm Edition, Roll 4, Minnesota Historical Society.

William H. Wallace to Board of Pardons dated July 6, 1897. Northfield, Minnesota, Bank Robbery of 1876. Selected Manuscripts Collections and Government Records, Microfilm Edition, Roll 3, Minnesota Historical Society.

E.D. Wheelock to Warden Henry Wolfer dated July 7, 1897, Northfield, Minnesota, Bank Robbery of 1876. Selected Manuscripts Collections and Government Records, Microfilm Edition, Roll 3, Minnesota Historical Society.

Bishop Henry B. Whipple undated letter to C.M. Start. Northfield, Minnesota, Bank Robbery of 1876. Selected Manuscripts Collections and Government Records, Microfilm Edition, Roll 4, Minnesota Historical Society.

D.J. Whiting affidavit dated July 7, 1897. Northfield, Minnesota, Bank Robbery of 1876. Selected Manuscripts Collections and Government Records, Microfilm Edition, Roll 3, Minnesota Historical Society.

F.J. Wilcox affidavit dated June 10, 1897. Northfield, Minnesota, Bank Robbery of 1876. Selected Manuscripts Collections and Government Records, Microfilm Edition, Roll 3, Minnesota Historical Society.

H.T. Williams to Governor Van Sant dated April 10, 1901. Northfield, Minnesota, Bank Robbery of 1876. Selected Manuscripts Collection and Government Records, Microfilm Edition, Roll 4, Minnesota Historical Society.

H.B. Wilson to Governor Marshall (i.e. Merriam) dated June 22, 1889. Northfield, Minnesota, Bank Robbery of 1876. Selected Manuscripts Collections and Government Records, Microfilm Edition, Roll 3, Minnesota Historical Society.

George P. Wilson to Warden Henry Wolfer dated July 10, 1897. Northfield, Minnesota, Bank Robbery of 1876. Selected Manuscripts Collections and Government Records, Microfilm Edition, Roll 3, Minnesota Historical Society.

John C. Wise to Governor Merriam dated July 12, 1889. Northfield, Minnesota, Bank Robbery of 1876. Selected Manuscripts Collections and Government Records, Microfilm Edition, Minnesota Historical Society.

Henry Wolfer to Roland H. Hartley filed July 22, 1897, with enclosures. Northfield, Minnesota, Bank Robbery of 1876. Selected Manuscripts Collections and Government Records, Microfilm Edition, Minnesota Historical Society.

Marshall P. Wright affidavit dated August 6, 1898. Northfield, Minnesota, Bank Robbery of 1876. Selected Manuscripts

Collections and Government Records, Microfilm Edition, Roll 4, Minnesota Historical Society.

B.G. Yates to Governor Merriam dated July 8, 1889. Northfield Minnesota, Bank Robbery of 1876. Selected Manuscripts and Government Records, Minnesota Historical Society.
B.G. Yates to Governor Merriam dated July 15, 1889. Northfield, Minnesota, Bank Robbery of 1876. Selected Manuscripts Collections and Government Records, Microfilm Edition, Roll 3, Minnesota Historical Society.

B.G. Yates to Governor Knute Nelson dated December 14, 1894. Northfield, Minnesota, Bank Robbery of 1876. Selected Manuscripts Collections and Government Records, Microfilm Edition, Roll 3, Minnesota Historical Society.

Cole Younger to M.J. Daly dated March 26, 1899. Original letter property of Mary Shasky; copies The History Museum of East Otter Tail County, Perham.

Cole Younger letter to M.J. Daly dated March 1901. Mary Shasky and The History Museum of East Otter Tail County, Perham.

Jim Younger to Warden Henry Wolfer, undated, Stillwater State Prison Case File: Younger brothers, Selected Manuscripts Collection and Government Records, Microfilm Division, Minnesota Historical Society.

T.J. Younger to W.H. Harrington dated August 17, 1887. Northfield, Minnesota Bank Robbery of 1876. Selected Manuscripts and Government Records, Microfilm Edition, Roll 3, Minnesota Historical Society.

Interviews

Carl Hage with author, Madelia, Minnesota, February 27, 1982.

Brent Peterson telephone interview with author, August 24, 2001.

Newspapers

Butler (Missouri) *Times,* June 12, 1889.
Cincinnati Commercial Gazette, July 23, 1889.
Cincinnati Enquirer, April 17, 1889.
Creede Candle, April 22, 1892.
Crookston Journal, March 2, 1899.
Denver Republican, June 9, 1892.
Fairmont Daily, 1899.
Faribault Democrat, November 17, 1876; November 24, 1876.
Faribault Republican, November 9, 1876.
Harper's Weekly, May 6, 1899.
House Journal, 1877.
Kansas City Star, February 7, 1899; July 11, 1901.
Kansas City Times, February 27, 1923.
Lake Crystal Union, February 22, 1899.
Lee's Summit Journal, July 3, 1981.
Lexington Morning Herald, August 9, 1903.
Liberty Tribune, July 31, 1891.
Mankato Free Press, February 17, 1899.
Mankato Record, November 18, 1876.
Martin County Sentinel, September 29, 1876.
Midway News, July 10, 1897.
Minneapolis Journal, July 9, 1897; January 19, 1901; February 11, 1901; March 25, 1901; May 8, 1901; May 11, 1901; May 14, 1901; May 17, 1901; June 28, 1901; July 8, 1901; July 9, 1901; July 10, 1901; July 11, 1901; July 13, 1901.
Minneapolis Tribune, January 23, 1876.
Minneapolis *Star Tribune,* August 2, 1998.
Minnesota Chronicle & Register, April 20, 1850.
Nevada (Missouri) *Daily Mail,* October 7, 1884; March 6, 1885; March 23, 1885; April 13, 1885; September 23, 1885; October 6, 1885; November 6, 1885; January 25, 1886; April 2, 1886; August 21, 1886; February 28, 1887; March 1, 1887; May 2, 1887; June 10, 1887; August 28, 1888; June 18, 1992.
Nevada (Missouri) *Herald,* October 24, 1971.
Nevada (Missouri) *Noticer,* November 11, 1886.
Northfield News, July 17, 1897.
The (Minneapolis) *Representative,* 1899.
St. James Plain Dealer, November 1926.
St. Louis Post-Dispatch, May 19, 1901; March 22, 1916.
St. Louis Republican, October 22, 1902.

St. Paul Daily Globe, January 27, 1884.

St. Paul Daily News, June 26, 1936.

St. Paul Dispatch, June 5, 1874; June 24, 1874.

St. Paul Pioneer Press, January 20, 1874; November 20, 1876; November 1879; July 23, 1886; July 24, 1886; August 1, 1886; August 13, 1886; September 17, 1889; September 19, 1889; July 13, 1897; July 14, 1897; July 15, 1897; July 10, 1901; July 11, 1901; April 9, 1904.

St. Paul & Minneapolis Pioneer Press, November 16, 1876; November 21, 1876; November 23, 1876; November 30, 1876; January 9, 1884; January 26, 1884; January 27, 1884; July 26, 1886.

Stillwater Democrat, February 19, 1887; September 19, 1889.

Stillwater Gazette, February 7, 1877; September 17, 1889; September 18, 1889; December 4, 1890; May 10, 1894; February 11, 1899; July 12, 1901; November 9, 1979.

Stillwater Messenger, May 22, 1874; January 12, 1884; January 26, 1884; February 2, 1884; May 25, 1889; June 22, 1889; August 3, 1889; March 28, 1891; June 9, 1894; July 13, 1901; February 7, 1903.

Stillwater *Prison Mirror,* August 10, 1887; August 17, 1887; September 19, 1889; October 10, 1889; October 17, 1889; October 24, 1889; December 26, 1889; January 16, 1890; Anniversary Edition, Vol. 103, No. 1, August 11, 1989, "Mirror Turns 103."

White Bear Lake *St. Croix Valley Press,* July 2001.

Personal Accounts

Charles F. Batchelder Papers, in collection of Chris Batchelder.

Records

Board of State Prison Managers Resolution forwarded to Board of Pardons (no date). Northfield, Minnesota, Bank Robbery of 1876. Selected Manuscripts Collections and Government Records, Microfilm Edition, Roll 4, Minnesota Historical Society.

Frank Bronaugh Obituary, January 1937, Louis Woodford Bronaugh/Pamela Luster Phillips Collection.

Warren Carter Bronaugh Obituary, February 1923, Louis Woodford Broanugh/Pamela Luster Phillips Collection.

Regular Meeting of the Board of Pardons, July 12, 1897. Summary in Northfield, Minnesota, Bank Robbery of 1876. Selected Manuscripts Collections and Government Records, Microfilm Edition, Roll 3, Minnesota Historical Society.

C.W. Deaton, "Plot to Free the Youngers Failed," published in Northfield Independent, Date Unknown, Collection of Northfield Public Library.

"The Enos Murders," Enos Family Records.

Daily Medical Records. Northfield, Minnesota, Bank Robbery of 1876. Selected Manuscripts Collections and Government Records, Microfilm Edition, Roll 3, Minnesota Historical Society.

Deed for Frank James house, Vernon County Missouri Deed Book 36.

Document signed by Warden John A. Reed for receipt of prisoners from A. Barton of Rice County. Author's Collection.

"In the Matter of the Parole of Coleman and James Younger." Northfield, Minnesota, Bank Robbery of 1876. Selected Manuscripts Collections and Government Records, Microfilm Edition, Roll 4, Minnesota Historical Society.

"Life in Minnesota in St. Paul's First Hundred Years," undated newspaper article, Northfield Public Library collection.

A.R. McGill, Statement. December 28, 1898. Northfield, Minnesota, Bank Robbery of 1876. Selected Manuscripts Collections and Government Records, Microfilm Edition, Roll 4, Minnesota Historical Society.

Medical Examination File. Northfield, Minnesota, Bank Robbery of 1876. Selected Manuscripts Collections and Government Records, Microfilm Edition, Roll 3, Minnesota Historical Society.

Minnesota Beginnings: Records of St. Croix County Wisconsin Territory, 1840-1849, Stillwater, Washington County Historical Society, 1999.

Parole Applications of Thomas Coleman Younger and James Hardin Younger to the State Prison Board of Managers dated May 6, 1901. Northfield, Minnesota, Bank Robbery of 1876. Selected Manuscripts Collections and Government Records, Microfilm Edition, Roll 4, Minnesota Historical Society.

Regular Meeting of the Board of Pardons, July 12, 1897. Summary in Northfield, Minnesota, Bank Robbery of 1876. Selected Manuscripts Collections and Government Records, Microfilm Edition, Roll 3, Minnesota Historical Society.

"Stillwater State Prison," Agency Record Group Administrative History, Minnesota Historical Society.

Gideon W. Thompson, Statement, March 5, 1898. Northfield, Minnesota, Bank Robbery of 1876. Selected Manuscripts Collections and Government Records, Microfilm Edition, Roll 4, Minnesota Historical Society.

U. S. Census for 1860.

Washington County Historical Society Files, Stillwater.

Unpublished Manuscripts

George T. Barr, "Account of Northfield Bank Robbery in 1876," in archives of Blue Earth County Historical Society, Mankato, Minnesota.

W.H. Harrington, "Justice," Northfield, Minnesota, Bank Robbery of 1876. Selected Manuscripts Collections and Government Records, Microfilm Edition, Roll 3, Minnesota Historical Society.

A.E. Hedback, M.D., June 7, 1921, "Cole Younger's Story of the Northfield Raid in his own Handwriting," William Watts Folwell and Family Papers, Northfield, Minnesota, Bank

Robbery of 1876. Selected Manuscripts Collections and Government Records, Microfilm Edition, Minnesota Historical Society.

Lyndon Irwin, "Bronaugh, Missouri History."

Charles A. Lamb, "Stillwater State Prison History," Minnesota Historical Society.

Northfield Historical Society Files.

Pam Phillips, "The Bronaugh Family," papers of Louis Woodford Bronaugh.

Afterword

Bob Boze Bell

Executive Editor, True West Magazine

Many times history reduces events to shorthand. In the case of the outlaw Younger Brothers, after their capture at Hanska Slough, history turned them into footnotes. Their problem (and ultimately our problem) is that legend and popular history followed the James Boys after the Minnesota manhunt and, consequently, the prison years of the Youngers have been glossed over, misremembered, or in many cases simply forgotten.

Author and first-class researcher, John Koblas has dug deep into the collective basements (both literally and figuratively) of the nation's repositories to come up with a fresh look at these men's lives after they were thrown behind bars. No one has bothered to document, or put together a year-by-year look at their prison years. For the first time, we feel the Younger's isolation and pain. They paid dearly for their crimes. Fortunately, Koblas took the time to find the truth about their journey. This is a most valuable book for anyone who wants the truth about Old West outlaws and the lives they led. I, for one, am looking forward to his next project, wherein he tracks the life of Cole Younger after his release from prison. Thank you, John Koblas!

Index